Mental Health Promotion in Schools: Foundations

Edited By

Raymond J. Waller

Troy University
USA

CONTENTS

FOREWORD

I became involved in school mental health in 1991, right out of graduate school and my pre-doctoral internship, with no prior background of working in schools. My job was of an assistant professor in the Department of Psychiatry at the University of Maryland, School of Medicine, and my assignment was to provide mental health services at a large inner-city high school in Baltimore serving over 2000 students. Initially, I was overwhelmed by the assignment and honestly spent some time being fairly confused on how to proceed. However, I immersed myself in the work, and soon began to really like it. I also worked with some university-based community mental health centers (CMHCs), and began to notice stark differences between my work in them and my work in the schools. With colleagues we came to a pretty straightforward, three point realization:

1. Children, adolescents and families were not getting to the CMHCs, with many barriers (*e.g.,* transportation, stigma, stress in families, lack of knowledge of mental health or mental health services) getting in the way, and even if a connection was made (after considerable burden and a long waiting period), this was usually only for one or a very few sessions,

2. The schools were overburdened with tremendous unmet mental health needs of youth, and limited resources and staff to address mental health needs, and

3. If we joined staff and programs from the CMHCs with staff and programs from the schools, we could reach many more youth and we would help both the mental health centers and the schools in achieving their missions.

This realization, and increasing strong collaborative relations with a great group of colleagues from multiple universities and youth serving systems in Baltimore and the state of Maryland, helped our team to develop the expanded school mental health (SMH) framework, involving a *shared agenda* (see Andis *et al.,* 2002) of schools, families, and community systems working together to develop and implement a full continuum of effective mental health promotion and intervention for youth in general and special education (see Weist, 1997; Weist, Evans, & Lever, 2003). In the early 1990s we explored dimensions of effective expanded SMH in Baltimore, with an overriding emphasis on quality. By asking youth and families, school, community, and government leaders what they wanted in quality SMH, clear themes emerged of moving toward proactive, preventive and more flexible mental health care, delivered by committed and caring professionals who would eliminate bureaucratic barriers and work to rapidly provide help to youth in need (Flaherty & Weist, 1999).

Immersion in this work led to an important opportunity to apply and receive funding for one of two national centers for mental health in schools in 1995, with initial funding from the Maternal and Child Health Bureau, which has continued through 2010 to support the work of the University of Maryland, Center for School Mental Health (CSMH; see http://csmh.umaryland.edu; www.school mentalhealth.org). It has been a great privilege for me to participate in the progressive development of the SMH field, and the CSMH, which has responded to thousands of technical assistance requests, held 15 national conferences on Advancing SMH, held 8 regional conferences on integrated school health and mental health services (the School Health Interdisciplinary Program), developed and widely disseminated over 150 documents and publications, and contributed to significant collaboration at local, state, national, and international levels (see the National Community on Collaborative School Behavioral Health, www.sharedwork.org; the International Alliance for Child and Adolescent Mental Health and Schools, www.intercamhs.org; the international journal, Advances in School Mental Health Promotion, www.schoolmentalhealth.co.uk).

Mental health programs and services in school have been around for a long time (see Sarason, 1996), but the norm has been for specific disciplines operating in schools, often without a lot of interaction, and often with constraints on their positions. Citing two examples, in spite of the fact that many have training as mental health professionals, school psychologists and counselors are often constrained into roles emphasizing evaluation and academic advisement (respectively), training and support for these staff members are often limited, and ratios of these staff members to students are far below those recommended by professional associations (see Flaherty *et al.,* 1998; DuPaul, 2007; Weist *et al.,* 2007). In contrast, the SMH field emerging and gaining strength in the last two decades emphasizes on an interdisciplinary and inter-systems (*e.g.,* education, mental health, child welfare, juvenile services) approach that is actively guided by youth and families, and other key stakeholders such as teachers and community leaders (see Lever *et al.,* 2003). While the research literature is still developing, advantages for SMH are being documented, including improving access to care (Burns *et al.,* 1995; Catron, Harris, & Weiss, 1998; Rones & Hoagwood, 2000), enhancing preventive services (Elias, Gager, & Leon, 1997; Weare, 2000), increasing early problem identification (Weist, Myers, Hastings, Ghuman, & Han, 1999), decreasing stigma (Atkins, Adil, Jackson, McKay, & Bell, 2001; Nabors & Reynolds, 2000), and increasing generalization of intervention impacts across settings (Evans, Langberg, & Williams, 2003).

The federal government in the United States is providing significant support to the SMH field (see Anglin, 2003) through major policy reports, including Surgeon General's reports on transforming mental health and children's mental health services (U.S. Department of Health and Human Services, 1999; U.S. Public Health Service, 2000) and the Achieving the Promise Report (President's New Freedom Commission, 2003), which emphasized SMH services as one of 19 prioritized recommendations (recommendation 4.2). There are also many federal grants supporting SMH, including those focused on Systems of Care (led by the Substance Abuse and Mental Health Services Administration [SAMHSA]), Safe Schools/Healthy Students (led by the U.S. Department of Education [DOE] and SAMHSA), Mental Health Integration into the Schools (led by DOE), Capacity Building for SMH (led by the Centers for Disease Control and Prevention), and strong support for SMH research from the National Institute of Mental Health, and the Institute for Education Sciences.

Indeed, in the U.S., school mental health programs and services are showing progressive growth, even in these economically challenging times. However, in spite of this progress, there is much to be done, in building the research base; and increasing implementation support for high quality, evidence-based practices (see Evans & Weist, 2004; Fixsen *et al.,* 2005; Weist *et al.,* 2009); broadening training opportunities at pre-service and in-service levels, especially effective interdisciplinary training that embraces principles of adult learning (Mellin, 2009); building policy support for SMH (Weist *et al.,* 2007); and increasing connections among training, practice, research and policy realms (Paternite, Weist, Burke, & Flaspohler, 2008). There is also a critical social marketing agenda to pursue increasing public awareness and involvement in the SMH agenda, supporting work that promotes students' wellness, reduces academic and non-academic barriers to their learning, and increases the likelihood of academic and subsequent career success.

To promote progress in all of the above there is a need to broaden the knowledge base in the field and to promote collaboration among the diverse stakeholders who have a vested interest in improving and expanding SMH (see President's New Freedom Commission, 2003). To that end, I am very pleased to provide the introduction of this book published by Bentham Science, and edited by leader in the field, Raymond J. Waller. This book, the first in a series and focused on Foundations, will be an important resource in the compelling school mental health field.

Mark D. Weist
University of South Carolina
USA

PREFACE

Wide agreement exists among those in mental health and allied fields that mental health needs are increasing and that needs far exceed the resources needed to address them. This is true, perhaps especially, for children. This public health tragedy is made more poignant by virtue of the availability of effective interventions for many mental health conditions. Even if the resources were obtainable for the treatment of those with mental health conditions, however, successful intervention does not prevent the stigma, syncopation in development, social isolation, cost incurring, and other potential negative outcomes associated with both the conditions and the labels applied in the process of typical treatment. Prevention of the incidence of these disorders (primary prevention) is thus clearly preferable to treatment (secondary prevention) or amelioration (tertiary prevention).

Among the more practical and effective tools in pursuit of this goal is mental health promotion, and there is a broad and expanding appreciation for the school being a foremost focal point of attention and intercession. The school setting offers many advantages, two of the most prominent being:

1. Universality of access: compulsory education laws ensure that children in wealthy countries—and in many economically developing nations, as well—are required to attend school, and

2. School already promotes, and some would contend in a manner consistent with the quality commensurate with best practices, health and health behavior. Broadening this endeavor to include promoting mental health is a manageable, though logical, modification to current goals and curricula.

This book, the first in a planned series, includes issues and considerations deemed to be fundamental in successful mental health promotion in the school setting. The scholarship of experts and premier practitioners has been sought in providing the most progressive knowledge currently prevailing throughout in the area. There are now professional journals dedicated to the topic (*e.g., Advances in School Mental*

Health Promotion) as well as prestigious centers of research and practice (National Center for Mental Health in Schools at UCLA and Clifford Beers Foundation). There are likewise numerous texts on the subject (*e.g.,* Waller, 2006). However, this book and the subsequent installments in the series are believed to be unique in the scope offered in one resource, though there are undoubtedly numerous topics of importance that are not covered. In any case, the topic is worthy of the level of attention it now receives, but in dissemination of the current state of the knowledge base and in the continued inquiry into the gaps in what remains unknown. Continued investigation will uncover unknown and ensure that needs and best interests of children are supported by the best research, policy, and practice that society can offer.

It is fair and right to acknowledge the help, assistance, and patience of Miss Asma Ahmed at Bentham Science eBooks, who has supported and guided this project from the outset. It is likewise imperative to thank, with a heart of respect and appreciation, the scholars and practitioners who contributed their time and expertise, with little offered in return except a means to further disseminate their valuable work and my personal gratitude.

Raymond J. Waller
Associate Professor and Director
Social Work, Human Services, and Rehabilitation
Troy University-Dothan
USA

REFERENCES

Andis, P., Cashman, J., Praschil, R., Oglesby, D., Adelman, H., Taylor, L., & Weist, M. D. (2002). A strategic and shared agenda to advance mental health in schools through family and system partnerships. *International Journal of Mental Health Promotion, 4,* 28-35.

Anglin, T. (2003). Mental health in schools: Programs of the federal government. In: Weist, M.D., Evans, S.W., Lever, N.A. (Eds.), *Handbook of school mental health programs: Advancing practice and research* (pp. 89-106). New York, NY: Springer.

Atkins, M., Adil, J., Jackson, M., McKay, M., & Bell, C. (2001). *An ecological model for school-based mental health services.* 13th Annual Conference Proceedings: A System of Care for

Children's Mental Health: Expanding the Research Base. Tampa: University of South Florida.

Burns, B. J., Costello, E. J., Angold, A., Tweed, D., Stangle, D., Farmer, E., & Erkanli, A. (1995). Data watch: Children's mental health service use across sectors. *Health Affairs, 13,* 147-159.

Catron, T., Harris, V. S., & Weiss, B. (1998). Posttreatment results after 2 years of services in the Vanderbilt school-based counseling project. In M. H. Epstein, K. Kutash, & A. Ducknowski (Eds.), *Outcomes for children and youth with behavioral and emotional disorders and their families: Programs and evaluation best practices* (pp. 633-656). Austin, TX: Pro-Ed.

DuPaul, G. (2007). School-based mental health: Current status and future directions. In S. Evans, M. Weist, & Z. Serpell (Eds.), *Advances in school-based mental health interventions: Best practices and program models, Volume II* (pp. 25-1 – 25-8). New York: Civic Research Institute.

Elias, M. J., Gager, P., Leon, S. (1997). Spreading a warm blanket of prevention over all children: Guidelines for selecting substance abuse and related prevention curricula for use in the schools. *Journal of Primary Prevention, 18*, 41-69.

Evans, S. W., Langberg, J., & Williams, J. (2003). Achieving generalization in school-based mental health. In M.D. Weist, S.W. Evans, & N.A. Lever (Eds.), *Handbook of school mental health: Advancing practice and research* (pp. 335-348). New York, NY: Springer.

Evans, S. W. & Weist, M. D. (2004). Implementing empirically supported treatments in the schools: What are we asking? *Clinical Child and Family Psychology Review, 7*, 263-267.

Fixsen, D. L., Naoom, S. F., Blase, K. A., Friedman, R. M., & Wallace, F. (2005). *Implementation Research: A Synthesis of the Literature.* (FMHI Publication #231). Tampa, FL: University of South Florida, Louis de la Parte Florida Mental Health Institute, The National Implementation Research Network.

Flaherty, L. T., Garrison, E., Waxman, R., Uris, P., Keyes, S., Siegel, M. G., & Weist, M. D. (1998). Optimizing the roles of school mental health professionals. *Journal of School Health, 68,* 420-424.

Flaherty, L. T., & Weist, M. D. (1999). School-based mental health services: The Baltimore models. *Psychology in the Schools, 36*, 379-389.

Lever, N. A., Adelsheim, S., Prodente, C., Christodulu, K. V., Ambrose, M. G., Schlitt, J., & Weist, M. D. (2003). System, agency and stakeholder collaboration to advance mental health programs in schools. In M.D. Weist, S.W. Evans, & N.A. Lever (Eds.), *Handbook of school mental health: Advancing practice and research* (pp. 149-162). New York, NY: Springer.

Mellin, E. A. (2009). Unpacking interdisciplinary collaboration in expanded school mental health: A conceptual model for developing the evidence base. *Advances in school mental health promotion, 2*, 4-14.

Paternite, C. E., Weist, M. D., Burke, R., & Flaspohler, P. (2008). Mental health issues in schools. *Encyclopedia of counseling, Volume 1: Changes and challenges for counseling in the 21st century (pp. 288-293).* New York: Sage.

Nabors, L. A., & Reynolds, M. W. (2000). Program evaluation activities: Outcomes related to treatment for adolescents receiving school-based mental health services. *Children's Services: Social Policy, Research, and Practice, 3*, 175-189.

President's New Freedom Commission on Mental Health (2003). *Achieving the Promise: Transforming Mental Health Care in America. Final Report for the President's New Freedom Commission on Mental Health (SMA Publication No. 03-3832).* Rockville, MD: Author.

Rones, M. & Hoagwood, K. (2000). School-based mental health services: A research review. *Clinical Child and Family Psychology Review, 3*, 223-241.

Sarason, S. B. (1996). *Barometers of change: Individual, educational, and social transformation.* San Francisco, CA: Jossey-Bass.

U.S. Department of Health and Human Services (1999). *Mental health: A report of the Surgeon General-Executive Summary.* Rockville, MD: U.S. Department of Health and Human Services, Substance Abuse and Mental Health Services Administration, Center for Mental Health Services, National Institute of Health, National Institute of Mental Health.

U. S. Public Health Service (2000). *Report on the Surgeon General's Conference on Children's Mental Health: A national action agenda.* Washington, DC: U.S. Government Printing Office.

Waller, R. J. (Ed.) (2006). *Fostering child and adolescent mental health in the classroom.* Thousand Oaks, CA: Sage.

Weare, K. (2000). *Promoting mental, emotional and social health: A whole school approach.* London: Routledge.

Weist, M. D. (1997). Expanded school mental health services: A national movement in progress. In T. Ollendick & R. J. Prinz (Eds.). *Advanced in Clinical Child Psychology* (Vol. 19, pp. 319-352). New York: Plenum Press.

Weist, M. D., Evans, S. W., & Lever, N. A. (2003). *Handbook of school mental health: Advancing practice and research.* New York: Springer.

Weist, M. D., Lever, N., Stephan, S., Youngstrom, E., Moore, E., Harrison, B., Anthony, L., Rogers, K., Hoagwood, K., Ghunney, A., Lewis, K., & Stiegler, K. (2009). Formative evaluation of a framework for high quality, evidence-based services in school mental health. *School Mental Health. 1(3)*, 196-211.

Weist, M. D., Myers, C. P., Hastings, E., Ghuman, H., & Han, Y. (1999). Psychosocial functioning of youth receiving mental health services in the schools *vs*. community mental health centers. *Community Mental Health Journal, 35*, 69-81.

Weist, M. D., Stephan, S., Lever, N., Moore, E., Flaspohler, P., Maras, M., Paternite, C., & Cosgrove, T. J. (2007). Quality and school mental health. In S. Evans, M. Weist, & Z. Serpell (Eds.), *Advances in school-based mental health interventions (pp. 4:1 – 4:14).* New York: Civic Research Institute.

List of Contributors

Howard Adelman, PhD

Co-director of the School Mental Health Project and its national Center for Mental Health in Schools at UCLA (USA). Their long-term focus is on youngsters in school settings who manifest learning, behavior, and emotional problems. The Center's policy and practice emphasis is on systemic reforms to enhance school and community efforts to address barriers to learning and enhance healthy development.

Angeleque Akin-Little, PhD, BCBA

Behavioral Educational and Research Consultants is a private psychology practice located in Gulf Harbour, New Zealand that provides a full array of psychological services to children, youth, families, and schools including teacher training and research consultation.

Carol L. Albertini, MEd

Teacher-Special Education, Gwinnett County Schools, USA

Dawn Anderson-Butcher, PhD, LISW

Professor in the College of Social Work, The Ohio State University, USA

Elise Cappella, PhD

Assistant Professor of Applied Psychology, New York University, USA

Joshua Couperus

Massey University, New Zealand

Melissa R. Dvorsky

Research Specialist, Department of Psychology, University of South Carolina, USA

Joetta Gonzales, EdD

Director of the Equity Alliance, Arizona State University, USA

Denise M. Green, PhD, LCSW

Assistant Professor and Chair, Social Work, Human Services, and Rehabilitation, Troy University, USA

Aidyn L. Iachini, PhD

Assistant Professor in the College of Social Work, University of South Carolina, USA

Daisy Jackson, MEd, PhD Cand.

Counseling Psychology neuropsychology extern, New York University, USA

Nancy Kupfrian, MEd

School Counselor, A.J. Belmonte Middle School, USA

Steven G. Little, PhD, BCBA

Associate Professor (Note: U. S. equivalent of full professor), School of Education, Massey University New Zealand

Allison Nealy, EdD

Lecturer, Department of Communication Sciences and Special Education, University of Georgia, USA

Kim Sheffield, MEd

Teacher-Special Education, Gwinnett County Schools, USA

Sarah E. Twill, PhD

Assistant Professor of Social Work, Wright State University, USA

Leslie K. Taylor

University of South Carolina, USA

Linda Taylor, PhD

Co-director of the School Mental Health Project and its national Center for Mental Health in Schools at UCLA (USA). Their long-term focus is on youngsters in school settings who manifest learning, behavior, and emotional problems. The

Center's policy and practice emphasis is on systemic reforms to enhance school and community efforts to address barriers to learning and enhance healthy development.

Raymond J. Waller, PhD, LCSW, BCSCR

Associate Professor and Director/Social Work, Human Services, and Rehabilitation, Troy University, USA

Mark D. Weist, PhD

Professor, Department of Psychology, University of South Carolina, USA

1

2

CHAPTER 1

Mental Health Treatment or Promotion in Resource Allocation: Two Topical Considerations Elucidate the Road Less Traveled

Raymond J. Waller[1,*], Carol L. Albertini[2] and Nancy L. Kupfrian[3]

[1]College of Health and Human Services, PO Box 8368, Troy University-Dothan, Dothan, AL 36304, USA; [2]Sugar Hill Elementary School, 939 Level Creek Road Buford, GA 30518, USA and [3]Belmonte Middle School, 25 Dow Street, Saugus, Massachusetts 01906, USA

Abstract: As a group of strategies, mental health promotion may better serve the needs of children than the treatment of a mental disorder already manifested. The school setting is more amenable to promotion than treatment, and more aligned with the mission of schools as well for several reasons. The purpose of this chapter is to discuss two of the criteria often involved in the complex decisional matrix involved in resource allocation regarding mental health outcomes: 1) which option provides the best outcome for the investment and 2) which alternative conveys the highest probability of accurate diagnosis/effective treatment selection. Finally, a case study involving mental health promotion strategies in schools to support and assist in the reduction of symptomatology in a diagnosed mental disorder is provided.

Keywords: Intervention, mental health promotion, mental health treatment, school counseling, selective mutism.

INTRODUCTION

Among the adages commonly heard espoused by supervisory personnel in many impecunious worksites affected by current economic challenges is the exhortation for employees to do more with less. If pondered briefly, this axiom, as are so many that presume to resolve complex issues with jejune solutions, bears the unfortunate pall of insensibility. One can only do less with less. The sting of failure resulting from overuse of pseudo-wisdom aside, many find maintaining employment during fiscal dearth is often contingent on being willing to accept the job responsibilities of former coworkers. Historically, human service endeavors

***Address correspondence to Raymond J. Waller:** College of Health and Human Services, PO Box 8368, Troy University-Dothan, Dothan, AL 36304, USA; Tel: 334-983-6556; Email: rjwaller@troy.edu

are curtailed when tax revenues decline. Those in mental health fields have long been in the position of being presumed more expendable, perhaps, than other professional undertakings supposedly bringing more value to the worksite or the world at large.

Resisting the temptation to discourse on the insight of political expedience and priorities, it is prudent to concede that resource allocation is important and that the wise administrator pursues the best outcomes for the most efficient investment of capital. In mental health, it could be said that a golden period predominates. A sound knowledge base exists which indicates that many diagnosable mental conditions associated with children and adolescents are either clearly treatable or the symptomatology of the condition, as a result of intervention, is assuaged.

However, even if many such conditions can be treated effectively, successful treatment does not resolve that the most efficient investment is currently purchasing the most advantageous outcomes. When speaking of health conditions, few would argue that prevention of disorder is a more optimal outcome and may be a better investment than treatment of a manifest condition. Who, for example, would decry that prevention of heart disease is a better and more cost effective goal than treating heart attacks and providing subsequent rehabilitation? This is true even if effective treatment exists for heart attack for many people.

When discussing health outcomes, however, making determinations related to resource allocation can be complex. There are many factors that impact health outcomes, and this certainly continues to be the case in mental health outcomes. The causative variable that ultimately cascades to disorder might be missed entirely, overlooked, or misinterpreted. While very high levels of cholesterol are considered to be a risk factor for having a heart attack, very low levels of cholesterol do not guarantee the prevention of heart attack. There is a complex array of intersecting factors that combine synergistically to bring about individual outcomes. This is, as mentioned above, true of mental health outcomes just as with physical health outcomes. Also true is that generally, prevention costs less than treatment.

Some in the mental health fields may be unable to resist the temptation of assuming that many of these confounding factors impact mental health more so than physical health outcomes, but distinguishing the best of two psychosocial treatment options gets harder yet. In both cases, language is typically heavily relied upon during the process of differential diagnosis—not to mention treatment. Classic research by Rosenhan (1973) informed us—among other valuable lessons—that, once deceit is infused into the assessment process, the diagnosis may be affected with the likely result being decreased diagnostic accuracy. All mental health conditions are not treated effectively using the same intervention any more than a topical cream that relieves unsavory dermatological symptoms is likely to facilitate healing of a broken femur. A faulty diagnosis can be expected to lead to ineffective interventions. The complexity grows exponentially from these points. The conclusion is the same, though the route to the conclusion more circuitous—prevention costs less than treatment.

In child and adolescent mental health, a mechanism of great interest that facilitates prevention as the outcome rather than treatment for disorder is mental health promotion in schools. The intention of the remainder of this chapter is to provide clarification *vis-à-vis* the question of whether, given the theoretical ability to choose the better of two options and preferentially allocate resources, there is greater face validity with emphasizing mental health treatment or promotion based on the two foci above: investment efficiency and diagnosis/intervention selection.

The field of school counseling is discussed to highlight ways an allied education profession can be redefined and reassigned in response to external forces rather than strict sensitivity to the needs of persons served. Selective mutism is presented so that challenges in accurately diagnosing and selecting an effective mental health condition might be better realized. Finally, a case study of intervention for a young male student in the school setting in which he was given support based on foundational mental health promotion strategies, resolving his symptoms of selective mutism.

A BRIEF HISTORY OF SCHOOL COUNSELING

Since the inception of the profession of school counseling, the role of these professionals has been redefined and modernized, often to meet the needs of a changing society or in response to societal events (Beesley, 2004; Burnham & Jackson, 2000; Gysbers & Henderson, 2001; Paisley & Borders, 1995). The role, position, and duties of school counselors have historically been muddled by the many influences that have shaped the very profession itself over the last century. As stated succinctly by Dahir (2004), "The history of school counseling has depicted a profession in search of an identity" (p. 345).

Throughout the years, there have been trends both towards and away from the use of guidance counselors in the school setting. Although the addition of giving attention to the social, personal and educational aspects of a student's life in addition to focusing on their vocational needs came into trend in the 1920's and 30's, the Great Depression led to the restriction of funds for counseling programs (Board, 2008). This occurred arguably at a time when students had increased need for social, personal, and educational issues. Allied educational fields continue to be among the first professionals scrutinized for cost reduction during times of resource scarcity in schools.

Although the 1980s were a significant time for the development of training standards and criteria for school counseling, the 1970s and 1980s were two decades where counselors found themselves at risk for having positions eliminated. In contrast to the idea that guidance counselors were not essential staff, it was during this time that school counselors were called upon to once again take broader responsibilities in the lives of students (Schimmel, 2008); furthermore, school counselors often have additional duties assigned to them in which they are supporting other functions, including but not limited to:

- Data entry,
- Clerical record keeping,
- Registration and scheduling of all new students,
- Coordinating or administering cognitive, aptitude and achievement tests,
- Responsibility for signing excuses for students who are tardy or absent,
- Performing disciplinary actions,

- Sending students home who are not appropriately dressed,
- Covering classes when teachers are absent, and
- Computing grade-point averages.

Currently, the school counselor's role in student mental health is outlined by the American School Counselor Association (ASCA) under the guidelines of a comprehensive school counseling program. According to the ASCA "comprehensive school counseling programs span the continuum of care provided to students and their families, and are consistent with professional school counselors' commitment to student success". The ASCA website provides the following summary of the professional school counselor's role in student mental health:

> Students' unmet mental health needs pose barriers to learning and development. Because of professional school counselor's training and position, they are uniquely qualified to provide education, prevention, intervention and referral services to students and their families. Although professional school counselors do not provide long-term therapy in schools, they provide a comprehensive school counseling program designed to meet the developmental needs of all students. As a component of this program, professional school counselors collaborate with other educational professionals and community service providers to assist with the mediation of student mental health issues and to promote healthy lifestyle choices.

SUMMARY

It is evident that school counselors, like school social workers and school psychologists—and, likely, most other professional educators as well—must adapt to resource constraints as well as societal expectations, cultural changes, and numerous other variables, in frequently redefining their roles and contributions in order to be professionally viable. Many school counselors have found themselves the coordinators of mandatory testing. For example, the list of common additional duties reported above could easily require several fulltime employees in a large school.

Simultaneously, the knowledge requirements necessary simply to meet the mental health expectations is formidable, and meeting this level of student need risks necessitating a fulltime commitment, thus compromising the counselor's availability to make copies for other employees. It is enough to dismay the discerning guidance counselor planning a graduate educational program in this field, deciphering whether graduate course instructional time might be best spent training candidates on evidence based interventions or on fine tuning technique on the most contemporary paper duplicating technology. The special training received (or not) obtained by school counselors may not be of interest to every educational profession. The topic may, however, serve as a clarifying example by which the difficulty of having the financial means, the available expertise, and the discernment to employ professionals qualified to treat the breadth of mental health conditions that can impair the functional status of the student body is a daunting challenge.

In the example of school counseling, which is ultimately similar to other professions involving emotional and behavioral intervention with children, the brief history above discusses the constriction of the field during times of economic duress. It progresses to discourse on additional duties taken on by school counselors, presumably so that the funds needed to hire office support can be redirected for other uses. Perhaps it is not the value of the saved dollar that is the being leveraged when professional time is squandered, but the value placed on mental health, quality of life, and the various mental health professions' ability to have a meaningful effect on those outcomes that is doubted.

Manipulation or Anxiety? Theoretical Perspectives and Other Treatment Choice Intricacies Related to Selective Mutism

Selective mutism (SM) is a psychiatric disorder categorized by an extreme manifestation of anxiety in which a child persistently refrains from speaking in one or more environments, but can converse normally in others (Yeganeh, Beidel, & Turner, 2006). Categorized as an anxiety disorder and often co-existing with social phobia, SM occurs most often in children that are of normal intelligence, and who are capable of hearing and communicating in comfortable situations (Yeganeh). Although the diagnosis is considered to be rare, affecting less than 1 percent of children, recent findings suggest that this condition has prevalence rates that are similar to other childhood disorders (Bergman, Piacentini, & McCracken, 2002; Elizur & Perednik, 2003).

Despite being clinically depicted over a century ago, only recently has research suggested that SM may not be an intentional act of manipulation on the part of the child, but rather, a real and overwhelming disorder. *Aphasia voluntaria* was the term that was used to describe what is now referred to as SM when it was first identified in the late 1800's (Krysanski, 2003). This idiom implied that the child was choosing not to speak. In 1934, Moritz Tramer, a Swiss pioneer in child psychology, began using the term *elective mutism*, but these words still suggested that an intentional decision was being made by the child to withhold conversation (Steinhausen, Wachter, Laimbock, & Winkler- Metzke, 2006). *The Diagnostic and Statistical Manual of Mental Disorders* (DSM-IV) changed the name of the disorder from elective to *selective mutism* in 1994. The new term eliminated the purposefulness of the act of withholding speech. Even so, the *International Classification of Diseases* (ICD-10) continues to call this condition elective mutism (Steinhausen *et al.,* 2006).

CLINICAL PRESENTATION

A child with selective mutism (SM) has normal receptive and expressive language skills, but abstains from speaking in certain environments (Cohan, Shavira, & Stein, 2006). The most common setting in which this disorder becomes evident is elementary school; often the first place where the child is expected to verbally respond to directives and questions by persons other than close family and friends (Bergman, Piacentini, & McCracken, 2002). Kaakeh and Stumpf (2008) reported that a diagnosis of SM is normally made between the ages of six and eight, but it may be diagnosed well into adolescence, as was the case with the Virginia Tech Massacre shooter- Seung-Hui Cho (Kearney & Vecchio, 2007). True onset of the disorder, however, is thought to occur sometime during the preschool years. Prior to entrance into elementary school, parents often attribute the child's symptoms to shyness or separation anxiety (Vecchio & Kearney, 2005).

According to the Diagnostic and Statistical Manual of Mental Disorders, Fourth Edition (DSM-IV-TR), a diagnosis of SM requires that the child exhibit a persistent lack of speech in specific social situations, while conversing normally in other environments (American Psychiatric Association, [DSM-IV-TR] 2000). The disorder must interfere with social communication and may sometimes impede academic or occupational success, although Manassis and colleagues (2003) and Pionek-Stone, Kratochwill, Sladezcek, and Serlin (2002) suggested that evaluative studies could not be found on the direct effects SM had on academic progress. The DSM–IV-TR diagnostic criteria that must be met for a child to be diagnosed with SM can be summarized as:

- A consistent failure to speak in specific social situations that has duration lasting more than one month,
- An interference with educational or occupational achievement or with social communication,
- A failure to speak in social situations that is not due to a lack of knowledge or comfort with spoken language, and
- In addition, the disturbance cannot be better accounted for by any other disorder.

THEORY GUIDING PRACTICE

Theory might be thought of as the road map that guides practice. Several theories have evolved over the years to explain the development of SM, but no consensus exists as to why children experience this condition. Hypotheses with varying levels of support have focused on psychodynamic factors, behavioral inhibition, neuro-developmental problems, and childhood social phobias (Manassis, Fung, Tannock, Sloman, Fiksenbaum, & McInnes, 2003). Although many researchers and practitioners agree on theoretical etiology, there are those that conceptualize the behaviors associated with SM as oppositional or a form of manipulation. Regardless of the school of thought, SM is a real and debilitating disorder that will benefit from more studies and research emphasizing proper assessment, diagnosis, and treatment.

Early psychodynamic and family-systems views of SM emphasized exposure to trauma, unresolved intra-psychic conflicts, or controlling/oppositional behavior

(Dow, Sonies, Scheib, Moss, and Leonard 1995). Giddan, Ross, Sechler, and Becker (1997) conceptualized SM as a form of unresolved conflict. SM, according to this conceptualization, becomes a way to cope with anger or anxiety or may be used to achieve a goal of punishing the parent(s) or other targeted individual(s). More recently psychodynamic conceptualizations have lost favor as anxiety-related theories have gained popularity (Krysanski, 2003).

Behavioral theorists see SM as a method to manipulate the environment, as a learned behavior which often develops as either an escape from anxiety or as a way of gaining attention from others (Cohan *et al.,* 2006), citing the findings of Labbe and Williamson (1984) that regardless of the cause for the behavior, there is a gain for the child that promotes the continued behavior over time. Behaviorists view the silent behavior of the child as serving a function that is supported and maintained by the environment (Krysanski, 2003). In fact, often parents and educators will negatively reinforce the behavior of the selective mute by speaking for him/her or giving up on requests for the child to speak for himself/herself (Yeganech *et al.,* 2006).

Other indications of SM include those that resemble behavioral inhibition (Shamir-Essakow, Ungerer, Rapee, & Safier, 2004). Behavioral inhibition (BI), is characterized by the predisposition to be irritable as an infant, overly shy and fearful as a toddler, and quiet, cautious, and withdrawn during the primary school years, with marked behavioral restraint and physiological arousal in unfamiliar settings (Shamir-Essakow *et al.,* 2004). Not surprisingly, this is linked to multiple anxiety disorders in middle childhood. Additional signs of BI are the absence of spontaneous smiles and lack of spontaneous speech with unfamiliar individuals (Manassis *et al.,* 2003; Kagan, Reznick, & Snidman, 1988).

Several research studies have reported that neuro-developmental disorders such as speech and language impairments and cognitive delays are also related to SM (Kristensen & Oerbeck, 2006; Manassis *et al.,* 2003). Neurological insult is thought to possibly arise from complications of pregnancy, sleep disorders, motor coordination problems, and eating difficulties (Kristensen, 2002). In addition, some studies have suggested that SM is a result of speech and language impairments, creating communication difficulties that cause anxiety within the child.

More recently, social anxiety inhibitions have been postulated to have a link with SM (Cunningham, McHolm, & Boyle, 2006). The Harvard Mental Health Letter (2004) stated that SM is characterized as a distinct disorder in the American Psychiatric Association's diagnostic manual, but many experts regard this condition as a rare symptom of a social anxiety disorder. Emerging case reports have concurred that there may be a relationship between social phobias and SM (Kristensen, 2000; Vecchio & Kearny, 2005. There is a high prevalence of children with SM that also meet the diagnostic criteria for social phobia or social anxiety disorder according to a compilation of research done by Cunningham, McHolm, and Boyle (2006). According to Dunaway (2005), common signs that often manifest in small children with SM include:

- Extreme shyness,
- Separation anxiety,
- Tantrums,
- Moodiness, and
- Often a severely inhibited temperament.

Interestingly, Dunaway (2006) also proposes that the threshold of excitability is dramatically decreased in those with SM. This decreased threshold sets off a series of defensive reactions to protect the individual. In a child with SM, daily social interactions instigate that extreme protective response.

Several psychopharmacological treatments have been used in the treatment of children with SM using the social anxiety model (Standart & LeCouteur, 2003). According to Schwartz and Shipon-Blum (2005) Fluoxetine (Prozac™) has shown efficacy for treating individuals with SM that experience social anxiety. Seventy percent of children with SM respond rapidly to such drugs, experiencing a reduction in anxiety that facilitates nonverbal and verbal communication and socialization (Schwartz & Shipon-Blum; Black & Uhde, 1994). Wright and colleagues (1995), Lake and colleagues (2000), and Velosa and Riddle (2000), found that other serotonin uptake inhibitors and monoamine oxidase inhibitors had also been effective in treating children with SM, although mild to severe side effects had been noted. These studies suggest efficacy for pharmacological treatment, although several studies cautioned that children may experience shyness and social anxiety into adulthood even with the use of medication (*e.g.*, Standart & LeCouteur, 2003).

With a diversity of symptoms and a competing number of theories as to their causes, theoretical perspectives often facilitate intervention selection. Some in the psychiatric community believe that low doses of anxiety medications are effective in the treatment of SM while others prefer psychodynamic treatments behavioral and cognitive therapy, parent-based practices, family therapy interventions, or other multi-modal approaches.

INTERVENTION OPTIONS PSYCHODYNAMIC

Psychodynamic treatments were the first to be used in the treatment of SM and are still being used today (Krysanski, 2003). For young children, this practice involves play and art therapy (Cohan *et al.*, 2006). The goal of these psychodynamic interventions is to allow the child to express his or her inner conflicts. The purpose is to understand the meaning of the child's mutism and the origins it has in the child's unconscious, rendering the need for silence obsolete. According to Cohan and colleagues, the outcomes of this type of therapy are unclear, principally because no experimental controls were in place in the case examples, making strong inferences about generalizing treatment effectiveness impossible. A similar criticism that Krysanksi advanced for this treatment approach was related to the limited research available and, as a result, also cautioned against generalizations being made that treatments from this perspective could be deemed effective.

TALK THERAPY

Counseling goals include changing the perceptions surrounding communication that negatively reinforce the child's self-concept as one who can't speak (Dunaway, 2005), encouraged ancillary parent and teacher roles (after they were trained) to:

- Aid the child in identifying negative beliefs,
- Encouraging new ways of thinking through action plans and scripted role-play, and
- Make necessary modifications that will create relaxed opportunities in which the child is encouraged to speak.

Krysanski (2003) noted that this type of therapy is normally quite lengthy and the research results endorsing this course of action were supported by limited supportive evidence, stressing that it is unknown if the practice is truly effective or if time eases the problem.

BEHAVIORAL TECHNIQUES

Systematic desensitization therapy involves practicing audible words in a comfortable setting and slowly affording opportunities for the child to speak in more anxiety-provoking settings, (Cohan *et al.,* 2006), or similarly to bring another person(s) into a controlled environment where the child is already comfortable speaking audibly. Stimulus fading is a technique involving the gradual increase in the number of people and places in which speech is rewarded (Grover *et al.,* 2006). Once the child becomes comfortable with these techniques in a controlled environment, they are generalized to the classroom and outside settings (Grover, 2006; Cohan *et al.,* 2006). Although these are several research-based practices that have been reported effective in a limited body of existing evidence, most therapists from this school of thought agree that using one behavioral technique is insufficient. Rather, multi-method approaches are supported by current literature (Krysanski, 2003).

GENERAL SUPPORTIVE STRATEGIES

Parent-based practices involve positive reinforcement of desired behavior in different settings (Kearney & Vecchio, 2007). Educators can play an important role in aiding parents and reciprocal assistance, depending on knowledge regarding SM. Grover and colleagues agreed, stressing the importance of including input from adults knowledgeable about the child when designing and implementing reinforcement systems.

The goal is to help the child feel comfortable enough to speak in new and different environments. Emphasizing this point, Kearney and Vecchio (2007) cautioned that a child should never be "shamed" or punished for not speaking; alternatively, a token economy or reward system should be developed and used to shape the desired behavior through rewards.

FAMILY SYSTEMS

Although not as popular, the premise of the family systems approach is one in which the family is viewed as an interactive unit where each individual seeks to get his or her needs met through family members (Cohan *et al.,* 2006). It is believed that the mutism serves as a way of getting those needs met. This approach focuses on identifying faulty family relationships or communication patterns that have caused or maintained the mutism. The family meets with the therapist in order to promote more positive and constructive family functioning, eliminating the conditions that promote the undesired behavior.

MULTIMODAL

The treatment of symptoms associated with SM must focus on the context under which the behaviors exist, the severity of the mutism, and the duration of symptomatology of the disorder. Multi-modal approaches, therefore, combine methods from psychodynamic, cognitive, behavioral, speech/language, and family therapy interventions to improve the symptoms associated with SM. Cohan and others (2006) reviewed multi-modal approaches and reported efficacy in a limited number of studies. Moldan (2005) combined stimulus fading, play therapy, parent training, and socialization to address the internal anxiety that children feel. Krohn, Weckstein, and Wright (1992) combined family involvement and empathic dynamic psychotherapy with response initiation procedures based on escape-avoidance principles. Promising results have been documented using contingency management with positive reinforcement. This involves receiving positive rewards for verbalizations, and not reinforcing pointing or using other non-verbal cues (Moldan).

SCHOOL SETTING

There are many studies combining intervention approaches, but no definitive treatment has received consensus or appears to correspond to a comprehensive theoretical framework such that it is universally endorsed by the mental health fields. Krundwell (2006), however, has highlighted five key elements of intervention with a child showing signs of SM in the academic setting.

- First, involve individuals with whom the child speaks outside of the school setting and invite them for conversational visits during the school day.

- Second, as the child becomes more comfortable, transfer the conversational visits to new locations, peers, and activities.

- Third, develop a reward system to motivate the child which involves a hierarchy to encourage movement to the next step.

- Fourth, focus on increasing opportunities for the child to interact and involve peers in conversation.

- Finally, monitor and evaluate the interventions.

The importance of parental involvement and support in the design and implementation of positive behavior interventions has repeatedly been stressed in research (Grover, Hughes, Bergman, & Kingery, 2006; Omdal, 2008). The information provided by the parents is often pivotal in determining the type of strategies that are opt to be most successful. Parent-based practices must be in alignment with the ultimate goal of generalizing speech through positive means. Requiring the child to speak or speaking for the child can actually reinforce the undesired behavior, negating the intention of the treatment process (Kearney & Vecchio, 2007). Collaboration between parent, teacher, and other individuals involved in the intervention should not cease when the child begins to speak. According to McHolm, Cunningham, and Vanier (2005) progress may be slow, but small steps often lead to success.

Can You Hear Me Now? Increasing Audibility of Vocalizations in a Fourth-Grade Student with Selective Mutism

Case Example: Parents, school personnel, and an autonomous therapist were all involved in the current case study involving a fourth-grade student diagnosed with

SM. The purpose of this section is to report on the implementation an effective intervention commensurate with school mental health promotion practices in an attempt to reduce symptomology and improve school functioning.

METHODS

Participant and Setting: This study involved one student that had been independently diagnosed with extreme anxiety and SM, showing significant behavioral changes with an inability to speak and function within the school environment. "Evan" was a ten-year-old student in the fourth grade. Although parent interviews signified that Evan was soft-spoken, no indication of total silence or academic difficulty had been noted prior to the end of third grade.

At three-years-old, Evan's parents divorced and Evan has since shared time between two home environments. He stays with mom, stepdad, and older brother for one week, and then travels 30 minutes away to spend a week with dad, stepmom, brother, and baby stepsister. No changes had been made to this arrangement immediately prior to intervention. Although Evan currently conversed with family members in the home environment, parents disclosed that they were observing similar symptoms to those reported in school when he was asked to complete homework and other school assignments.

Through third grade, Evan had satisfactory grades and met or exceeded in all areas of district and state testing. Toward the end of third grade, the teacher noticed a withdrawal from participation, but stated that no significant changes in academic functioning occurred. This student attended a writing institute during the summer prior to entering fourth grade and published a writing piece that was of a quality commensurate with his peers. During the first nine weeks of fourth grade, a significant and distinct decline in both academic standing and verbal communication was noted by the general classroom and Inter-related Resource co-teachers. Evan continued to functionally decline to the point of failing all subjects for the academic term.

Parents, administrators, and teachers met to determine the necessary course of action. Parents were asked to complete a parent interview and a parent Behavior Assessment for Children-second edition (BASC) questionnaire (see Reynolds,

2010). It was also requested that the educators complete a teacher BASC. The results suggested that Evan was in the clinically significant range for anxiety and withdrawal with secondary features including depression and attention difficulties.

Administration of the Weschler Intelligence Scale for Children, Fourth Edition, was attempted but discontinued due to Evan's inability to respond. The results were considered to be a severe underestimate of Evan's capabilities.

INTERVENTION PLANNING: FIRST ATTEMPT

Averting the Response to Intervention process, Evan was crisis-assigned special education services with an eligibility of Emotional Behavior Disorder. It was decided that the Interrelated Resource program would serve Evan in a small-group setting for reading, written expression, math, and social studies.

The autonomous therapist suggested that the school initially concentrate on helping Evan communicate rather than focusing on academic achievement. Few assignments were independently attempted by the student over the next several months. Progress reports, along with district and state assessments, confirmed that Evan did not meet passing level expectations in any academic areas. As a result, Evan was retained in the fourth grade.

YEAR TWO

At the beginning of the following year, Evan was placed with the same Resource teacher from the prior year. He preferred using gestures to indicate his desires, but did occasionally whisper answers when required to respond to questions. Work completion started slowly, but Evan completed all classroom assignments and homework. Although his grades had improved, Evan continued to avoid speaking. He acclimated well to the new students in his classroom, often smiled, and silently laughed, although he rarely conversed.

Experimental Design, Behavioral Definition, Measurement, and Inter-observer Agreement: The authors used an ABBC changing criterion design to measure the effectiveness of the intervention on audible vocalizations. The baseline was measured during small-group reading on three separate occasions. Each vocal response to a teacher question or prompt served as the dependent variable. The vocalization was considered audible if the word, sentence, or paragraph could be clearly understood from a distance of approximately seven feet while Evan's side was to the observer. The observer recorded the first 40 responses given by both a control student and Evan. Responses did not have to be accurate to be recorded; they just needed to be audible. If the initial vocalization was inaudible to the teacher, who was facing Evan and less than three feet away, further instructions were provided and Evan was given another opportunity to respond in an audible voice.

Data were collected by three speech and language pathologists who were skilled in completing direct observations. The observers collected data during a 25 minute reading segment, with two of the three segments lasting almost 30 minutes. These observations occurred every other day for three days. Inter-observer agreement could not be calculated, as only one teacher was collecting data during each segment. The normal classroom operations and location of reading groups would have been compromised had the teacher of record collected data, alerting Evan that he was being observed.

On each occasion, a small-group phonics lesson was reviewed, with Evan and selected control students taking turns responding to questions. The two students then took turns reading an individual paragraph from a chapter book. On each of the three observations, of the first forty responses, Evan spoke an audible vocalization two times, nine times, and seven times respectively. The control was heard thirty-seven times, thirty-nine times, and forty times. During a regular classroom segment, Evan would not be heard from a distance of seven feet without asking several times to repeat himself.

Intervention Development: Results from past functional behavior analyses and direct observations provided evidence that the function of behavior (SM) was to avoid school work and attention from peers and teacher. Although Evan was whispering and speaking softly and academic performance had significantly improved from the prior year, intervention modifications were necessary to help him increase audible vocalizations.

A positive reward system already existed within the Resource classroom environment. It had proven to be a very effective behavior management system in which students earned school dollars for desired behaviors such as classroom participation and work completion (Boniecki & Moore, 2003). Evan was quite successful at earning points and enjoyed shopping with the money he accumulated. With this in mind, the teacher and Evan discussed the possibility of earning additional dollars he could bank for purchasing a desired item contingent on increasing the volume of audible responses—creating a contingency management plan.

Evan's contingency management plan was combined with positive reinforcement and planned ignoring. A reward dollar was earned each time Evan reached a predetermined rate based on the criteria that was set. The rules required that the volume and clarity of Evan's vocalizations be heard from a distance of approximately seven feet. It was also agreed upon that gestures were no longer a means of communication. Each gesture was ignored until Evan verbally requested the desired item or activity.

Intervention Evaluation Procedures: Baseline data was collected under normal instructional circumstances with the exception of slightly extended the reading group segment, which lasted approximately five minutes longer than usual. This afforded the teacher the opportunity to ask a sufficient number of questions for the observers to gather enough data. The results were reviewed and the intervention was implemented the following week during two segments in the Resource setting.

A changing criterion design was used, the goal being to gradually increase the number of audible vocalizations that Evan was required to attempt during the intervention phase. Baseline data indicated that Evan had a mean vocalization rate of six out of forty responses. After a discussion with the student, the teacher set a goal of four audible vocalizations per segment, making the daily goal eight audible vocalizations as the first performance criterion. Evan's voice had to be heard from at least seven feet away and would only be counted as an audible vocalization if he was heard without being asked to repeat his response. This initial criterion was set for a two-week period. The second criterion raised the number of responses to six per segment. This criterion was also set for a period of two weeks.

RESULTS

Fig. **1** shows the data collected during baseline and the intervention phases.
During baseline, a mean of six responses out of forty attempts was recorded. He met the criterion of four responses per reading and social studies segment on each day during the two-week period of intervention 1. The mean response rose from a baseline of six to 9.7 responses during the first intervention. Throughout intervention 2, Evan was able to maintain the minimum six responses per segment and often exceeded the goal that had been set, rising to a mean of 14.8 responses.

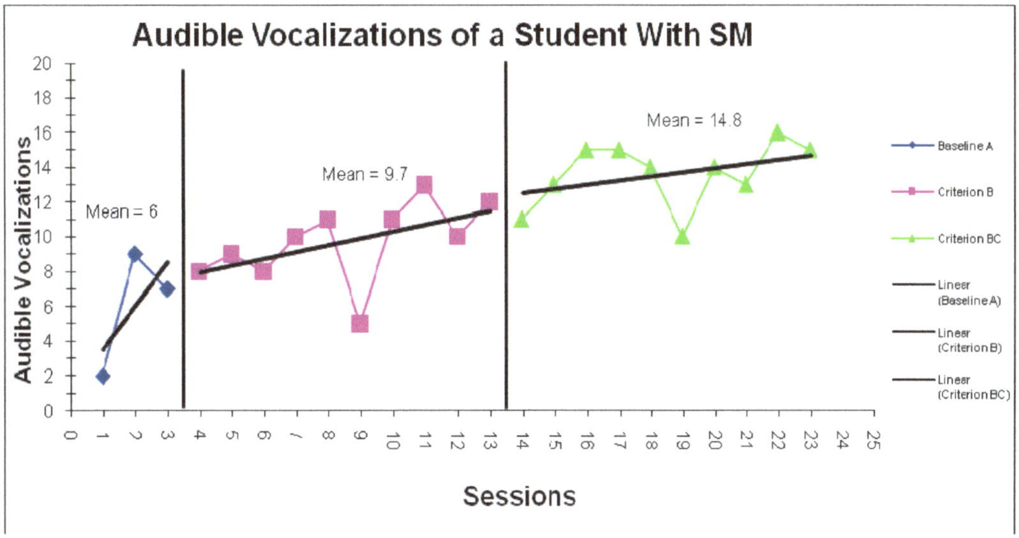

Figure 1: Audible Vocalizations of a Student with Selective Mutism.

DISCUSSION

There were several factors that may have fostered maintenance of SM prior to the intervention phase for several reasons. First, the teacher had grown so accustomed to straining to hear Evan that her assumption was that he was performing at optimal level. Academic improvement from last year to this year was significant, fostering in the teacher a fear of putting undue pressure on Evan lest his success be derailed because past experience had shown that Evan would completely shut-down when stressed. Lastly, other students would conjecture Evan's needs and ask questions or make statements on his behalf, accommodating the non-vocal environment in which he felt comfortable.

During the student interview done prior to intervention, Evan disclosed that he had always been quiet but that he was willing to try and improve the audibility of his vocalizations as long as he was not expected to speak in the general education setting. Since he had input in the treatment plan, he was able to discuss what he thought were reasonable goals, contributing to a situation in which he had control over exposure to anxiety-provoking situations. He could, therefore, influence the pace of exposure to his fear. As a result, Evan not only met achieved the set criterion but exceeded them during each day of the intervention phase.

Mondays still continued to be troublesome for Evan, possibly due to fatigue. His father admitted that Evan's schedule was altered on the weeks spent with him, and this appeared to affect global participation. Up until the intervention phase, Evan would revert to symptoms similar to the extremes witnessed during the 3rd grade year. Once reminded that he was working for a reward, Evan would attempt to respond more audibly.

Due to ethical considerations, there was no attempt to return to baseline. Evan's ability to communicate improved, not only with his teacher, but also his peers and at home. To risk reducing gains by returning to baseline could have compromised the success and confidence that the student had gained prior to and during the intervention phases.

CONCLUSION

The discerning reader may have already identified the false dichotomy suggested by juxtaposing the case example above with the earlier suggestion that treatment and mental health promotion are separate, mutually exclusive options. The case involves practices corresponding with mental health promotion strategies and treatment components. In fact, a good continuum of care focused on optimizing student outcomes based on individual needs serves student and societal best interests. Regardless of the level of prevention programming implemented, human physiological and behavioral complexity will ensure that some diagnosable mental health conditions will emerge nonetheless.

We do not know the answer of many questions related to the case example. We do not know if more aggressive mental health promotion may have dissuaded Evan from his developmental progression toward symptomology. We do not know how treatment was being administered during the 3rd grade year, though some intervention was attempted. We do not know with certainty that the intervention reported in the case reported above was a causative factor in symptom reduction. If it was, we do not know what role, if any, which components commensurate with mental health promotion impacted his progress.

Actually, we know some answers. We know that Evan had symptoms of SM that occurred for a long time without symptom remediation. We know that previous attempts at intervention had not succeeded. We know that the school system made a significant investment in this young man, involving parents, teachers, administrators, an independent therapist, speech therapists, and an occupational therapist in the intervention. We know that, whatever combination of variables was actually curative, Evan *did* get better.

Less worthy of immodesty, we *suspect* some answers as well. Prior documentation reported that Even would 'shut down when stressed'. We suspect if his classroom support had been highly prescriptive, less inclusive of his input, or addressed by means of rigid enforcement of classroom management policies enforced through coercion, a high rate of 'shutting down' would have been the likely response. We suspect that the supportiveness described during the intervention process served as a more therapeutic example for Evan's classmates, who imitated the supportive models the adults presented themselves to be. Often, coercive approaches to behavior management models from adults precede coercion and ostracism from students. We also suspect, though admit extrapolation, that mental health promotional techniques applied while prodromal or immediately upon observation that he was withdrawing from a previous level of social and academic interaction *could* have ameliorated or even prevented the manifest condition.

The school environment is amenable to the endeavor of mental health promotion, and a large and expanding body of knowledge informs many practices that facilitate the goal. Evidence such as the case example above suggests that the classroom may also serve as a focal point of effective intervention for manifest mental health conditions as well. The two pursuits complement each other rather than compete for prominence. Success in both efforts requires access to the resources, expertise, stamina, and sensitivity too purposefully program for optimal student outcomes and opportunities.

This chapter started with the false suggestion that mental health promotion or treatment were options to select. In fact, they are part of a continuum of care that greatly increases the likelihood of desirable mental health, functional, and quality of life outcomes. If truly confronted with the authority and responsibility to choose one option for your school, there are complicated algorithms that may assist you in doing a cost-benefit analysis. Perhaps a simpler and better method than reverting to mathematical modeling is to ask one question, "How much is not spending an extra year in the 4th grade worth?"

ACKNOWLEDGEMENT

Declare none.

CONFLICT OF INTEREST

The author(s) confirm that this chapter content has no conflict of interest.

REFERENCES

Allison, S, Roeger, L, & Abbot, D. (2008). Overcoming barriers in referral from schools to mental health services. *Child and Adolescent Psychiatry, 16*(1), 44-47.

American Psychiatric Association (1994). *Diagnostic and statistical manual of mental disorders (4th ed. Rev.).* Washington, DC: Author.

American School Counselor Association. (2011). Accessed 4Jan11 from www. schoolcounselor.org

Board, J. (2008). *Guidance and school counseling - a brief history of school guidance and counseling in the united states.* Retrieved from Guidance and School Counseling - A Brief History of School Guidance and Counseling in the United States.

Bergman, R. L., Piacentini, J., & McCracken, J. T. (2002). Prevalence and description of selective mutism in a school-based sample. *Journal of the American Academy of Child and Adolescent Psychiatry, 41 (8),* 938 – 946.

Black B., & Uhde, T. (1995). Psychiatric characteristics of children with selective mutism: A pilot study. *Journal of the American Academy of Child and Adolescent Psychiatry, 34 (7),* 847 – 856.

Black B., & Uhde, T. (1994). Treatment of elective mutism with fluoxetine: A double-blind, placebo-controlled study. *Journal of the American Academy of Child and Adolescent Psychiatry, 33 (7),* 1000 – 1007.

Boniecki, K. A., & Moore, S. (2003). Breaking the silence: Using a token economy to reinforce classroom participation. *Teaching of Psychology, 30 (3),* 224 – 227.

Carlson, J. S., Mitchell, A. D., Segool, N. (2008). The current state of empirical support for the pharmacological treatment of selective mutism. *School Psychology Quarterly, 23 (3),* 254 - 372.

Cohan, S. L., Shavira, D. A., & Stein, M. B. (2006). Practitioner review: Psychosocial interventions for children with selective mutism: A critical evaluation of the literature from 1990 – 2005. *Journal of Child Psychology and Psychiatry, 47 (11),* 1085 – 1097.

Cunningham, C. E., McHolm, A. E., & Boyle, M. H. (2006). Social phobia, anxiety, oppositional behavior, social skills, and self-concept in children with specific selective mutism, generalized selective mutism, and community controls. *European Child and Adolescent Psychiatry, 20,* 1-11.

Dahir, C. A. (2004). Supporting a nation of learners: The role of school counseling in educational reform. *Journal of Counseling & Development, 82(3),* 344-353.

Davies, Douglas. (2004). *Child development: a practitioner's guide.* New York: The Guilford Press.

Dorman, S. (1998). Web resources in school mental health services. *Journal of School Health, 68(10),* 447.

Dow, S. P., Sonies, B. C., Scheib, D., Moss, S. E., & Leonard, H. L. Practical guidelines for the assessment and treatment of selective mutism. *Journal of the American Academy of Child and Adolescent Psychiatry, 34(7),* 857-862.

Dummit, S. E., Klein, R. G., Tancer, N. K., Asche, B., Martin, J., & Fairbanks, J. A. (1997). Systematic assessment of 50 children with selective mutism. *Journal of the American Academy of Child and Adolescent Psychiatry, 36 (5),* 653 – 660.

Dunaway, C. (2005). *Using a counseling approach when working with children selective mutism.* Available from: www.selectivemutism.org/articleofthemonth/UsingCounselingApproach.pdf

Elizur, Y. & Perednik, P. (2003). Prevalence and description of selective mutism in immigrant and native families: A controlled study. *Journal of the American Academy of Child and Adolescent Psychiatry, 42 (12),* 1451 – 1459.

Friedrich, A. A., Mendez, L. M., & Mihalas, S. T. (2010). Gender as a factor in school-based mental health service delivery. *School Psychology Review, 39(1),* 122-136.

Giddan, J. J., Ross, G. J., Sechler, L. L., & Becker, B. R. (1997). Selective mutism in elementary school: Multidisciplinary interventions. *Language, Speech, and Hearing Services in the Schools, 28,* 127-133.

Grover, R. L., Hughes, A. A., Bergman, R. L., & Kingery, J. N. (2006). Treatment modifications based on childhood anxiety diagnosis: Demonstrating the flexibility in manualized treatment. *Journal of Psychotherapy: An International Quarterly, 20 (3),* 275 – 286.

Gysbers, N. C. (2004). Comprehensive guidance and counseling programs: the evolution of accountability. *Professional School Counseling, 8(1),* 1-14.

Gysbers, N. C. (2001). School guidance and counseling in the 21st century: Remember the past into the future. *Professional School Counseling, 5,* 75.

Gysbers, N. C., & Henderson, P. (2001). Comprehensive guidance and counseling programs: A rich history and a bright future. *Professional School Counseling, 4,* 246-256.

Hultquist, A. M. (1995). Selective mutism: Causes and interventions. *Journal of Emotional and Behavioral Disorders, 3 (2),* 100 – 108.

Kaakeh, Y., & Stumpf, J. L. (2008). Treatment of selective mutism: Focus on selective serotonin uptake inhibitor. *Pharmacotherapy, 28 (2),* 214 – 224.

Kagan, J., Reznick, J. S., & Snidman, N. (1988). Biological bases of childhood shyness. *Science, 240,* 167-171

Kearney, C. A., & Vecchio, J. L. (2007). When a child won't speak. *The Journal of Family Practice, 56 (11),* 917 -921.

Kearney, C. A., & Vecchio, J. L. (2006). Functional analysis and treatment of selective mutism in children. *The Journal of Speech and Language Pathology, 1 (2),* 141 – 148.

Kristensen, H. (2000). Selective mutism and comorbidity with developmental disorder/delay, anxiety disorder, and elimination disorder. *Journal of the American Academy of Child and Adolescent Psychiatry, 39,* 249-256.

Kristensen, H. (2002). *Selective mutism in children: Comorbidity and clinical characteristics: Dissertation.* Oslo: Faculty of Medicine, University of Oslo.

Kristensen, H., & Oerbeck, B. (2006). Is selective mutism associated with deficits in memory span and visual memory? An exploratory case-control study. *Depression and Anxiety, 23(2),* 71-76.

Kristensen, H., & Torgersen, S. (2001). MCMI-II personality traits and symptom traits in parents of children with selective mutism: A case-control study. *Journal of Abnormal Psychology, 110 (4),* 648 – 652.

Krohn, D, D., Weckstein, S. M., & Wright, H. L. (1992). A study of the effectiveness of a specific treatment for elective mutism. *Journal of the American Academy of Child and Adolescent Psychiatry, 31(4),* 711-718.

Krundwell, R. M. A., (2006). Identifying and teaching children with selective mutism. *Teaching Exceptional Children, 38 (3),* 48 – 54.

Krysanski, V. (2003). A brief review of selective mutism literature. *Journal of Psychology,* 137 (1), 29 – 40.

Kumpulainen, K. (2002). Phenomenology and treatment of selective mutism. *CNS Drugs, 16 (3),* 175 – 180.

Kumpulainen, K., Rasanen, E., Raaska, H., & Somppi, V. (1998). Selective mutism among second-graders in elementary school. *European Child and Adolescent Psychiatry, 7 (1),* 24 – 29.

Labbe, E. E., & Williamson, D. A. (1984). Behavioral treatment of elective mutism: A review of the literature. *Clinical Psychology Review, 4(3),* 273-292.

Lavoritano, J. E., & Segal, P. B. (1992). Evaluating the efficacy of short-term counseling on adolescents in a school setting. *Adolescence, 27(107)*, 535-543.

Manassis, K., Fung, D., Tannock, R., Sloman, L., Fiksenbaum L., & McInnes, A. (2003). Characterizing selective mutism: Is it more than social anxiety? *Depression and Anxiety, 18 (3),* 153 – 161.

Manning, A. R. (2009). Bridging the gap from availability to accessibility: Providing health and mental health services in schools. *Journal of Evidence Based Social Work, 6*, 40-57.

McHolm, A. E., Cunningham, C. E., & Vanier, M. K. (2005). *Helping your child overcome selective mutism or a fear of speaking: A parent's guide.* Oakland, CA: New Harbinger Publications, Inc.

McInnes, A., Fung, D., Manassis, K., Fiksenbaum, L., & Tannock, R. (2004). Narrative skills in children with selective mutism: An exploratory study. *American Journal of Speech-Language Pathology, 13 (4),* 304 – 315.

Moldan, M. B. (2005). Selective mutism and self-regulation. *Clinical Social Work Journal, 33 (3),* 291–307.

Nastasi, R. K., Moore, R. B., & Varjas, K. M. (2003). *School based mental health services: Creating comprehensive and culturally specific programs*. Washington, D. C.: American Psychological Association.

Omdal, H. (2008). Including children with selective mutism in mainstream schools and kindergartens: Problems and possibilities. *International Journal of Inclusive Education, 12 (3),* 301 – 315.

Pionek-Stone, B., Kratochwill, T. R., Sladezcek, I., & Serlin, R. C. (2002). Treatment of selective mutism: A best-evidence synthesis. *School Psychology Quarterly*, *17(2),* 168 – 190.

Reynolds, C. R. (2010). Behavior assessment system for children. *Corsini encyclopedia of psychology.* 1-2.

Richburg, M. L. & Cobia, D. C. (1994). Using behavioral techniques to treat elective mutism: A case study. *Elementary School Guidance & Counseling, 28 (3),* 214 -221.

Rosenhan, D. L. (1973). On being sane in insane places. *Science, 179,* 250-258.

Samuels, C. A. (2007). Schools' role in mental-health care uneven, experts say. *Education Week, 26(35),* 14.

Schallert, L. E. (2005). Lessons learned in developing school-based mental health services. *Behavioral Health Management*, 48-52.

Schimmel, C. (2008). *School counseling a brief historical overview (dissertation summary).* Unpublished manuscript, College of Education and Human Services, Marshall University, Huntington, West Virginia. Retrieved from http://www. marshall.edu/etd/doctors/schimmel-christine-2008-phd.pdf

Schwartz, R. H., & Shipon-Blum, E. (2005). "Shy" child? Don't overlook selective mutism. *Contemporary Pediatrics, 22(7),* 30-53.

Shamir-Esskow, G., Ungerer, J. A., Rapee, R. M., & Safier, R. (2004). Caregiving representations of mothers of behaviorally inhibited and uninhibited preschool children. *Developmental Psychology, 40(6),* 899-910.

Standart, S. & LeCouteur, A. (2003). The quiet child: A literature review of selective mutism. *Child and Adolescent Mental Health, 8 (4),* 154 – 160.

Steinhausen, H. C., Wachter, M., Laimbock, K., & Winkler-Metzke, C. (2006). The long-term outcome study of selective mutism in childhood. *Journal of Child Psychology and Psychiatry*, *47 (7),* 751 - 756.

Vecchio, J. L., & Kearney, C. A. (2005). Selective mutism in children: Comparison to youths with and without anxiety disorders. *Journal of Psychopathology and Behavioral Assessment*, *27 (1),* 31 – 37.

Wright, H. H., Cuccaro, M. L., Leonhardt, T. V., Kendall, D. F., & Anderson, J. H. (1995). Case study: Fluoxetine in the treatment of a preschool child with selective mutism. *Journal of the American Academy of Child and Adolescent Psychiatry*, *34(7),* 857-862.

Yeganeh, R., Beidel, D. C., Turner, S. M. Pina, A. A., & Silverman, W. K. (2006). Clinical distinctions between selective mutism and social phobia: An investigation of childhood psychopathology. *Journal of the American Academy of Child and Adolescent Psychiatry*, *42 (9),* 1069 – 1075.

CHAPTER 2

Increasing School Attendance: The First Step in Promoting Mental Health

Steven G. Little[1,*], Angeleque Akin-Little[2] and Joshua Couperus[3]

[1]School of Education, Massey University, Private Bag 11 222, Palmerston North, 4442, New Zealand; [2]Behavioral Educational and Research Consultants, 68 Nautilus Drive, Gulf Harbour; Auckland, New Zealand and [3]New Zealand Ministry of Education, 1-3 Oxford Street, Palmerston North 4410, PO Box 1154, Palmerston North 4440, New Zealand

Abstract: Among the variety of topics that are keystones for the promotion of mental health in schools, an issue that may go unaddressed-perhaps because it seems so elementary-is this: before student mental health can be supported in school, students must be in school. Evidence of failure to get students in school is seen not only in daily attendance rates, but is reflected in other sources of evidence including the surprisingly low high school graduation rates and in truancy data. Absenteeism is among the most serious threats impacting school success and has been shown to be associated with a variety of factors such as the school environment, home environment, and individual student characteristics. The goal of this chapter is to explicate the influences impacting attendance such that educators can effectively plan for success in this most basic requirement for promoting mental health in schools.

Keywords: Absenteeism, drop out, graduation, school refusers, truancy, school mental health, high school, minorities and school, school attendance, school environment, home environment, IQ and absenteeism, mental health and absenteeism, school refusal, school reorganization, community partnerships.

INTRODUCTION

To paraphrase Yogi Berra, school success is "90 percent showing up; the other half is mental" (Reeve, 2008, p.90). In spite of the attempted humor of the remark, there is no question that a lack of consistent school attendance is a serious concern. Lack of consistent attendance in school is a major barrier to academic achievement which can lead to poor mental health (Goldstein, Little, & Akin-Little, 2003; Gottfried,

***Address correspondence to Steven G. Little:** Private Bag 902 104, Albany 0930, Auckland, New Zealand; Tel: 64 9 414 0800 ext 41595; Email: S.Little@massey.ac.nz

Raymond J. Waller (Ed)

2009). Overall, American students with higher rates of attendance perform better on standardized achievement tests and have lower rates of dropping out of school, are less likely to engage in delinquent or destructive behaviors (Sheldon, 2007), and are more likely to graduate from high school (Gewertz, 2007). To that end, the *No Child Left Behind* legislation (*NCLB*, 2002) included attendance as one of the criteria in a school's evaluation for adequate yearly progress.

There is an extensive literature base addressing the problem of absenteeism dating back over 60 years. Many attempts to increase attendance rates have been successful; however, many of the methodologies used have had notable disadvantages including cost, drainage of faculty resources, difficulty of implementation, or time consumption (DeKalb, 1999; Goldstein *et al.,* 2003; Lamdin, 1996). Interventions for this problem have been community-based (McPartland & Nettles, 1991; Reid & Bailey-Dempsey, 1995), family-based (Copeland, Brown, & Hall, 1974; Volkman, 1996), and school-based (Noonan & Thibeault, 1974), or a combination of all of these (Sheldon, 2007), as well as the use of interventions psychotherapeutic in nature (Enea & Dafiniou, 2009). This chapter reviews the literature on issues surrounding school attendance (*e.g.,* importance of high school graduates, variables related to absenteeism) and the lack thereof. Specific variables influencing absenteeism are discussed. The concluding sections provide a detailed response in attempts to alleviate the problem with the ramifications of failing to respond implicit throughout.

HIGH SCHOOL GRADUATION

Maintaining a high percentage of high school graduates is an important part of a nation's economy (Goldstein *et al.,* 2003). Individuals who fail to graduate from high school can have enduring effects on the economy because they are more likely to be unqualified to perform duties in an increasing technical and service related economy. Nationally, only 78 percent of white students, 56 percent of African American students, and 52 percent of Hispanic students graduate from high school 4 years after they enter 9th grade (Greene, 2009). In New York City, only 9 percent of African American students and around 10 percent of Latino students earn Regents diplomas in 4 years (Gewertz, 2005). Additionally, only 45 percent of African-American male students graduate from high school in 4 years, compared with 70 percent of white male students (Gewertz, 2006). The states with the worst high school graduation rates are Georgia, which graduated only 54 percent of its students in 4 years, Nevada (58 percent), and Florida, Arizona, and the District of Columbia (all 59 percent) (Greene). Additionally, students in predominantly black and Latino *schools* are less likely to earn a *high school diploma* or equivalent (Goldsmith, 2009). Attendance is a major factor in high school graduation success (Pinkus, 2009). When children and youth are in school, they have the opportunity to succeed academically, an opportunity not afforded to them when not in attendance. A study by the Consortium on Chicago School Research indicated that 9th grade grades and attendance are two of the most important indicators of high school graduation (Gewertz, 2007).

***Attendance and Graduation*:** Graduation from high school is accomplished by successfully passing specific classes and, in most states, a state exit exam. In order to do this, students must attend classes to learn the content needed to pass exams and complete assignments. Freshman-year grades and *attendance* were found to be the two most reliable predictors of high school completion and *graduation* in Chicago (Gewertz, 2007). Gewertz also found that freshmen who missed 10 to 14 days of classes per semester had a 40 percent chance of completing *high school* in 4 years compared to 63 percent for those who missed only 5 to 9 days and 87 percent for those who missed fewer than 5 days. These data imply that increasing attendance in school might have a direct relationship to the successful completion of school, resulting high school graduation.

ABSENTEEISM

Absenteeism from school has been labeled a serious public health issue for mental health professionals and educators (Kearney, 2008a). Truancy has been identified as one of the top 10 major problems in American schools, and rates of absenteeism have reached as high as 30 percent in some cities. In the largest school district in the United States, New York City, an estimated 150,000 out of 1,000,000 students are absent daily (DeKalb, 1999). Data accumulated over the past 15 years (1995-1996 to 2009-2010) indicate an overall attendance rate of only 88.7 percent of students across all grades (New York City Department of Education, 2010). The problem is even more dramatic when data from high school students are analyzed alone, with an attendance rate of only 82 percent across the same period.

The second largest school district in the United States, Los Angeles Unified School District (LAUSD), reports that on an average day approximately 10 percent of its students are absent and only one half of absences are accompanied with written excuses (DeKalb, 1999). Data from 2004 indicate that the district-wide attendance rate was 93. 49 percent but the high school attendance rate was only 89.9 percent (Baresh, 2004). The third largest school district in the United States, Chicago Public Schools (2010), reports overall attendance rates of 91.2 percent for the 2006-2007 school year with a rate as low as 83.7 percent for 9th graders.

Although school officials are unsure as to the proportion of legitimate verses illegitimate absences, nationwide estimates have ranged from 1 percent to 22 percent for illegitimate absences (Guevermont, 1986). These data may actually underestimate non-illness related absences due to the large margin of error likely to be found in self-report data of this nature. It is quite possible that the proportion of illegitimate absences has changed since these data were reported; however, no recent estimates are available. Additionally, the proportion of illegitimate absences may vary substantially among school districts in different parts of the country.

Based on norms for adults in the workplace, DeLeonibus (1978) estimated an attendance rate of 96 percent as an adequate rate; a rate most schools fail to attain (Goldstein *et al.,* 2003). For example, on a day selected at random in June 2010, data indicated only 90 of more than 1600 schools in New York City met the criteria set by DeLeonibus, a rate of approximately 5 percent (New York City Department of Education, 2010). Attendance rates from other parts of the country may differ, and it is possible that DeLeonibus' criterion is too stringent an expectation for school children. Still, even taking these things into consideration, it is apparent that lack of attendance at the largest school districts in the country is a problem which can have many negative consequences.

Students with lower rates of attendance may not do as well in academic areas such as grades and standardized tests. Researchers have consistently found grades, achievement tests, and standardized tests to be positively correlated with individual attendance records. Lamdin (1996) compared attendance rates with California Achievement Test scores, reading grade level scores, and math grade level scores. Even while holding teacher/pupil ratio and socioeconomic status constant, attendance rates were positively correlated with all three scores.

Other consequences of poor attendance can be far reaching (Wilkins, 2008). Children who have high rates of absenteeism are more likely to drop out of school before completing high school (see discussion above) (DeRosier, Kupersmidt, & Patterson, 1994; Gerics & Westheimer, 1988; Gerwitz, 2006, 2007). Given the relationship between academic attainment and monetary income (US Census Bureau, 2010), chronic absences from school may eventually lead to less or lower level employment and the inability to sustain oneself or his/her family as they enter young adulthood. Absenteeism has also been found to be a predictor of future criminality, alcoholism, and occupational difficulty (Kearney, 2008b).

A survey of school administrators (Neill, 1979) indicated a concern about potential effects on their schools from high degrees of truancy. Absenteeism was seen as contributing to the overall lowering of academic standards of a school. Administrators were concerned about the extra time teachers needed to spend working with students who were absent. Administrators felt high degrees of absenteeism lead teachers to become frustrated, and morale problems are more likely to be experienced when this occurs. Another concern was that high rates of absenteeism could have a negative effect on the school's relationship with the community as a whole, as the school institution may ultimately be viewed as burdensome rather than as a resource to assist children and adolescents in becoming educated and responsible adults. Overwhelmingly, administrators (95 percent) believed that truancy was a major problem in their school districts. Although these data are over 30 years old, they are used as these are the only data from administrators found on this important issue. Anecdotal report alone would suggest that today's school administrators have these same sorts of concerns and at the same levels.

Clearly, as indicated from the administrators' responses above, school absenteeism has been a persistent problem for educators and society for years. The long term consequences can be substantial, and decades of research have been dedicated to understanding the etiology of absenteeism (Goldstein *et al.*, 2003). Understanding the etiology is essential for planning effective intervention for low attendance rates.

MEDIATING FACTORS

School absenteeism appears to be related to a number of diverse factors. Studies have suggested that factors from three major domains contribute to higher rates of absenteeism (Goldstein *et al.,* 2003): School related variables, family environment, and personal characteristics of the student.

School Environment: A number of studies have examined elements specifically related to schools. Eaton (1979), for example, found relationships between teachers and students as the most significant factor related to absenteeism. Other studies have supported this notion, suggesting that conflict in teacher/student relationships contributes to absenteeism (Bealing, 1990; Harte, 1994). Corville-Smith, Ryna, Adams, and Dalicandro (1998) found evidence that student's negative perceptions of school and school personnel may be a predictor of future absenteeism. Pasternicki, Wakefield, Robertson, and Edwards (1993) found that *truancy* was influenced by a combination of class management, lesson content, and physical facilities. Noaks and Noaks (2000) discuss attempts to avoid victimization from bullies as an additional factor in absenteeism. The Illinois State Board of Education (2010) lists nine school factors that are related to absenteeism. They are:

a) Uninteresting and irrelevant curriculum;

b) Improper class placement (above or below abilities);

c) Failure to identify and provide services for problem students;

d) Poor pupil-teacher relationships;

e) Insufficient counseling and guidance staff;

f) High student/teacher ratio;

g) Low teacher expectations;

h) Lack of parent - school communication and involvement; and

i) Too weak, or too rigid administration of policies.

Home Environment: Neilson and Gerber (1979) also found factors related to students' home environments that may have contributed to their absenteeism.

They found that truants had a number of family-related psychosocial stressors. For example, 41 percent had a family member with a serious illness; 40 percent had experienced the divorce or separation of their parents; 40 percent had moved within the past 2 years; 38 percent had unemployed parents; 27 percent were from single-parent families; and alcoholism was present in 19 percent of families in the sample. Only 35 percent of the truants ate regularly with their family, and 57 percent had at least one parent who did not graduate from high school. It did not appear to the authors, however, that parents were directly encouraging truancy, as 90 percent of the parents reported anger about their children's truancy.

Other studies have examined factors related to students' home environments, as well. For example, Hunt and Hopko (2009) found that having a less educated mother as well as disruption to the home environment as leading causes of absenteeism in their sample from the Appalachian south. York and Kearney (1993) found greater levels of family conflict in families of school avoiders compared to normative controls. Additionally, Corville-Smith and others (1998) found that absentee subjects were more likely to perceive parental discipline as lax or inconsistent, were more likely to perceive stronger attempts by parents at control, and were more likely to experience family conflict than students with regular attendance. Finally, the Illinois State Board of Education (2010) lists nine home factors that are related to absenteeism:

a) Parents lack appreciation for value of education;

b) Parents are high-school dropouts;

c) Financial difficulties (lack of adequate nutrition, clothing, transportation; inability to pay fees);

d) Ineffective parenting; lack of parental control and supervision;

e) Familial instability (one-parent household, parental discord, poor parent-child relationship, frequent moving);

f) Inappropriate role models;

g) Child abuse and/or neglect (physical, psychological, sexual);

h) Substance abuse; alcoholic parent; and

i) Parental convenience (older sibling kept home to babysit for young children).

Individual Characteristics: A number of child related factors appear to be associated with truancy, as well. As far back as 1963,Greene found correlations between IQ, grades, and absenteeism. Children with lower IQs tended to have higher rates of absenteeism, and children with lower grades also had higher rates of absenteeism. Other researchers have found that children who have lower degrees of social competence in their relationships with peers also have higher rates of absenteeism (Corville-Smith *et al.,* 1998; Eaton, 1979; Reid, 1984; Southworth, 1992). DeRosier and colleagues (1994) found that rejected peers tend to have more externalizing behavior problems, more teacher-rated internalizing problems, and higher degrees of absenteeism. Students with lower self-esteem and poorer academic self-concept have also been found to have higher absenteeism rates (Corville-Smith *et al.,* 1998; Southworth, 1992) as have children who are overweight (Grier *et al.,* 2007). Research has also shown that truants are more likely than nontruants to have higher levels of anxiety (Reid; Southworth) and substance abuse (Enberg & Morral, 2006). The Illinois State Board of Education (2010) lists 17 student factors that are related to absenteeism:

a) Poor self-concept; low self-esteem;

b) Low academics; particularly in reading and math;

c) Socially isolated; poor inter-personal skills; lack of positive peer relationships at school;

d) Feeling of not belonging at school, of being different;

e) Feeling of lack of control over life (*i.e.,* "No matter how hard I try I will not succeed.");

f) Little or no extra-curricular involvement;

g) Mental and/or emotional instability; childhood depression;

h) Unidentified learning disabilities;

i) Vision and/or auditory problems that have gone undiagnosed;

j) Language barriers;

k) Poor health;

l) Negative peer relationships and older, non-school oriented, friends;

m) Substance abuse;

n) Fear of school, teachers, and/or administrators;

o) Experienced recent traumatic event (divorce, death of a loved one);

p) Fear of physical protection going to or at school; and

q) Teenage pregnancy and/or parenting.

Overall, the literature concerned with the etiology of absenteeism suggests that the factors associated with absenteeism are heterogeneous in nature but, in many respects, related. In as many as 17 of the factors related to absenteeism indicated above, mental health issues such as school refusal, a specific anxiety disorder, and antisocial behavioral issues (*e.g.,* conduct disorder) are often implicated.

MENTAL HEALTH AND ABSENTEEISM

Dube and Orpinas (2009) state that in order to improve rates of school absenteeism due to school refusal and avoid negative associated factors we must first understand the rationale for the behavior. The authors discuss two major functions of school refusal:

- Avoidance in which avoiding aversive elements of school provides negative reinforcement and

- Positive reinforcement in which the student attains parental attention or other positive benefit from avoiding school.

This behavioral explanation of school refusal also provides an overall framework to understand the reasons behind school absenteeism and proffers a structure to understand behavior patterns that may persist into adulthood. For example, if a child discovers the easiest way to provide an immediate positive outcome is to avoid tasks or activities that he or she finds unpleasant, they may continue this in their personal and vocational activities into adulthood.

Guevermont (1986) distinguished between chronic school absence based on antisocial and delinquent activity from those with an affective basis (*e.g.,*anxiety or depression) without coexisting antisocial behavior. Guevermont termed the former definition "truancy" and the latter definition "school refusal". This discrimination has been widely used by researchers exploring absenteeism (Berg *et al.,* 1993; Guevermont, 1986; Huffington & Sevitt, 1989; Mattison, 2000; Neilson & Gerber, 1979). Using the behavioral framework discussed above, truants would be those who missed school for primarily the positive reinforcement attained in non-school related activities while school refusers would be those whose behavior is influenced more by negative reinforcement.

From a legal perspective, a persistent and unjustifiable pattern of absence from school is referred to as truancy. In contrast to truants who are likely to spend time away from school with peers, school refusers were more likely to stay home when absent (Dube & Orpinas, 2009). Swimmer (2008) identified anxiety, depression, and physical complaints as factors that interfered with school attendance. These students typically valued high grades and appropriate classroom behavior (Neilson & Gerber, 1979). They were more often satisfied with teachers, had parents who were aware of their absences, and engaged in little antisocial behavior. Their fear was generally associated with a specific circumstance at school, or was related to separation anxiety from their primary caregiver.

Berg and colleagues (1993) found that of the 80 frequently absent students in their sample, 32 percent had a *DSM-III-R* diagnosis of disruptive behavior disorders (including oppositional defiant disorder and conduct disorder). Additionally, 17 percent of their sample had been diagnosed with a mood/anxiety disorder. Although a little over 50 percent of this sample had no psychological diagnosis, the data still indicate the utility of addressing mental health concerns in interventions designed to increase attendance.

INTERVENTIONS

In a review of truancy interventions from 1990 to 2007, Sutphen, Ford, and Flarerty (2010) assessed 16 studies and concluded that, because of methodological shortcomings, inconsistent definitions and lack of replication, there is a need for more and better research with regard to the efficacy of truancy interventions. They did, however, identify interventions that they termed "useful and promising". These interventions included:

- Contingency management,
- School reorganization,
- Community partnerships, and
- Family-oriented activities.

The problem of absenteeism has been addressed using a variety of intervention techniques based primarily on likely contributing factors. Attempts have been made to implement programs based on school, family, and community partnerships (Sheldon, 2007; Volkmann, 1996), to use psychotherapeutic techniques (Enea & Dafiniou, 2009; Newsome, 2004; Shechtman, 1993), and individual incentives such as money (Reid & Bailey-Dempsey, 1995), exemption from semester exams (Sturgeon, 1990), and qualifying for a special party (Barber & Kagey, 1977). A number of interventions have been directed specifically towards truants with behavior problems, and others have been focused on anxiety-based school refusers (Goldstein *et al.,* 2003). Although many successful interventions have been implemented, the majority have had notable disadvantages in terms of cost, complexity, time consumption, drainage of faculty resources, or level of overall improvement (Sutphen *et al.,* 2010).

Kearney (2008b) proposes a comprehensive interdisciplinary model of school absenteeism. He describes four criteria that must be incorporated into any successful model of absenteeism:

a) The use of common terminology and definitions,

b) Comprehensiveness,

c) Fluidity and flexibility, and

d) "User friendliness" for assessment and treatment.

Of particular importance is the emphasis on a multi-axial assessment approach. Instead of the current approach in which assessors emphasize a particular set of variables depending on their perspective on the problem, his recommended approach covers all aspects of the individual child's case (*e.g.,* child, parent, family, peer, community factors). If one identifies key factors for each specific child, then it would increase the likelihood of developing an efficacious approach for that given child.

He further proposed five levels of intervention. At the *primary level* of absenteeism, the causes are limited to the child. Intervention at this level could be psychotherapeutic to attempt to alleviate anxiety or depression; behavioral (*e.g.,* operant techniques, gradual reintegration); education, and/or parent-school cooperation. The *secondary level* involves parent and/or family variables as well as those focused on the child. Interventions at this level would involve an increased role for the parents, conflict resolution, peer mentors, and/or increased supervision in addition to the primary level intervention previously mentioned. The *tertiary level* adds peer factors to the mix. Interventions at this level include primary and secondary strategies as well as increased therapist-school collaboration, an Individual Education Plan (IEP) or 504 plan, and enhanced coordination of services. The *quaternary level* includes school-based factors such as a poor school climate. In addition to primary, secondary, and tertiary interventions this level adds an increased emphasis on the child's educational and safety needs which may include systemic interventions aimed at problems within the school. Finally, at the *quinary level*, in addition to all the issues identified at the other levels, severe community factors contribute to extensive absenteeism at the school. Interventions at this level add intensive home and community-based interventions.

A community based approach, project RAISE (Raising Ambition Instills Self-Esteem), was evaluated by McPartl and Nettles (1991). This intervention focused on students at risk for dropping out and began with sixth grade students and continued through high school. The program assigned volunteers within the community to at-risk students to provide after school tutoring as well as conflict resolution. Results indicated that attendance rates and English grades improved, however, no differences in grade retention or standardized test scores were observed. Unfortunately only one study on this program is reported in the professional literature and the cost, over 2 million dollars for only 420 students over a 7 year period, leads to questions of the overall utility of the program.

Sheldon (2007) compared schools utilizing a school-wide program of school, family, and community partnerships with similar control schools on student attendance. Believing that family and community involvement is an important component when considering absenteeism, they recognized that efforts to improve family and community involvement in school often tend to be uncoordinated and based more on "trial and error" than as part of an organized strategy. To this end the authors examined whether the implementation of the National Network of Partnership Schools (NNPS) program, which involved organized action teams and planned community and parent involvement, reduced absenteeism in schools. NNPS member schools all receive "tools and guidelines for establishing, maintaining, and improving school-wide partnership programs that reach out to the families of all students" (p. 268). Schools implementing NNPS during the 2000-2001 school years were compared with a matched sample of schools not implementing the program (both samples were in Ohio). Results indicated that schools who implemented the program showed an improvement in attendance rates of .5 percent, while schools not implementing the system showed a slight decline in attendance rates. Sheldon concluded that the schools that had strong implementation of the NNPS program and which actively sought to reach out to parents and remove barriers to attendance were more likely to experience an increase in student attendance; however, the magnitude of improvement was relatively small. While the results suggested that length of time the school had implemented the program was not an important variable (treatment integrity was) little discussion involved cost in time and money to implement the program.

Other community and school related approaches have been somewhat less costly, and similarly effective. Reid and Bailey-Dempsey (1995) evaluated a program called PAY, which used monetary incentive contracts. Although there was concern that monetary incentives might undermine intrinsic motivation (see Akin-Little & Little, 2009 for a complete discussion of this issue), the incentive was viewed as analogous to earning wages for going to a job. Results indicated that the program had a modest positive effect on grades and a larger effect on improving attendance. While not in the professional literature, monetary incentives have been found to be successful in improving attendance in improving school attendance for girls in rural areas of Yemen (UN Office for the Coordination of Humanitarian Affairs, 2010) and have been used in various school districts in the United States such as Washington DC and Chelsea, Massachusetts.

Volkman (1996) used a very simple intervention that involved sending invitations to parents to attend school with their child for 1 hour, 1 day per month. Results indicated significant improvement in attendance. This method was neither costly nor time consuming, however, it was noted that having a parent in the classroom may become disruptive to the educational process and some children may feel excluded if their parents are not available to attend the class.

A classic study by Copeland, Brown, and Hall (1974) utilized a school-based behavioral approach. They found that when the school principal called the parents of three chronically absent kindergarten and first grade students to praise them for having their children come to school, the students' attendance improved. The researchers conducted a second experiment and found that when the principal praised the students in the classroom each day for coming to school, attendance improved dramatically. These findings have the advantage of simplicity and cost-effectiveness.

Volkman and Bye (2006) investigated the impact on attendance of pairing elementary school students with adult volunteer reading partners. They hypothesized that by improving reading proficiency, a vital skill for academic achievement, there may be a positive influence on reducing absenteeism as well as improving academic achievement. While results indicated no significant changes in total attendance, students were more likely to attend school on the days when they were scheduled to meet with their adult reading partner. Unfortunately the results on reading proficiency were equivocal. While children in the third grade showed improvement, there was a slight decrease in scores for students in the fifth grade. Volkman and Bye concluded that one step in improving attendance rates in schools could involve a positive mentoring system but the results are by no means definitive.

McCluskey, Bynum, and Patchin (2004) assessed a small component of the U. S. Department of Justice's (2004) "Weed and Seed" program aimed at improving attendance in elementary schools with chronic absenteeism issues. The parents of children who had been absent more than 20 percent of the school term were sent a letter that detailed the number of days the child was absent from school, the importance of attending school, and informed the parents of the state laws regarding school attendance. After two weeks, if improvements were noted a congratulatory letter was sent. If no improvements were noted then a series of steps were taken, beginning with involvement of mental health or social work agencies and escalating to punitive action (*i.e.,* prosecution for truancy). Results indicated that this intervention was successful in reducing absenteeism and that the most improvements were seen after the initial lower lever steps (a letter home to the parents). This program was simple and low in cost, though the longitudinal effects on those prosecuted is unclear.

Psychotherapeutic techniques are more likely to be used with school refusers than with chronic truants. Blagg and Yule (1984) successfully treated school refusers using a flooding technique and contingency management. They simply had the participants in their study attend school, often with escorts to keep the children in their classrooms. Parents were taught a contingency management system to encourage positive attendance related behavior and to ignore negative behavior such as complaints and temper tantrums. Results indicated that 93 percent of those students who received this intervention were attending school at a one year follow-up, compared to 10 percent of a comparison group who received home psychotherapy.

More recently cognitive behavioral treatments have been utilized successfully to treat truants and school refusers. A variety of techniques including graduated *in vivo* exposure, anxiety hierarchies, and cognitive self-statement training (Hargett & Webster, 1996; King *et al.,* 1998; Last, Hansen, & Franco, 1997) have been implemented with positive results. For example, King and colleagues implemented a 4-week program where school refusing subjects were given six, 50-minute individual therapy sessions. Children were taught cue-controlled relaxation and modification of self-talk as strategies to deal with stressors such as caregiver separation, peer bullying, and teasing. Imaginal and *in vivo* anxiety-provoking situations were presented during the last three sessions so the children could learn to apply the skills. Additionally, parents were given five, 50-minute behavior management training sessions. One meeting was also held with the students' teachers to discuss facilitation of regular classroom attendance. Percentage of days present increased from 62 to 94 and these gains were maintained at 3-month follow-up. Although this intervention successfully increased attendance rates, the time involvement, over 9 hours per student, was considerable.

Enea and Dafiniou (2009) assessed the efficiency of a package of motivational/solution focused group counselling techniques for reducing school truancy rates among adolescents in Romania. This intervention used a combination of motivational stimulation strategies with behavioural strategies (*e.g.,* reinforcement, behaviour contracts). Enea and Dafiniou compared 19 students who completed this program with 19 control students. Results indicated a 61 percent reduction in truancy for the experimental group with no change in the truancy for the controls. While no attempts were made to determine the relative weight which individual components of the intervention contributed to the success of the intervention, a study using a solution-focused brief therapy group intervention with junior high school students (Newsome, 2004) found no differences between experimental and control groups on school attendance. This leads to the possibility that the behavioral components of the program may have contributed the greater about of variance to the results. In fact, the most successful programs with the least significant disadvantages for improving attendance rates appear to be the behavioral interventions (Goldstein *et al.,* 2003).

CONCLUSION

Absenteeism has been and continues to be a significant problem in American schools. Attendance rates appear to vary substantially across different areas of the country; however, it is doubtful that more than a few are at an acceptable rate. DeLeonibus (1978) suggested a 96 percent criterion rate for adequate attendance based on adult standards in the workplace, which may be somewhat unrealistic given attendance rates in major school districts in the United States. Still, few districts, as exemplified by data from the three largest school districts in the country, come anywhere near this workplace suggested rate.

Absenteeism has been found to correlate significantly with a number of achievement indicators. Additionally, students are more likely to drop out of school and are more at risk for criminal behavior, alcoholism, and social, emotional, and occupational difficulties in adulthood (Kearney, 2008b). A substantial research base has accrued over the past 60 years focused primarily on the etiology of absenteeism. While there is some research that has addressed interventions, the literature is sparse, particularly considering the importance of the problem.

Factors related to schools, to students' home environments, and to students' them selves appear to be related to absenteeism (Corville-Smith *et al.,* 1998; Southworth, 1992). Upon examining absenteeism and individual characteristics, different types of frequently absent students have been identified: truants and school refusers. Information gathered concerning the etiology of absenteeism has assisted researchers in developing interventions to improve attendance rates. Interventions have focused on a variety of etiological factors and have included many different treatment techniques. Behavioral interventions appear to have the least significant disadvantages in terms of cost, complexity, and ease of implementation but as Kearney (2008b) points out all aspects of the child's environment (child, parent, family, peer, and community) must be identified to increase the likelihood of developing an efficacious intervention for any given child.

In conclusion, poor attendance continues to be a pervasive problem at a large number of American schools. A combination of community-based and school-based programs may be the most effective way to address this issue over the long term. With limited resources, however, the most direct and efficient methods available to most schools appear to be behavioral, school-based interventions. Due to the many negative individual and community outcomes associated with chronic absenteeism, this is a problem that must be addressed if we are to meet the mental health needs of all children.

ACKNOWLEDGEMENT

Declare none.

CONFLICT OF INTEREST

The author(s) confirm that this chapter content has no conflict of interest.

REFERENCES

Akin-Little, A., & Little, S.G. (2009). The true effects of extrinsic reinforcement on "intrinsic" motivation. In A. Akin-Little, S. G. Little, M. Bray, & T. Kehle (Eds.), *Behavioral interventions in schools: Evidence-based positive strategies* (pp. 73-91). Washington, DC: APA Books.

Barber, R. M., & Kagey, J. R. (1977). Modification of school attendance for an elementary population. *Journal of Applied Behavior Analysis, 10,* 41-48.

Baresh, T. (2004). *Student attendance initiation: Los Angeles Unified School District.* Retrieved June 10, 2010 from www.lausd.k12.ca.us/lausd/hrc/Student percent20 Attendance percent20Initiative.pdf.

Bealing, V. (1990). Pupil perception of absenteeism in the secondary school. *Maladjustment and Therapeutic Education, 8,* 19-34.

Berg, I., Butler, A., Franklin, J., Hayes, H., Lucas, C., & Sims, R. (1993). DSM-III-R disorders, social factors and management of school attendance problems in the normal population. *Journal of Child Psychology and Psychiatry,34,* 1187-1193.

Blagg, N., & Yule, W. (1984). The behavioral treatment of school refusal—A comparative study. *Behavior Research and Therapy, 22,* 119-127.

Chicago Public Schools (2010). *Monthly attendance by school and grade.* Retrieved June 10,2010 from http://research.cps.k12.il. us/cps/accountweb/Reports/allschools.html

Copeland, R., Brown, R., & Hall, V. (1974). The effects of principal-implemented techniques on the behavior of pupils. *Journal of Applied Behavior Analysis, 7,* 77-86.

Corville-Smith, J., Ryan, B., Adams, R., & Dalicandro, T. (1998). Distinguishing absentee students from regular attenders: The combined influence of personal, family, and school factors. *Journal of Youth and Adolescence, 27,* 629-640.

DeKalb, J. (1999). Student truancy. *ERIC Digest, 125.* [On-line], Retrieved June 4, 2010 from http://eric.uoregon.edu/publications/digests/digest125.html

DeLeonibus, N. (1978). *Absenteeism: The perpetual problem. The practitioner.* Reston, VA: National Association of Secondary School Principals. (ERIC Document Reproduction Service No. ED 162 424).

DeRosier, M. E., Kupersmidt, J. B., & Patterson, C. J. (1994). Children's academic and behavioral adjustment as a function of the chronicity and proximity of peer rejection. *Child Development,65,* 1799-1813.

Dube, S, R., & Orpinas, P. (2009). Understanding excessive school absenteeism as school refusal behavior. *Children & Schools, 31*, 87-95.

Eaton, M. J. (1979). A study of some factors associated with the early identification of persistent absenteeism. *Educational Review, 31,* 233-242.

Enberg, J., & Morral, A. R. (2006). Reducing substance use improves adolescents' school attendance. *Addiction, 101,* 1741-1751.

Enea, V., & Dafinoiu, I. (2009). Motivational/solution-focused intervention for reducing school truancy among adolescents. *Journal of Cognitive and Behavioral Psychotherapies, 9*, 185-198.

Gerics, J., & Westheimer, M. (1988). Dropout Prevention: Trinkets and gimmicks or Deweyan reconstruction? *Teachers College Record, 90,* 41-59.

Gewertz, C. (2005). N.Y.C. schools report lower rates of graduation for blacks and Latinos. *Education Week, 25(15),* 4-10.

Gewertz, C. (2006). Outgoing governor cites progress. *Education Week, 25(19),* 22.

Gewertz, C. (2007). Graduation predictors. *Education Week, 27(1),* 5.

Goldsmith, P. (2009). Schools or neighborhoods or both? Race and ethnic segregation and educational attainment. *Social Forces, 87*, 1913-1941.

Goldstein, J. S., Little, S. G., & Akin-Little, K. A. (2003). Increasing attendance in the public schools: A review of most effective techniques. *The California School Psychologist, 8*, 127-139.

Gottfried, M. A. (2009). Evaluating the relationship between school attendance and achievement in urban elementary and middle schools: An instrumental variables approach. *American Educational Research Journal*, November 17, 2009, doi:10. 3102/0002831209350494.

Greene, J. E., Sr. (1963). Factors associated with absenteeism among students in two metropolitan high schools. *Journal of Experimental Education, 31,* 389-393.

Greene, J. P. (2009). *High school graduation rates in the United States.* New York: Manhattan Institute for Policy Research, Inc. Retrieved June 4, 2010 from http://www.manhattan-institute.org/html/cr_baeo.htm.

Grier, A. B., Foster, G. D., Womble, L. G., McLaughlin, J., Borradaile, K. E., Nachmani, J., Sherman, S., Kumanyika, S., & Shults, J. (2007). The relationship between relative weight and school attendance among elementary schoolchildren, *Obesity, 15*, 2157-2161.

Guevremont, D. C. (1986). Truancy and school absenteeism. *Interventions for Achievement and Behavior Problems, 26,* 581-591.

Hargett, M., & Webster, R. (1996). Treatment integrity and acceptability with families: A case study of a child with school refusal. *Psychology in the Schools, 33,* 319-324.

Harte, A. J. (1994). *Improving School Attendance: Responsibility and Challenge.* Toronto:Canadian Education Association.

Huffington, C., & Sevitt, M. (1989). Family interaction in adolescent school phobia. *Journal of Family Therapy, 11,* 353-375.

Hunt, M. K., & Hopko, D. R. (2009). Predicting high school truancy among students in the Appalachian south. *The Journal of Primary Prevention, 30*, 549-567.

Illinois State Board of Education (2010). Causes/contribution factors to truancy. Received June 16, 2010 from http://mcdonough.k12.il.us/optionaleducation/TAOEP/truancy.htm.

Kearney, C. A. (2008a). School absenteeism and school refusal behavior in youth: A contemporary review. *Clinical Psychology Review, 28*, 451-471.

Kearney, C. A. (2008b). An interdisciplinary model of school absenteeism in youth to inform professional practice and public policy. *Educational Psychology Review, 20*, 257-282.

King, N., Tongue, B., Heyne, D., Pritchard, M., Rollings, S., Young, D., Myerson, M., & Ollendick, T. (1998). Cognitive-behavioral treatment of school-refusing children: A controlled evaluation. *Journal of the American Academy of Child and Adolescent Psychiatry, 37,* 395-403.

Lamdin, D. J. (1996). Evidence of student attendance as an independent variable in education production functions. *Journal of Educational Research, 89,* 155-162.

LaRowe, L. N., Tucker, R. D., & McGuire, J. M. (1980). Lunchroom noise control using feedback and group contingent reinforcement. *Journal of School Psychology, 18,* 51-57.

Last, C., Hansen, M., & Franco, N. (1997). Cognitive-behavioral treatment of school phobia. *Journal of the American Academy of Child and Adolescent Psychiatry, 37,* 404-411.

Mattison, R. E. (2000). School Consultation: A review of research on issues unique to the school environment. *Journal of the American Academy of Child and Adolescent Psychiatry, 39,* 402-413.

McCluskey, C. P., Bynum, T. S., & Patchin, J. W. (2004). Reducing chronic absenteeism: An assessment of an early truancy initiative. *Crime & Delinquency, 50*, 214-234.

McPartland, J., & Nettles, S. (1991). Using community adults as advocates or mentors for at-risk middle school students: A two-year evaluation of project RAISE. *American Journal of Education, 99,* 568-586.

Neill, S. (1979). *Keeping students in school: Problems and solutions. AASA Critical Issues Report.* Arlington, VA: American Association of School Administrators. (ERIC Document Reproduction Service No. ED 177 704).

Neilson, A., & Gerber, D. (1979). Psychosocial aspects of truancy in early adolescence. *Adolescence, 54,* 1-26.

Newsome, S. W. (2004). Solution-focused brief therapy groupwork with at-risk junior high students: Enhancing the bottom line. *Research on Social Work Practice, 14,* 336-343.

New York City Department of Education (2010). *Attendance*. Retrieved June 10, 2010 from http://schools.nyc.gov/AboutUs/data/stats/attendance/default.htm.

No Child Left Behind Act of 2001 (2002). Pub. L. No. 107-110, 115 Stat. 1425.

Noaks, J., & Noaks, L. (2000). Violence in school: Risk, safety, and fear of crime. *Educational Psychology in Practice, 16*, 70-73.

Noonan, R., & Thibeault, R. (1974). Primary prevention in Appalachian Kentucky: Per reinforcement of classroom attendance. *Journal of Community Psychology, 2,* 260-264.

Pasternicki, G., Wakefield, D., Robertson, J., & Edwards, L. (1993). A school-based action research project on truancy: Within-school factors. *Support for Learning, 8*, 3-6.

Pinkus, L. M. (2009, April). *Action required: Addressing the nation's lowest-performing high schools. Policy brief.* Washington, DC: Alliance for Excellent Education. Retrieved June 4, 2010 from www.all4ed.org/files/ActionRequired.pdf.

Reeve, D. B. (2008). Improving school attendance. *Educational Leadership, 65(8)*, 90-91.

Reid, K. (1984). Some social, psychological, and educational aspects related to persistent school absenteeism. *Research in Education, 31,* 63-82.

Reid, W. J., & Bailey-Dempsey, C. A. (1995). The effects of monetary incentives on school performance. *Families in Society: The Journal of Contemporary Human Services, 76,* 331-340.

Shechtman, Z. (1993). School adjustment and small-group therapy: An Israeli study. *Journal of Counseling and Development, 72,* 77-81.

Sheldon, S. B. (2007). Improving student attendance with school, family and community partnerships. *The Journal of Educational Research, 100*, 267-275.

Southworth, P. (1992). Psychological and social characteristics associated with persistent absence among secondary aged school children with special reference to different categories of persistent absence. *Personality and Individual Differences, 13,* 367-376.

Sturgeon, R., & Beer, J. (1990). Attendance reward and absenteeism in high school. *Psychological Reports, 66,* 759-762.

Sutphen, R.D., Ford, J. P., & Flaherty, C. (2010). Truancy interventions: A review of the research literature. *Research on Social Work Practice, 20*, 161-171.

United Nations Office for the Coordination of Humanitarian Affairs (2010). Yemen: Paying girls is paying off for school attendance. Retrieved June 26, 2010 from http://www.irinnews.org/Report.aspx?ReportId=89381

U. S. Census Bureau (2010). Earnings by occupation and education. Retrieved June 15, 2010 from http://www.wwwcensusgov.zuom.info/hhes/www/income/earnings.html.

U. S. Department of Justice (2004). *The weed and seed strategy*. Retrieved June 27, 2010 from http://www.ojp.usdoj.gov/ccdo/ws/manuals.html.

Volkman, B. (1996). *You can't educate an empty chair: Increasing student attendance through parent involvement in regular classroom lessons.* (ERIC Document Reproduction Service No. ED 415 466).

Volkmann, B., & Bye, L. (2006). Improved school attendance through adult volunteer reading partners. *Children & Schools, 28*, 145-152.

Wilkins, J. (2008). School characteristics that influence student attendance: Experiences of students in a school avoidance program. *The High School Journal, 91*, 12-24.

Wimmer, M. (2008). School refusal. *Principal Leadership, 8*, 10-14.

York, T., & Kearney, C. (1993, April). *Familial factors and the function of school refusal behavior in children and adolescents.* Paper presented at the annual meeting of the Western Psychological Association, Phoenix, AZ.

CHAPTER 3

Student Engagement and Disengagement: An Intrinsic Motivation Perspective and a Mental Health Concern

Howard Adelman[1,*] and Linda Taylor[2]

[1]UCLA Department of Psychology, 1285 Franz Hall, Box 951563, Los Angeles, CA 90095-1563, USA and [2]Center for Mental Health in Schools, UCLA Department of Psychology, Box 951563, Los Angeles, CA 90095-1563, USA

Abstract: The recognition that school is a necessary cite in the positive mental health of children has become widespread, though the importance of mental health promotion in schools is not as universally understood and appreciated. A difficult reality is that students enter school with a variety of behavioral, emotional, and learning needs, complicating the goals and expectations placed on professional educators. Nonetheless, the manner in which children engage in the relationships, environment, and societal and cognitive requirements faced in school are not always acknowledged and addressed in educational programming. This chapter discusses challenges and opportunities for educational professionals within the context of the best current information available on effective and positive engagement of students in the global school experience.

Keywords: Engagement, intrinsic motivation, motivation, reengagement, school improvement.

INTRODUCTION

The U.S. Department of Health and Human Services (2001) stresses that:

> *Growing numbers of children are suffering needlessly because their emotional, behavioral, and developmental needs are not being met by the very institutions and systems that were created to take care of them.*

One of those institutions is the school.

The irony is that in many schools the need to attend to matters such as mental health is a common topic. And there is growing advocacy for mental health in

***Address correspondence to Howard Adelman:** UCLA Department of Psychology, 1285 Franz Hall, Box 951563, Los Angeles, CA 90095-1563, USA; Tel: 310-825-1225; Email: Adelman@psyche.ucla.edu

Raymond J. Waller (Ed)

schools. Nevertheless, mental health concerns continue to receive only marginal attention in schools, and advocates are pushing a variety of agenda items that compete with each other (Adelman & Taylor, 2010).

Our efforts to enhance mental health in schools emphasize the need for *fundamental systemic changes and system building* (Adelman & Taylor, 2007). We recognize that some students come to school with mental health problems and that schools should have the capacity to play a role in addressing the needs of such youngsters. At the same time, we recognize that schools are a source of mental health problems both by what they do and what they don't do. And, we stress that a significant facet of what they *don't do* is to:

a) Facilitate positive social and emotional development with the same commitment they make to cognitive development,

b) Address barriers to teaching and learning comprehensively, and

c) Concentrate on intrinsic motivation as they strive to enhance student engagement and re-engage disconnected students.

In this chapter, our focus is on engagement and re-engagement because these are fundamental concerns for mental health in schools. Engagement is a critical buffer against learning, behavior, and emotional problems; disengagement is related to a host of student and school problems.

We begin with a brief discussion of student engagement and re-engagement. Then, we highlight the following:

- Motivation in the context of school improvement policy and practice,
- Motivation beyond reinforcement theory,
- Understanding the motivational bases for disengagement,
- Intrinsic motivation and the challenge of re-engaging students in school learning.

While our focus here is on students, any discussion of motivation has applications to family members and school personnel. Think about the challenge of home involvement in schooling, and think about teacher burnout and dropout; think about systemic change.

ABOUT ENGAGEMENT AND RE-ENGAGEMENT OF STUDENTS

It is given that teachers are faced with a complex continuum of learner motivation. This fact requires schools to provide a range of ways to enhance engagement. Student engagement involves not only engaging and maintaining engagement, but also *re-engaging* those who have disconnected from classroom instruction. For school personnel to do all this effectively they must broaden their understanding of both extrinsic and intrinsic motivation and the complex relationship between extrinsics and intrinsics (see Exhibit **1**). To this end, there is a growing body of literature to draw upon (*e.g.,* see Brophy, 2004; Center for Mental Health in Schools, 2010a; Deci, 1975; Deci & Flaste, 1995; Deci & Ryan, 1985; Dweck, 2007; National Research Council and the Institute of Medicine, 2004; Pink, 2009; Stipek, 1998; Vansteenkiste, Lens, & Deci, 2006; Wehrmeyer & Sands, 1998).

Exhibit 1

Sources of Motivation and Intervention Concerns

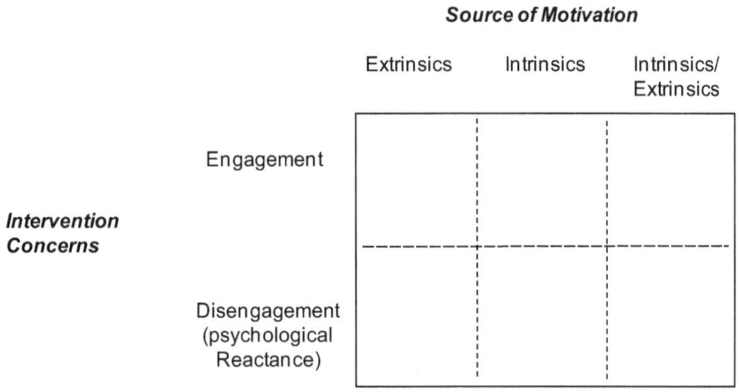

As applied to schools, Fredricks, Blumenfeld, and Paris (2004) indicate that engagement is defined in three ways in the research literature:

- ***Behavioral engagement*** draws on the idea of participation; it includes involvement in academic and social or extracurricular activities and is considered crucial for achieving positive academic outcomes and preventing dropping out.

- ***Emotional engagement*** encompasses positive and negative reactions to teachers, classmates, academics, and school and is presumed to create ties to an institution and influences willingness to do the work.

- ***Cognitive engagement*** draws on the idea of investment; it incorporates thoughtfulness and willingness to exert the effort necessary to comprehend complex ideas and master difficult skills.

Their review of the research underscores that engagement is associated with positive academic outcomes, including achievement and persistence in school; and it is higher in classrooms with supportive teachers and peers, challenging and authentic tasks, opportunities for choice, and sufficient structure.

Unfortunately, maintaining engagement is a widespread problem for schools. And, for those students who become actively disengaged from classroom learning, the disconnection is both symptomatic of one or more causal factors and an additional factor exacerbating student and school problems.

From a motivational perspective, disengagement from proactive classroom learning often is associated with situational threats to feelings of competence, self-determination, and/or relatedness to valued others. The demands producing such threats may be from school staff, peers, or instructional content and processes. Psychological disengagement can be expected to result in internalized behavior (*e.g.,* boredom, emotional distress) and/or externalized behavior (misbehavior, dropping out).

The importance of attending to all this is well-understood, but not readily addressed. As the National Academy of Science′s Research Council (2004) has stressed:

> *Engaging adolescents, including those who have become disengaged and alienated from school, is not an easy task. Academic motivation decreases steadily from the early grades of elementary school into high*

> *school. Furthermore, adolescents are too old and too independent to follow teachers' demands out of obedience, and many are too young, inexperienced, or uninformed to fully appreciate the value of succeeding in school.*

Clearly, a prominent focus of school improvement efforts should be on how to

a) Motivate the many students who are hard to engage, and

b) Re-engage those who have totally disengaged from classroom learning.

Of particular concern is what teachers should do when they encounter a student who has disengaged and is misbehaving.

When students are not engaged in the schoolwork at hand, they tend to pursue other activity. As teachers and other staff try to cope with those who are disruptive, the foremost emphasis is on managing the behavior (*e.g.,* classroom management strategies). At one time, a heavy dose of punishment was the dominant approach. Currently, the stress is on more positive practices designed to provide behavior support in and out-of-the-classroom. For example, there is ongoing advocacy for social skills training, asset development, character education, and positive behavior support initiatives. The move from punishment to positive approaches is a welcome one, but most of the initiatives have not focused enough on providing systemic ways to help teachers deal with student engagement issues. And, too often, strategies aimed at directly stopping disruptive behavior are applied and experienced by students as a form of *social control.*

The reality is that an overemphasis on social control can be counterproductive to re-engaging students in classroom instruction. An often-stated assumption by those who teach social control as the key to classroom management is that just stopping misbehavior will make the student amenable to teaching. In a few cases, this may be so. However, the assumption ignores all the work that has led to understanding *psychological reactance.* As John Holt said, only half in jest: *I suspect that many children would learn arithmetic, and learn it better, if it were illegal.*

It is important to recognize that an emphasis on intrinsic motivation in re-engaging students rarely is a prominent part of pre or in-service preparation and seldom is the focus of interventions pursued by professionals whose role is to support teachers and students. It is time to ensure that all school personnel are brought up to date on what has been learned about human motivation in general and intrinsic motivation in particular over the last 50 years. As we will emphasize, re-engagement depends on use of interventions that help minimize conditions that negatively affect intrinsic motivation and maximize conditions that have a positive motivational effect.

MOTIVATION IN THE CONTEXT OF SCHOOL IMPROVEMENT POLICY AND PRACTICE

Prevailing school improvement planning tends to marginalize strategies for addressing behavior and emotional problems at school. For the situation to significantly shift, school improvement policy and practice must move from a two- to a three-component blueprint (Center for Mental Health in Schools, 2010b). The intent of the third component is to provide a unifying concept and umbrella under which all resources currently expended for student and learning supports are woven together. The goal is to develop a comprehensive and cohesive system for addressing barriers to learning and teaching and re-engaging disconnected students. Such a system involves much more than enhancing availability and access to mental and physical health and social services or limiting the focus to any other piecemeal and ad hoc initiatives aimed at preventing and correcting learning, behavior, and emotional problems (Adelman & Taylor, 1997, 2006a, 2006b).

To guide establishment of a comprehensive system, we stress developing integrated *systems* within and across a *continuum of interventions.* That continuum includes systems for:

a) Promoting healthy development and preventing problems,

b) Responding as early after problem onset as is feasible, and

c) Providing for those whose serious, pervasive, and chronic problems require more intensive assistance and accommodation.

And we also stress that, just as efforts to enhance instruction emphasize well delineated and integrated curriculum content, so must efforts to address external and internal factors that interfere with students engaging effectively with that curriculum. At schools, the *content* (or curriculum) for addressing a full range of interfering factors can be coalesced into six classroom and school-wide arenas (Adelman & Taylor 2006a, 2006b). These focus on:

1) Enhancing regular classroom strategies to enable learning(*e.g.*, improving instruction for students who have become disengaged from learning at school and for those with mild-moderate learning and behavior problems),

2) Supporting transitions (*i.e.* assisting students and families as they negotiate school and grade changes and many other transitions),

3) Increasing home and school connections,

4) Responding to, and where feasible, preventing crises,

5) Increasing community involvement and support (outreaching to develop greater community involvement and support, including enhanced use of volunteers),

6) Facilitating student and family access to effective services and special assistance as needed.

The framework created by combining the continuum and the content is highlighted in Exhibit **2**.

Exhibit 2

Intervention Framework Highlighting the Scope and Content of a Component to Address Barriers to Learning*

Scope of Intervention

Organizing around the **Content/ Curriculum** (for addressing barriers to learning & promoting healthy development)	System for Promoting Healthy Development & Preventing Problems	System for Early Intervention (Early after problem onset)	System of Care
Classroom-Focused Enabling			
Crisis/ Emergency Assistance & Prevention			
Support for transitions			
Home Involvement in Schooling			
Community Outreach/ Volunteers			
Student and Family Assistance			

Accommodations for differences & disabilities Specialized assistance other intensified interventions (*e.g.*, Special Education & School-Based Behavioral Health).

*Note that specific school-wide and classroom-based activities related to positive behavior support, prereferral interventions, and the eight components of Center for Prevention and Disease Control's Coordinated School Health Program are embedded into the six content (curriculum) arenas.

Running throughout all of this is an emphasis on the importance of enhancing motivational readiness, focusing on motivation as a fundamental process concern, and enhancing intrinsic motivation as an intervention outcome. And of course each of these motivational concerns has mental health implications.

Motivation: Beyond Reinforcement Theory

> *External reinforcement may indeed get a particular act going and may lead to its repetition, but it does not nourish, reliably, the long course of learning by which [one] slowly builds in [one's] own way a serviceable model of what the world is and what it can be.*
>
> Jerome Bruner (1966)

Those who argue schools must focus on basics are right. But, the basics for the 21st century involve much more than the 3 Rs. A particularly important basic outcome of schooling is enhanced intrinsic motivation for learning and problem solving.

Concern about student engagement and re-engagement must be more about how to enhance motivation to learn in and out of school and less about managing behavior and must include a strong emphasis on intrinsic motivation. What many of us have been taught about dealing with students runs counter to what we intuitively understand about human motivation. School staff and parents, in particular, often learn to over depend on reinforcement theory despite the appreciation they have for the importance of intrinsic motivation.

Because motivation is fundamental to all that schools do, a broadened understanding is essential to clarifying how best to facilitate student learning and school improvement. For example, such a broadened understanding underscores that engagement requires.

a) Providing significant opportunities for choice and self-determination, and

b) Avoiding processes that limit options, make students feel controlled and coerced, and narrowly focus on remedying problems.

Of course, teachers, parents, and support staff cannot control all factors affecting motivation. Indeed, when any of us address learning and behavior concerns, we only have direct control over a relatively small slice of the physical and social environment. Using what is accessible, we try to maximize the likelihood that opportunities to learn are a good fit with the current *capabilities* of a given youngster. So, with student engagement in mind, we try to match individual differences in motivation which means attending to the following concerns.

Motivation as a Readiness Concern: Optimal performance and learning require motivational readiness. The absence of such readiness can cause or maintain problems. If a learner does not have enough motivational readiness, strategies must be implemented to develop it (including ways to reduce avoidance motivation). Readiness should not be viewed in the old sense of waiting until an individual is interested. Rather, it should be understood in the contemporary sense of establishing environments that are perceived by students as caring, supportive places and as offering stimulating activities that are valued and challenging, and doable.

Motivation as a Key Ongoing Process Concern: Many learners are caught up in the novelty of a new subject, but after a few lessons, interest often wanes. Some students are motivated by the idea of obtaining a given outcome but may not be motivated to pursue certain processes and thus may not pay attention or may try to avoid them. For example, some are motivated to start work on overcoming their problems but may not maintain that motivation. Strategies must be designed to elicit, enhance, and maintain motivation so that a youngster stays mobilized.

Minimizing Negative Motivation and Avoidance Reactions as Process and Outcome Concerns: Teachers and others at a school and at home not only must try to increase motivation, especially intrinsic motivation, but also take care to avoid or at least minimize conditions that decrease motivation or produce negative motivation. For example, care must be taken not to exclusively depend on extrinsics to entice and reward because to do so may decrease intrinsic motivation. At times, school is seen as unchallenging, uninteresting, over demanding, overwhelming, over controlling, nonsupportive, or even hostile. When this happens, a student may develop negative attitudes and avoidance related to a given situation, and over time, related to school and all it represents.

Enhancing Intrinsic Motivation as a Basic Outcome Concern: It is essential to enhance motivation as an outcome so the desire to pursue a given area (*e.g.*, reading, good behavior) increasingly is a positive intrinsic attitude that mobilizes learning and behaving outside the teaching situation. Achieving such an outcome involves use of strategies that do not overuse extrinsic rewards and that do enable youngsters to play a meaningful role in making decisions related to valued options. In effect, enhancing intrinsic motivation is a fundamental protective factor and is the key to developing *resiliency*.

Students who are intrinsically motivated to learn at school seek out opportunities and challenges and go beyond requirements. In doing so, they learn more and learn more deeply than do classmates who are extrinsically motivated. Facilitating the learning of such students is a fairly straightforward matter and fits well with school improvements that primarily emphasize enhancing instructional practices. The focus is on helping establish ways for students who are motivationally ready and able to achieve and, of course, to maintain and enhance their motivation. The process involves knowing when, how, and what to teach and also knowing when and how to structure the situation so they can learn on their own.

In contrast, students who manifest learning, behavior, and/or emotional problems often have developed extremely negative perceptions of teachers and programs. In such cases, they are unlikely to be open to people and activities that look like the same old thing. Major changes are required if the youngster is even to perceive things are different. Minimally, exceptional efforts must be made to have the student.

a) View the teacher and other interveners as supportive (rather than controlling and indifferent), and

b) Perceive content, outcomes, and activity options as personally valuable and obtainable.

Thus, any effort to re-engage disengaged students must begin by addressing negative perceptions. School support staff and teachers must work together to reverse conditions that led to such perceptions.

WHAT ARE THE MOTIVATIONAL BASES FOR DISENGAGEMENT?

Two common reasons people give for not engaging are

- It′ s not worth it, and
- I know I won′ t be able to do it.

These reflect two key concepts that help us understand motivation: *valuing and expectations.* In general, the amount of time and energy spent on an activity seems dependent on how much the activity is valued by the person and on the person′ s expectation that what is valued will be attained without too great a cost.

Conversely, nonproactive psychological disengagement from an activity seems dependent on how much the activity is devalued by the person and/or on the person′ s expectation that something that is valued can only be attained at too great a cost. Such psychological disengagement can be expected to result in internalized behavior (*e.g.,* boredom, emotional distress) and/or externalized behavior (*e.g.,* misbehavior, dropping out).

Increasing intrinsic motivation involves affecting a student′ s thoughts, feelings, and decisions. In general, the intent is to use procedures that can potentially reduce negative and increase positive feelings, thoughts, and coping strategies with respect to learning. For learning and behavior problems, in particular, this means identifying and minimizing experiences that maintain or may increase avoidance motivation.

ABOUT VALUING

What makes something worth doing? Prizes? Money? Merit awards? Praise? Certainly! We all do a great many things, some of which we don′ t even like to do, because the activity leads to a desired reward. Similarly, we often do things to escape punishment or other negative consequences that we prefer to avoid.

Rewards and punishments may be material or social. For those with learning, behavior, and emotional problems, there has been widespread use of such 'incentives' (*e.g.,* systematically giving points or tokens that can be exchanged for candy, prizes, praise, free time, or social interactions). Punishments have included loss of free time and other privileges, added work, fines, isolation, censure, and suspension. Grades have been used both as rewards and punishments. Because people will do things to obtain rewards or avoid punishment, rewards and punishment often are called *reinforcers*. Because they generally come from sources outside the person, they often are called *extrinsics*.

Extrinsic reinforcers are easy to use and can immediately affect behavior. Therefore, they have been widely adopted in the fields of special education and psychology. Unfortunately, the immediate effects are usually limited to very specific behaviors and often are short-term. Moreover, extensive use of extrinsics can have some undesired effects. And, sometimes the available extrinsics simply aren′t powerful enough to get the desired results.

It is important to remember that what makes an extrinsic factor rewarding is the fact that it is experienced by the recipient as a reward. What makes it a highly valued reward is that the recipient highly values it. If someone doesn′t like candy, there is not much point in offering it as a reward. Furthermore, because the use of extrinsics has limits, it is fortunate that people often do things even without apparent extrinsic reason. In fact, a lot of what people learn and spend time doing is done for intrinsic reasons. Curiosity is a good example. Curiosity seems to be an innate quality that leads us to seek stimulation, avoid boredom, and learn a great deal.

People also pursue some things because of what has been described as an innate striving for competence. Most of us value *feeling competent*. We try to conquer some challenges, and if none are around, we usually seek one out. Of course, if the challenges confronting us seem unconquerable or make us too uncomfortable (*e.g.,* too anxious or exhausted), we try to put them aside and move on to something more promising.

Another important intrinsic motivator appears to be an internal push toward things that make a person *feel self-determining*. People seem to value feeling and thinking that they have some degree of choice and freedom in deciding what to do. And, human beings also seem intrinsically moved toward establishing and maintaining relationships. That is, we value *feeling connected interpersonally.*

ABOUT EXPECTATIONS

Our expectations of outcome are shaped by our perceptions of how easy or hard it will be to obtain the outcome. Such expectations about these matters are influenced by past experiences. Sometimes we know we can easily do something, but it is not something that we value. At other times, we may value something a great deal but don't believe we can do it or can only obtain it by paying too great a personal price. Under such circumstances, we are likely to look for other valued activities and outcomes to pursue.

Previously unsuccessful areas usually are seen as unlikely paths to valued extrinsic rewards or intrinsic satisfactions. We may perceive past failure as the result of our lack of ability; or we may believe that more effort was required than we were willing to give. We may also feel that the help we needed to succeed was not available. If our perception is that very little has changed with regard to these factors, our expectation of succeeding now will be rather low. In general, then, what we value interacts with our expectations, and motivation is one product of the transactions (see Exhibit **3**).

EXHIBIT 3

A Bit of Theory

Motivation theory has many facets. At the risk of oversimplifying things, the following discussion is designed to make a few crucial points.

E x V

Can you decipher this? (Don't go on until you've tried.)
Hint: the 'x' is a multiplication sign.

In case the equation stumped you, don't be surprised. The main introduction to motivational thinking that many people have been given in the past involves some form of reinforcement theory (which essentially deals with extrinsic motivation). Thus, all this may be new to you even though motivational theorists have been wrestling with it for a long time, and intuitively, you probably understand much of what they are talking about.

E represents an individual's *expectations* about outcome (in school this often means expectations of success or failure). **V** represents *valuing,* with valuing influenced by both what is valued intrinsically and extrinsically. Thus, in a general sense, motivation can be thought of in terms of expectancy times valuing. *Such theory recognizes that human beings are thinking and feeling organisms and that intrinsic factors can be powerful motivators. This understanding of human motivation has major implications for learning, teaching, parenting, and mental health interventions.*

Within some limits (which we need not discuss here), high expectations and high valuing produce high motivation, while low expectations **(E)** and high valuing **(V)** produce relatively weak motivation as do high expectations **(E)** and low valuing **(V)**.

Low Expectations, High Valuing: Youngsters may greatly value the idea of improving their reading. They usually are not happy with limited skills and know they would feel a lot better about themselves if they could read. But, often they experience everything the teacher asks them to do as a waste of time. They have done it all before, and they *still* have a reading problem. Sometimes they will do the exercises, but just to earn points to go on a field trip or to avoid the consequences of not cooperating. Often, however, they try to get out of doing the work by distracting the teacher. After all, why should they do things they are certain won′t help them read any better.

Expectancy x Valuing = Motivation

0 x 1.0 = 0

High Expectations, Low Valuing: Similarly, high expectations paired with low valuing yield low approach motivation. Thus, the of cited remedial strategy of guaranteeing success by designing tasks to be very easy is not as simple a recipe as it sounds. Indeed, the approach is likely to fail if the outcome (*e.g.,* improved reading, learning math fundamentals, applying social skills) is not valued or if the tasks are experienced as too boring or if doing them is seen as too embarrassing. In such cases, a strong negative value is attached to the activities and contributes to avoidance motivation.

Expectancy x Valuing = Motivation

1.0 x 0 = 0

Appropriate appreciation of all this is necessary in designing a match for optimal engagement, learning, and performance.

ABOUT OVER-RELIANCE ON EXTRINSICS

Throughout this discussion of valuing and expectations, the emphasis has been on the fact that motivation is not something that can be determined solely by forces outside the individual. Others can plan activities and outcomes to influence motivation and learning; however, how the activities and outcomes are experienced determines whether they are pursued (or avoided) with a little or a lot of effort and ability. Understanding that an individual's perceptions can affect motivation has led researchers to important findings about some undesired effects resulting from over-reliance on extrinsics.

Because of the prominent role they play in school programs, grading, testing, and other performance evaluations are a special concern in any discussion of the over-reliance on extrinsics as a way to reinforce positive learning. Although grades often are discussed as simply providing information about how well a student is doing, many, if not most, students perceive each grade as a reward or a punishment. Certainly, many teachers use grades to try to control behavior to reward those who do assignments well and to punish those who don't. Sometimes parents add to a student's perception of grades as extrinsic reinforcers by giving a reward for good report cards.

A perspective on all this is found in a 2006 research review by Vansteenkiste, Lens, and Deci. In discussing autonomy-supportive *versus* controlling social environments, they suggest that in externally controlling contexts teachers emphasize overtly coercive strategies, such as salient reward contingencies, deadlines, and overtly controlling language. By way of contrast, in autonomy-supportive contexts teachers empathize with the learner's perspective, allow opportunities for self-initiation and choice, provide a meaningful rationale if choice is constrained, refrain from the use of pressures and contingencies to motivate, and provide timely positive feedback.

What research has shown is that an over-reliance on extrinsic rewards and external social control can undermine intrinsic reasons for doing things. Although this is not always the case and may not always be a bad thing, it is an important consideration in deciding to rely on extrinsic reinforcers and controlling environments in addressing learning, behavior, and emotional problems. The first preference in designing intervention intended to enhance intrinsic motivation as an outcome should be an emphasis on intrinsic motivation and autonomy-support.

Over-Reliance on Extrinsics Can Exacerbate Problems

Many individuals with learning problems also are described as hyperactive, distractible, impulsive, behavior disordered, and so forth. Their behavior patterns are seen as interfering with efforts to remedy their learning problems. Although motivation has always been a concern to those who work with learning and behavior problems, the emphasis in handling these interfering behaviors usually is on using extrinsics as part of efforts to directly control, and/or in conjunction with, direct skill instruction. For example, interventions are designed to improve impulse control, perseverance, selective attention, frustration tolerance, sustained attention and follow-through, and social awareness and skills. In all cases, the emphasis is on reducing or eliminating interfering behaviors, usually with the presumption that the student will then re-engage in learning. However, there is little evidence that these strategies enhance a student′ s motivation toward classroom learning.

Ironically, the reliance on extrinsics to control behavior may exacerbate student problems. Motivational research suggests that when people perceive their freedom (*e.g.,* of choice) is threatened, they have a psychological reaction that motivates them to restore their sense of freedom. (For instance, when those in control say: *You can′ t do that. you must do this.,* the covert and sometimes overt psychological reaction of students often is: *Oh, you think so!*) This line of research also suggests that with prolonged denial of freedom, people′ s reactivity diminishes; they become motivated and usually feel helpless and ineffective.

INTRINSIC MOTIVATION AND THE CHALLENGE OF RE-ENGAGING STUDENTS IN SCHOOL LEARNING

As we have noted, psychological scholarship over the last fifty years has brought renewed attention to intrinsic motivation as a central concept in understanding learning, attention, behavior, and emotional problems. This work is just beginning to find its way into applied fields and programs. One line of work has emphasized the relationship of learning and behavior problems to deficiencies in intrinsic motivation. This work clarifies the value of interventions designed to increase the following:

- Feelings of self-determination,

- Feelings of competence and expectations of attaining valued outcomes,
- Feelings of interpersonal relatedness,
- The range of interests and satisfactions related to learning.

The research also stresses the importance of minimizing interventions that threaten these basic psychological needs. All of this has implications for promoting positive mental health and preventing and correcting mental health problems.

EXAMPLES OF PRACTICES

Activities to correct deficiencies in intrinsic motivation may first be directed at

a) Increasing students′ awareness of personal motives and true capabilities and then helping them,

b) Learn to set valued and appropriate goals,

c) Learn to value and make appropriate and satisfying choices, and

d) Learn to value and accept responsibility for choice.

Examples of practices for maximizing intrinsic motivation are:

- Personalized (as opposed to individualized) instruction,
- Building relationships and planning instruction with an understanding of student perceptions and including a range of real life needs, as well as personal and cooperative experiences,
- Providing real, valued, and attainable options and choices ensuring shared decision making,
- Enhancing feelings of competence, self-determination, and relatedness to valued others.

Examples of minimizing threats to intrinsic motivation are:

- Welcoming, caring, safe, and just environment,
- Countering perceptions of social control and indifference including not relying too much on extrinsics,
- Motivated application as opposed to rote practice and deadening homework,
- Ensuring extra-curricular and enrichment opportunities,
- Providing regular feedback in ways that minimize use of evaluative processes that threaten feelings of competence, self-determination, and relatedness to valued others.

GENERAL STRATEGIES

With an emphasis on all this, we pursue the following four personalized intervention strategies in working with disengaged students:

1) Clarifying student perceptions of the problem,
2) Reframing school learning,
3) Renegotiating involvement, and
4) Reestablishing and maintaining an appropriate working relationship.

As will be evident from the following brief description, each of these requires an expanded focus in applying *Response to Intervention* (RtI) methodologies.

***Clarifying Student Perceptions of the Problem*:** It is desirable to create a situation where it is feasible to talk openly with students about why they have become disengaged. Such open interchange provides an invaluable basis for interpreting responses to intervention and formulating a personalized plan to alter current negative perceptions and prevent others from developing.

Reframing School Learning: As noted above, in the case of those who have disengaged, major reframing in teaching approaches is required so that these students (a) view the teacher as supportive (rather than controlling and indifferent) and (b) perceive content, outcomes, and activity options as personally valuable and obtainable. It is important, for example, to eliminate threatening evaluative measures; reframe content and processes to clarify purpose in terms of real life needs and experiences and underscore how current activity builds on previous learning; and clarify why it is reasonable to expect the procedures to be effective (especially those designed to help correct specific problems).

***Renegotiating Involvement in School Learning*:** New and mutual agreements must be developed over time through conferences with the student and including parents, where appropriate. The intent is to affect perceptions of choice, value, and probable outcome. The focus throughout is on clarifying awareness of valued options, enhancing expectations of positive outcomes, and engaging the student in meaningful, ongoing decision making. For the process to be most effective, students should be assisted in sampling new processes and content, options should include valued enrichment opportunities, and there must be provision for reevaluating and modifying decisions as perceptions shift.

***Reestablishing and Maintaining an Appropriate Working Relationship*:** This requires the type of ongoing interactions that create a sense of trust, open communication, and provide personalized support and direction. To maintain re-engagement and prevent disengagement, the above strategies are pursued using processes and content that:

- Minimize threats to feelings of competence, self-determination, and relatedness to valued others,
- Maximize such feelings (included here is an emphasis on a school taking steps to enhance public perception that it is a welcoming, caring, safe, and just institution),
- Guide motivated practice (*e.g.,* providing opportunities for meaningful applications and clarifying ways to organize practice),

- Provide continuous information on learning and performance in ways that highlight accomplishments,

- Provide opportunities for continued application and generalization (*e.g.,* ways in which students can pursue additional, self-directed learning or can arrange for additional support and direction).

Obviously, it is not an easy task to decrease well-assimilated negative attitudes and behaviors. And, the task is likely to become even harder with high-stakes testing policies (no matter how well-intentioned). It also seems obvious that, *for many schools, enhanced achievement test scores will only be feasible when the large number of disengaged students are re-engaged in learning at school.*

All this argues for:

1) Minimizing student disengagement and maximizing re-engagement by moving school culture toward a greater focus on intrinsic motivation, and

2) Minimizing psychological reactance and resistance and enhancing perceptions that lead to re-engagement in learning at school by rethinking social control practices.

Those designing and implementing RtI and Positive Behavior Support initiatives and those concerned with advancing mental health in schools need to incorporate the implications of the strategies discussed above in working with disengaged students.

ABOUT INCREASING OPTIONS

Reviews of the literature on human motivation suggest that providing students with options and involving them in decision making are key facets of addressing the problem of engagement in the classroom and at school. For example, numerous studies have shown that opportunities to express preferences and make choices lead to greater motivation, academic gains, increases in productivity and on task behavior, and decreases in aggressive behavior. Similarly, researchers report that student participation in goal setting leads to more positive outcomes (*e.g.*, higher commitment to a goal and increased performance).

A large proportion of individuals with avoidance or low motivation for learning at school are found among those with learning, behavior, and/or emotional problems. For such students, few currently available options at school may be appealing. How much greater the range of options needs to be depends primarily on how strong avoidance tendencies are. In general, however, working to re-engage disconnected students may require:

- Further expanding the range of options for learning (if necessary, this includes avoiding established curriculum content and processes),
- Primarily emphasizing areas in which the student has made personal and active decisions,
- Accommodating a wider range of behavior than usually is tolerated (*e.g.*, a widening of limits on the amount and types of differences tolerated).

ABOUT CHOICE AND DECISION MAKING

From a motivational perspective, one of the most basic concerns is the way in which students are involved in making decisions about available options. In general, all decision making processes have the potential to generate perceptions of coercion and control or perceptions of real choice (*e.g.*, being in control of one's decisions, being self-determining). As noted above, such differences in perception play a critical role in whether a student is mobilized to pursue or avoid planned learning activities and outcomes.

People who have the opportunity to make decisions among valued and feasible options tend to be committed to following through. In contrast, people who are not involved in decisions often have little commitment to what is decided. And, if individuals disagree with a decision that affects them, besides not following through they may react with hostility.

Thus, essential to programs focusing on motivation are decision making processes that affect perceptions of choice and probable outcome. Three special points should be noted about decision making:

- Decisions are based on current perceptions. As perceptions shift, it is necessary to reevaluate decisions and modify them in ways that maintain a learner′ s motivation,

- Effective and efficient decision making is a basic skill, and one that is as fundamental as the three Rs. Thus, if an individual does not do it well initially, this is not a reason to move away from learner involvement in decision making. Rather, it is an indication of a need and a reason to use the process not only for motivational purposes, but to improve this basic skill,

- Among students manifesting learning, behavior, and/or emotional problems, it is well to remember that the most fundamental decision some of these individuals have to make is whether they want to participate or not. That is why it may be necessary in specific cases to put aside (temporarily) established options and standards.

Clearly, re-engaging disconnected students requires interventions that maximize the likelihood that students will perceive the learning environment as positively different--and quite a bit so--from the one in which they had so much failure (see Exhibit **4**).

EXHIBIT 4

Re-engaging Students: Some Basic Intervention Considerations

Think in terms of

$ *Enhancing* feelings of

- Self-determination
- Competency
- Connectedness to others

$ *Minimizing threats to* feelings of

- Self-determination
- Competency
- Connectedness to others

Examples of Some Guidelines and Strategies that Capture an Understanding of Intrinsic Motivation

$ Minimize strategies designed only for social control and other coercive interactions

- Increase
  - ➢ Options (emphasizing real life interests and needs),
  - ➢ Choice (stress *real* options and choices),
  - ➢ Involvement in decision making (ensure a meaningful role in decision making).

$ Facilitate students' desires and abilities to share their perceptions readily (to enter into dialogues with the adults at school)

$ Provide enrichment opportunities (and be sure not to withhold them as punishment)

$ Provide a *continuum* of structure (*i.e.,* personalized communication, support, and guidance)

CONCLUDING COMMENTS ABOUT A RENEWED AND ENHANCED FOCUS ON MOTIVATION

> *Many students say that. they feel their classes are irrelevant and boring, that they are just passing time. (and) are not able to connect what they are being taught with what they feel they need for success in their later life. This disengagement from the learning process is manifested in many ways, one of which is the lack of student responsibility for learning. In many ways the traditional educational structure, one in which teachers "pour knowledge into the vessel" (the student), has placed all responsibility for learning on the teacher, none on the student. Schools present lessons neatly packaged, without acknowledging or accepting the "messiness" of learning-by-doing and through experience and activity. Schools often do not provide students a chance to accept responsibility for learning, as that might actually empower students. Students in many schools have become accustomed to being spoon-fed the material to master tests, and they have lost their enthusiasm for exploration, dialogue, and reflection -- all critical steps in the learning process.*
>
> American Youth Policy Forum (2000)

Student disengagement, acting out behavior, bullying, truancy, dropouts/pushouts—noone doubts that motivation plays a key role in all this. In many cases, it is a causal factor; in all cases, it is key to preventing and correcting problems.

Whatever the initial cause of someone′s learning and behavior problems, the longer the individual has lived with such problems, the more likely she or he will have negative feelings and thoughts about instruction, teachers, schools, and him or herself. The feelings may include anxiety, fear, frustration, anger, and a great deal of unhappiness. The thoughts may include strong expectations of failure and vulnerability and low valuing of many learning opportunities. Such thoughts and feelings can result in avoidance motivation or low motivation for learning and performing in many areas of schooling.

Low motivation leads to half-hearted effort. Avoidance motivation leads to avoidance behaviors. Individuals with avoidance and low motivation often also are attracted to socially disapproved activity. Poor effort, avoidance behavior, and active pursuit of disapproved behavior on the part of students are sure-fire recipes for failure and mental health problems.

It remains tempting to focus directly on student misbehavior. It also is tempting to think that behavior problems at least can be minimized by laying down the law. We have seen many administrators pursue this line of thinking. For every student who shapes up, ten others may be pushed out of school through a progression of suspensions, opportunity transfers, and expulsions.

Most official dropout figures don′t tell the tale. The reality seen in too many high schools in cities such as Los Angeles, Baltimore, Washington, D.C., Miami, and Detroit is that only about half those who were enrolled in Grade 9 are still around to graduate from Grade 12.

Most of these students entered kindergarten with a healthy curiosity and a desire to learn to read and write. By the end of Grade 2, we start seeing the first referrals by classroom teachers because of learning and behavior problems. From that point on, increasing numbers of students become disengaged from classroom learning, and most of these manifest some form of behavioral and emotional problems. It is not surprising, then, that many of us are heartened to see the shift from punishment to positive behavior support in addressing unwanted behavior. However, as long as factors that lead to disengagement are left unaffected, we risk perpetuating the phenomenon that William Ryan identified as blaming the victim.

While appreciation of motivational considerations is not new, we are detecting growing concern about what professional preparation and development programs teach and do not teach with respect to motivation. In particular, there is the matter of how well such programs distinguish between interventions that are oriented to intrinsic motivation *vs*. those that are oriented to extrinsic motivation. Generations of teachers and support staff have been trained in the use of reinforcement theory with its emphasis on extrinsic controlling strategies. This tends to be the major focus of strategies to 'manage' behavior. Just emerging is growing advocacy for professional preparation and development programs to incorporate a focus on applying what has been learned over many decades of research on intrinsic motivation and psychological reactance. Such a focus provides an essential foundation for personalizing instruction.

From a motivational perspective, we stress that personalization differs from individualization. Personalization requires establishing a good match in terms of *both* motivation and capability. And with specific respect to motivation, a good match requires factoring in the student's perceptions in determining the right mix of intrinsic and extrinsic factors. It also requires understanding the key role played by a student's perceived expectations related to outcomes.

Without a good match, social control strategies can temporarily suppress negative attitudes and behaviors, but re-engagement in classroom learning is unlikely. Without re-engagement in classroom learning, not only will gains in achievement test scores be elusive, suppressed behaviors can be expected to reappear. And this poignant state of affairs is a breeding ground for dropouts and mental health and juvenile justice problems.

ACKNOWLEDGEMENT

Declare none.

CONFLICT OF INTEREST

The author(s) confirm that this chapter content has no conflict of interest.

REFERENCES

Adelman, H.S., & Taylor, L. (1997). Restructuring education support services and integrating community resources: Beyond the full service school model. *School Psychology Review, 25,* 431–445.

Adelman, H.S., &Taylor, L. (2006a). *The school leader's guide to student learning supports: New directions for addressing barriers to learning.* Thousand Oaks, CA: Corwin Press.

Adelman, H.S., &Taylor, L. (2006b). *The implementation guide to student learning supports in the classroom and schoolwide: New directions for addressing barriers to learning.* Thousand Oaks, CA: Corwin Press.

Adelman, H.S, & Taylor, L. (2007). Systemic change for school improvement. *Journal of Educational and Psychological Consultation, 17(1)* 55-77.

Adelman, H.S., & Taylor, L. (2010). *Mental health in schools: Engaging learners, preventing problems, and improving schools.*Thousand Oaks, CA: Corwin Press.

American Youth Policy Forum (2000). *High Schools of the Millennium Report*, Washington, DC: American Youth Policy Forum.

Brophy, J. (2004). *Motivating students to learn* (2nd ed.). Mahwah, NJ: Erlbaum.

Bruner, J.S. (1966). *Toward a theory of instruction.* Cambridge, MA: Belknap Press.

Center for Mental Health in Schools (2010a). *Motivation Quick Find.* Los Angeles: Author at UCLA. http://smhp.psych.ucla.edu/qf/motiv.htm

Center for Mental Health in Schools (2010b). Turning around, transforming, and continuously improving schools: Federal proposals are still based on a two- rather than a three- component blueprint. Los Angeles: Author at UCLA.http://smhp.psych.ucla.edu/pdfdocs/turning.pdf

Deci, E.L. (1975). *Intrinsic motivation.* New York: Plenum.

Deci, E.L., with Flaste, R. (1995). *Why we do what we do.* New York: Penguin Books.

Deci, E.L., & Ryan, R.M. (1985). *Intrinsic motivation and self-determination in human behavior.* New York: Plenum Press.

Dweck, C.S. (2007).The perils and promises of praise. *Educational Leadership, 65,* 34–39.

Fredricks, J.A., Blumenfeld, P.C., & Paris, A.H. (2004). School engagement: Potential of the concept, state of the evidence. *Review of Educational Research, 74,* 59–109.

Holt, J. (1989). *Learning all the time.* Reading, MA: Addison Wesley.

Pink, D. (2009). *Drive: The surprising truth about what motivates us.*New York: Riverhead.

National Research Council and the Institute of Medicine (2004). *Engaging schools: Fostering high school students' motivation to learn.* Washington, DC: National Academies Press.

Stipek, D.J. (1998). *Motivation to learn: From theory to practice* (3rd ed.). Boston: Allyn & Bacon.

Vansteenkiste, M., Lens, W., & Deci, E.L. (2006). Intrinsic *versus* extrinsic goal contents in self-determination theory: Another look at the quality of academic motivation. *Educational Psychologist*, *41*, 19-31.

Wehrmeyer, M. L. & Sands, D. J. (1998). *Making it happen: Student involvement in education planning, decision making, and instruction.* Baltimore, MD: Paul Brookes Publishing Co.

CHAPTER 4

Teacher-Student Relationships in Mental Health Promotion

Melissa R. Dvorsky[1,*], Leslie K. Taylor[2] and Mark D. Weist[3]

[1]University of South Carolina, Department of Psychology, School Mental Health Team, Columbia, SC 29208, USA; [2]University of South Carolina, Department of Psychology, School Mental Health Team, Columbia, SC 29208, USA and [3]University of South Carolina, Department of Psychology, School Mental Health Team, Columbia, SC 29208, USA

Abstract: As more evidence has accumulated regarding child and adolescent development and school mental health promotion has promulgated, significant variables correlated with mental health promotion have emerged with repetition and replication. One such variable is the importance of teacher student relationships. High quality teacher student relationships are necessary components of school's mental health promotion and, more broadly, comprehensive school performance. Conversely, such matters as negative attributions toward student ability and behavior and teacher student conflicts both tend to constrain desirable student outcomes and are disposed to be highly recalcitrant to change. This chapter summarizes data on these issues, provides strategies for enhancing teacher student relationships that stimulate mental health and optimizing positive outcomes, discusses influences that hinder positive relationships and remediate negative relationships that may already exist, and concludes with a brief discussion of future investigation that will advance our knowledge of this important area.

Keywords: Academic needs, at risk, conflict, mental health needs, teacher-student relationships.

INTRODUCTION

Child and adolescent mental health has become a growing concern for policy makers and educators. Indeed, recommendations from the President's New Freedom Commission on mental health include improving and expanding school mental health services as well as promoting the mental health in young children (New Freedom Commission on Mental Health, 2003). Epidemiological data indicate that, at any given time, up to 15% of children in the United States

***Address correspondence to Melissa R. Dvorsky:** University of South Carolina, Department of Psychology, School Mental Health Team, Columbia, SC 29208, USA; Tel: 803-777-0449; Email: dvorsky@mailbox.sc.edu

Raymond J. Waller (Ed)

experience more serious mental health problems (Roberts, Attkisson, Rosenblatt, 1998), yet less than 1 in every 5 children actually receive help or mental health services (U. S. Department of Health and Human Services, 1999, 2000; Costello, Mustillo, Erkanli, Keeler, & Angold, 2003). This staggering number of youth with underserved mental health needs prompts an interest in promoting school mental health, especially through prevention practices.

Despite significant advances in school mental health (Evans, Weist, & Serpell, 2007), and the existence of school mental health programs in the majority of primary and secondary schools in the United States (Foster, Rollefsom, Doksum, Noonan, & Robinson, 2005), school interventions targeting student academic and mental health needs often occur in isolation of each other (Hoagwood *et al.,* 2007). This is disturbing given that schools have been identified as a critical environment for students to receive mental health services (Weist, Evans, & Lever, 2003).

Youth spend a great deal of their time in school, where they develop relationships with peers and teachers that shape their interpersonal competence, views of self and cultural values. Given that teachers interact with students regularly, they are often the key collaborators with mental health professionals for promoting mental health services and effective interventions to students. In particular, youth's relationships with their teachers can be influential to their school connectedness (Furrer & Skinner, 2003), classroom motivation (Roeser, Eccles, & Sameroff, 2000; Connell & Wellborn, 1991; Eccles, 1993; Wentzel, 2002), academic success (Birch & Ladd, 1997; Burchinal, Peisner-Feinberg, Pianta, & Howes, 2002; Pianta, La Paro, Payne, Cox, & Bradley, 2002; Pianta, Nimetz, & Bennett, 1997), andmental health (Birch & Ladd, 1997; Hughes, Cavell, & Jackson, 1999;Silver, Measelle, Armstrong & Essex, 2005).

Although research has increasingly highlighted the significance of teacher-student relationships for improving students' social adjustment (Pianta, 1999) and classroom functioning (Howes, Hamilton, & Philipsen, 1998; Pianta & Steinberg, 1992), the importance of this relationship to children's academic and social-emotional development (Gregory & Weinstein, 2004; Hamre & Pianta, 2001), is not typically capitalized on within school mental health (SMH) programs. In fact, the reality is that most school communities underutilize teachers as resources for SMH service delivery (Burke & Paternite, 2007; Lynn, McKay, & Atkins, 2003; Paternite, 2004).

The purpose of this chapter is to explore the utility of the teacher-student relationship in the development of youth's mental health and education outcomes. Specifically, we will review empirical findings regarding the impact of this relationship on student outcomes through discussing the development and implications of problematic teacher-student relationships, strategies for promoting positive relationships, effective interventions for relationship improvement, and recommendations for maximizing these relationships to promote healthy school practices.

THE IMPORTANCE OF QUALITY TEACHER-STUDENT RELATIONSHIPS

Within SMH, the impact of teacher-student relationships on students' emotional health, development, academic success, and classroom functioning is a critically important area of program development and research (see, Birch & Ladd, 1996; Eccles *et al.,* 1993; Pianta, 1999). Teacher-student relationships have been associated with students' positive school outlook, classroom motivation, and improved academic outcomes (Pianta, 1999; Roeser, Eccles, & Sameroff, 1998). Supportive relationships serve as a resource of resiliency for students by enhancing their emotional health by teaching social skills, self-regulatory capacities, and practicing basic developmental functions such as attachment, exploration, play and mastery (*e.g.,* Pianta, 1999). Further, supportive relationships are particularly critical for high-risk students experiencing compromised relationships outside of school (Roberts, 1996). This section will highlight the impact of the teacher-student relationship on both students' outcomes and for at-risk students.

Teacher-Student Relationships Influence Student Outcomes: Mental health problems in youth are paired with impairment in functioning across social, academic and family settings. These social, emotional, and behavioral challenges experienced in youth are highly stable and predictive of negative outcomes later in life such as school dropout, drug and alcohol abuse, and incarceration (*e.g.,*

Keenan & Wakschlag, 2000; Kellam, Ling, Merisca, Brown, & Lalongo, 1998; Lochman & The Conduct Prevention Research Group, 1995). However, school mental health services such as prevention and early intervention programs have the potential to alter these trajectories and contribute to positive outcomes for at-risk youth (*e.g.,* Conduct Problems Prevention Research Group, 2004). Further, classroom adjustment has shown to be critically influenced by adult-child relationships, including teacher-student relationships (Hamre & Pianta, 2001; Pianta, 1999). Evidence supporting high quality teacher-student relationships as strong contributors to both proximal (*e.g.,* peer relationships, academic motivation, classroom engagement) and distal (*e.g.,* academic achievement, grade retention) student outcomes (Baker, 2006; Hamre & Pianta, 2001; Roeser, Midgley & Urdan, 1996) are discussed in the proceeding paragraphs.

The majority of research on teacher-student relationships has focused primarily on students' social, emotional, and behavioral outcomes. For example, Howes and colleagues (2008) found that emotional support (*i.e.,* warmth, positivity, child-centeredness, sensitivity, and responsivity to students) from teachers was predictive of a range of task-oriented social competencies such as following directions. When the teacher-student relationship is characterized as supportive and sensitive, students show high levels of school adjustment (Birch & Ladd, 1997; Pianta, Steinberg, & Rollins, 1995). Similarly, Rimm-Kaufman and colleagues (2002) found that teacher sensitivity was effective in reducing negative behaviors in extroverted students such as being off-task during classroom activities. These findings indicate that teacher-student relationships are important correlates of students' social adjustment in the classroom.

Academic performance outcomes have also been investigated in association with teacher-student relationships. For instance, Birch and Ladd (1997) found that the quality of teacher-student relationships correlated with academic performance as assessed by the Metropolitan Readiness Test. They reported that among kindergarteners, both closeness and dependency contributed to visual and language skill performance.

Teacher-Student Relationships with At-Risk Students: Several factors influence social and emotional competence of youth including socioeconomic status, family stability, the number of caregivers, and the number of siblings (Zelli, Dodge, Lochman, Laird, & The Conduct Problems Prevention Research Group, 1999). In fact, many studies have reported the association between these factors and student school failure (see Pianta & McCoy, 1997). Raver and Knitzer (2002) summarized findings on preschoolers' mental health competence and reported that children with emotional and social challenges are less accepted by their peers and teachers, receive less positive feedback and instruction from teachers, have negative opinions of school, and learn less than their classmates. There is a widespread consensus that the quality of youth's social experiences at school with both peers and adults accounts for the links between stressors and poor outcomes (Pianta & McCoy, 1997).

Although child characteristics (*e.g.,* in-attentiveness, dependency, noncompliance) can create strain within the teacher-student dyad, there are specific teacher characteristics that can serve to ameliorate these influences. Emotional support from teachers has been associated with high academic achievement in the first grade among students at high functional risk (*i.e.,* those with early behavioral problems, inattentiveness, lack of social skills, and/or academic problems; see Liew, Chenm & Hughes, in press; Hamre & Pianta, 2005). For example, Hamre and Pianta (2005) found that students of teachers who were receptive and responsive to individual students' needs, and used effective behavior management strategies had higher levels of academic achievement than students in classes with teachers not showing these qualities.

Overall, these findings emphasize the importance of teacher-student relationships in influencing students' social adjustment in school. They also suggest that positive teacher-student relationships serve as a protective factor for children who experience risk conditions (Pianta, 1999) and more generally promote student resilience (Battistich, Solomon, Watson, & Schaps, 1997; Brophy & Good, 1986; Eccles & Roeser, 1998).

CHALLENGES TO ENGAGING TEACHERS IN SCHOOL MENTAL HEALTH PROMOTION

In spite of the increased appreciation for the role of social, behavioral and emotional factors in student learning and achievement (Metlife, 2002; Rose &

Gallup, 2000), many schools struggle with how to integrate SMH programs and services into the highly structured and busy school day (Begeny & Martens, 2006; Coalition for Psychology in the Schools and Education [CPSE], see Rollins, Subotnik, Bassford, & Smulson, 2008). Further, many SMH programs involve teachers in delivery. For teachers, this adds to existing pressures to meet the demands of academic instruction and this struggle has only increased in the past years due to mandates regarding standardized testing benchmarks. Given these pressures, a concern is that increased responsibility in areas related to students' mental health (see New Freedom Commission on Mental Health, 2003) will be viewed by teachers as burdensome *versus* helpful to students and themselves.

Some SMH programs have specifically targeted improvement in the student-teacher relationship (Pianta & Hamre, 2001; McIntosh, Rizza, & Bliss, 2000). However, related to the above, teachers may be reluctant to implement these programs due to increased demands on their time and to other factors such as limited support from school administrators for implementation.

Both individual (*e.g.,* burnout, belief about teaching efficacy) and organizational (*e.g.,* curriculum support, training and coaching, quality of school leadership) factors have been implicated as key factors influencing the quality of teacher's intervention delivery (Ransford, Greenberg, Domitrovich, Small, & Jacobson, 2009). In terms of individual factors, teachers' psychological experiences are important to consider. For example, teacher inability to effectively manage the classroom typically precedes deterioration of the classroom climate (*e.g.,* students showing low levels of on-task behavior, and increases in behavior problems; Marzano, Marzano, & Pickering, 2003), and this may trigger periods of emotional exhaustion, or teacher burnout (Osher, Dwyer, & Jackson, 2007).

Under the strain of emotional exhaustion, teachers may resort to reactive discipline practices, which contribute to the self-sustaining cycle of classroom disruption (Osher *et al.,* 2007). In addition, teachers dealing with burnout who decide to continue teaching may promote negative learning environments (Jennings & Greenberg, 2009). Attitudes characteristic of teacher burnout suggest that these teachers are resistant to implementing mental health programs, especially if they require additional responsibilities (see Ransford *et al.,* 2009).

In terms of organizational factors, teachers may be hesitant to be involved in school mental health promotion programs due to inadequate training and lack of familiarity with intervention content. For example, when examining the feasibility of a school wide mental health promotion program with teachers implementing curriculum modules, Evans, Mullett, Weist, and Franz (2005) found that teachers were less likely to support program implementation than counselors, school psychologists, and school social workers. Findings by Ransford and colleagues (2009) indicate that teachers who feel supported by their school administrators, and perceive training and coaching positively, are more likely to implement interventions with higher implementation quality.

The Impact of Conflict in Teacher-Student Relationships: Research indicates associations among teacher-student relationship quality and behavioral, emotional, and academic outcomes (Hamre & Pianta, 2001; Hamre & Pianta, 2005). These studies not only point toward how significant the relationship is, but toward identification of potential mediators and moderators leading to relationship deterioration. Examination of these factors is important for SMH programs given the critical role educators play in them (*e.g.,* Positive Behavior Intervention and Supports, PBIS, Office of Special Education Programs, 2010).

Negativity within the student-teacher relationship has been operationalized in several different ways, but is often conceptualized by discord and frustration between teachers and students (*e.g.,* Birch & Ladd, 1997, 1998; Hughes, Gleason, & Zhang, 2005; Pianta, 2001; Pianta, Steingberg & Rollins, 1995), and findings indicate that high conflict relationships predict poor outcomes (Birch & Ladd, 1997; 1998). For example, in a sample of kindergarten children, teacher-student conflict was associated with decreased classroom participation, negative school attitudes, lower academic achievement, and peer-reported aggression (Birch & Ladd, 1997).

Further, results suggest that once developed, negativity within teacher-student relationships shows longitudinal stability. An example of this can be drawn from results reported by Hamre and Pianta (2001) indicating that negativity within the teacher-student relationship (measured by teacher perception of student dependency and conflict) predicts a significant proportion of the variance in behavioral and academic outcomes for students from kindergarten to middle school. That is, relational negativity continued to predict behavioral (*i.e.,* number of suspensions, disciplinary actions) and academic outcomes (*i.e.,* standardized test scores, grades) from kindergarten to upper elementary school, with the association among relational negativity and behavioral and academic outcomes at these time points mediated by children's earlier performance in these domains, suggesting that particular children are not easily able to develop positive teacher-student relationships (Hamre & Pianta, 2001).

Research suggests that specific interactions within the teacher-student dyad contribute to and maintain relationship conflicts. For instance, students who display more behavioral, attention, academic, and social problems elicit a variety of interactions from teachers (*e.g.,* Arnold, McWilliams, & Arnold, 1998). Teachers are likely to attribute students' misbehavior as malicious intent and may respond with harshness (Poulou & Norwich, 2000). Teacher-student relationships characterized by verbal attacks on student ability (*i.e.,* name calling, yelling, or public ridicule) are associated with poor adjustment patterns over time, particularly for at-risk youth (Brendgen, Wanner, & Vitaro, 2006). For example, students displaying antisocial behaviors (*i.e.,* lying, fighting, destroying other students' things, hitting, kicking) and inattentiveness are at high risk of verbal abuse by teachers from kindergarten to grade four (Brendgren, *et al.,* 2006).

While this is consistent with research showing that teacher interactions with aggressive students are often characterized by a greater number of reprimands, commands, and negative affectivity (Fry, 1983; Van Acker & Grant, 1996), of further note is that these types of interactions are related to an increasing number of teacher-student conflicts (Howes, Phillipsen, & Peisner-Feinberg, 2000), suggesting continued and perhaps irreparable deterioration of the relationship. Findings also support the stability of teacher-student conflicts for inattentive students longitudinally, despite changes in classroom teachers upon grade level promotion (Brendgen *et al.,* 2006).

Given the stability of conflict within the dyad, a related concern for youth with low levels of attention is the extent to which this may impact long term academic achievement. Repeated verbal abuse by teachers from kindergarten to fourth grade has been associated with low academic achievement in early adolescence, especially for youth with low levels of attention and acting out behaviors. Although researchers are still untangling the relationships among teacher verbal abuse in childhood and adult adjustment, some have posited that youth evoke scolding or criticism from teachers in front of classmates, which may undermine motivation to achieve academically over time (Brendgen, Warner, Vitaro, Bukowski, & Trembley, 2007).

It should also be noted that teachers' responses not only affect a student at the individual level in terms of achievement, but in how they are perceived by their peers. Research suggests that even young children are aware of a teacher's differential interactions with students and use this information to make accurate inferences regarding the teacher's attitudes toward and liking for students (Lei *et al.,* 2007). Thus, it is not surprising that students who receive support from teachers, and from their peers, feel more comfortable in school, like school more, and participate more in classroom activities (Ladd, Birch, & Buhs, 1999; Pianta *et al.,* 1995; Silver, Measelle, Armstrong, & Essex, 2005).

Alternatively, it is also not surprising that students who are unable to develop quality relationships with teachers are more likely to be retained a grade, experience peer rejection, and participate less in classroom activities (Ladd *et al.,* 1999; Pianta *et al.,* 1995; Silver *et al.,* 2005). Further, peer rejection alone has been implicated as a predictor of school avoidance, conduct problems, and academic failure during adolescence (Parker & Asher, 1987; Roff, Sells, & Golden 1972). Taken together, these findings suggest that students with difficulties in the classroom exhibit the greatest need for supportive and accepting teacher and peer relationships, but are the least likely to experience these types of relationships.

PROMOTING POSITIVE RELATIONSHIPS BETWEEN TEACHERS AND STUDENTS THROUGH PREVENTION AND EARLY INTERVENTION INITIATIVE

Numerous developmentally informed theories suggest that positive and responsive interactions with adults (*e.g.,* parents, and teachers) contribute to youths' development including their ability to regulate emotions, social behavior, social skills, and emotional understanding (Birch & Ladd, 1998; Eccles, 1993; Howes, 2000; Wentzel, 2002). Evidence of this perspective is further supported through results indicating that positive classroom climates and sensitive teachers are associated with greater self-regulation in elementary and middle school students (Skinner, Zimmer-Gembeck & Connell, 1998) and greater social competence (Burchinal *et al.,* 2005; Howes, 2000; Pianta *et al.,* 2002).

***School-Wide Approach to Teacher-Student Relationships*:** With important implications for the SMH field, studies show that early intervention strategies have the potential to alter the negative trajectory for at-risk youth and produce positive outcomes for these individuals (*e.g.,* Hill, Coie, Lochman, & Greenberg, 2004). Effective interventions can be provided universally to all children, targeted toward groups of children who are found to be at-risk, or are given to children who are already in the clinical range and already meet criteria for a disorder (*e.g.,* Offord, 2000). School-wide Positive Behavior Intervention Support (PBIS) services are based on such a model, providing preventative interventions to all students (Sugai *et al.,* 2000), with more intensive services for students with greater problems severity (Eber, Sugai, Smith, & Scott, 2002). This type of intervention model reduces risk factors and increases protective factors thereby shifting the balance between the two and helping children to increase the odds of adaptive outcomes (Shonkoff & Phillips, 2000). Moreover, evidence suggests school interventions focusing on positive teacher-student interactions strategies are successful in diminishing student risks (*e.g.,* Catalano, Mazza, Harachi, Abbott, Haggerty, & Flemming, 2003; Greenberg, Domitrovich, & Bumbarger, 2001; Walker, Stiller, Severson, Feil, & Golly, 1998).

Within the PBIS model, teachers act as key change agents in the promotion of positive student behavior. Teacher-student interactions are characterized by three common practices:

1) Acknowledging instances of prosocial behavior with developmentally appropriate praise (Ialongo, Poduska, Werthamer, & Kellam, 2001),

2) Active supervision that incorporates the use of pre-correction, or reminding of an appropriate behavior before the child has an opportunity to make a behavior error (DePry & Sugai, 2002), and

3) More intensive strategies involving problem-solving with students, such as, the Check In-Check Out (CICO) program, which includes checking in with a mentor before and after school for review of goals, structured teacher-student feedback, and encouragement (Crone, Horner, & Hawkin, 2003).

Ultimately, use of these strategies promotes the development of high quality teacher-student relationships by increasing the ratio of positive to negative interactions within the dyad (Filter, McKenna, Benedict, Horner, Todd, & Watson, 2007; McIntosh, Campbell, Carter, & Dickey, 2009).

Salient to mental health promotion in schools, the PBIS model provides preventative intervention for and early detection of behavioral problems. When properly implemented, PBIS includes school-wide prevention of conflict resolution, violence prevention, and social skills programs (Lane, Wehby, Robertson, & Rogers, 2007). Thus, all students participate in these programs, and 80% typically respond at this level of intervention (Horner & Sugai, 2000). The remaining 20% of students are identified and monitored through school attendance and discipline referrals, with 5% of these students needing more intensive intervention services, such as wrap-around services (Eber, Breen, Rose, Unizycki, & London, 2008).

Further, PBIS practices improve school climate through enabling effective academic instruction and implementation of behavior management to occur (McIntosh, Filter, Bennett, Ryan, & Sugai, 2010). Given unsafe and chaotic schools are associated with low levels of academic learning (Kellam, Mayer, Rebok, & Hawkins, 1998), fostering safety and stability within schools is critical for promoting positive social and academic outcomes. Implementation of PBIS has been shown to improve school safety perceptions and academic achievement (Horner *et al.*, 2009). Changes in school disciplinary actions as a result of PBIS may contribute to this shift in school perception. As part of implementation, an overarching aim of school professionals is to reduce exclusionary discipline actions such as office discipline referrals, suspensions, and expulsions through monitoring school data.

In addition, proactive discipline approaches (*e.g.,* warning, incident debriefing, conferences, and behavior contracts) as opposed to reactive approaches (*e.g.,* suspension and detention) become established practices. Reactive discipline strategies can involve student removal from the classroom and may not be effective for those with long histories of detention and suspension (Netzel & Eber, 2003). Thus, incorporating proactive discipline strategies not only provides school staff with a greater number of alternatives for deterring problem behavior (Netzel & Eber, 2003), but also fosters a school environment more conducive to student learning and engagement (McIntosh *et al.,* 2010).

Classroom Climate Initiatives: Although the school-wide prevention and early intervention strategies described above contain classroom and individual level components, additional programs have focused exclusively on improving the classroom climate and quality of individual teacher-student interactions.

Curriculum-based programs that teach students social skills and emotional and behavioral regulation promote the development of healthy relationships by providing students with an open and supportive environment to discuss various feelings and situations. One such school program implemented throughout Australia (MindMatters; Mullett *et al.,* 2004) promotes mental health through a focus on strengthening life skills and community partnerships. Mind Matters aims to provide schools with a framework and resources to audit, plan, and implement mental health promotion practices by using the three "spheres" to create school health promotion:

1) Curriculum;

2) Teaching and learning; school organization, ethos, and environment; and

3) Partnerships and services (Wyn, Cahill, Holdsworth, Rowling, & Carson, 2000).

This program implements five curriculum modules for teachers to implement in the classroom including:

1) Enhancing Resilience part 1;
2) Enhancing Resilience part 2;
3) A Whole-School Approach to Dealing with Bullying and Harassment;
4) Understanding Mental Illnesses;
5) Loss and Grief.

Preliminary data have shown improvement in students' academic performance, attitudes of school personnel, and knowledge of school policies (Hazell, Vincent, Waring, & Lewin, 2002; Wyn *et al.,* 2000). Mind Matters was recently evaluated in four U. S. communities and involved group discussions with stakeholders and endorsement ratings of the program's relevance and impact (Evans *et al.,* 2005). Over 85% of the participants reported that the program would help students in their community to feel safe and valued, and they strongly endorsed the Mind Matters curriculum units targeting suicide prevention, bullying, and harassment.

Another program that promotes positive social-emotional relations in classroom settings is PATHS (*Promoting Alternative Thinking Strategies;* Greenberg, Kusche, Cook, & Quamma, 1995). The PATHS curriculum is a program that focused on the social experience of teachers and students in the classroom. It is designed to help elementary school aged children develop self-control, emotional awareness, and interpersonal problem-solving skills. Students learn to identify and label these skills, generate solutions and practice these solutions. PATHS aims to enhance social competence and social understanding in students, as well as create positive educational practices in the classroom. The Conduct Problems Prevention Research Group (1999) found PATHS to be effect in improving the quality of classroom relationships (*e.g.,* peer and teacher) and classroom climate. That is, in classrooms where teachers understood the importance of PATHS and generalized the lessons taught in PATHS to their daily interactions with students, reported a decrease in overall aggressive behavior. These results are consistent with the bi-directionality of teachers' perceptions and their behavior with students.

Components of both the Mind Matters and PATHS curriculums target the development of quality relationships in the classroom. The quality of the teacher-student relationship and the interactions between students and teachers that promote this relationship may also be the focus of efforts to promote students' well-being. Teachers can implement specific approaches to form quality relationships that are positive, supportive, and responsive to students. The following section will describe how quality interactions between teachers and students can foster resiliency and positive outcomes for students.

Quality of Interactions Between Teachers and Students: Beyond traditional academic teaching responsibilities, teachers also have a unique role in promoting youth's social experiences in the classroom. In recent years, researchers have examined how support from teachers may foster resiliency in students identified at risk for mental and academic problems (*e.g.,* Liew *et al.,* in press; Eccles & Roeser, 1998). Specifically, evidence supports that school interventions that focus on implementing strategies for positive teacher-student interactions are successful in diminishing student risks (*e.g.,* Catalano *et al.,* 2003; Greenberg *et al.,* 2001; Walker, Stiller, Severson, Feil, & Golly, 1998). Noam and Herman (2002) take a school-based prevention approach focusing on the importance of relationships with a school mentor (Noam, Warner, & Van Dyken, 2001). Such relationships function as resources and resilience mechanisms which compensate for the effects of risks, stressors and problems in family relationships.

A close examination of the teacher-student relationship may reveal key relationship elements that serve as protective mechanisms shielding students from risks factors. Supportive teachers by definition are sensitive, responsive, consistent, and positive to students (Rimm-Kaufman, Voorhees, Snell, & La Paro, 2003). Supportive teachers who display each of these characteristics increase social competence in students by teaching coping skills and offering behavioral support (Doll, 1996).

Specifically, sensitive teacher-student interactions promote both students' social, emotional and behavioral adjustment and academic skills (Pianta, 1999; Pianta *et al.,* 2002). Sensitive teachers are effective at responding to students' needs in a child-centered manner by taking on the students' perspective (Rimm-Kauffman *et al.,* 2003). These sensitive and responsive interactions between teachers and students help students to focus their attention, understand their emotions, and apply social skills to the classroom setting, all of which are critical to promoting the students' mental health and academic achievement in school (Thompson, 1994).

There is a sizable amount of research examining how positive daily interactions between teachers and students predict positive development for all children (Birch & Ladd, 1998; Hamre & Pianta, 2001; Ritchie & Howes, 2003). That is, positive relationships between teachers and students have been associated with better or improved outcomes for at-risk and non-risk samples of children (Pederson, Faucher & Eaton, 1978; Werner &Smith, 1980). For example, Ladd and Burgess (2001) found that positive relationships help foster resources for students at risk for failing school. Similarly, Pianta and colleagues (1995) found positive teacher-student relationships to prevent grade retention and future referral to special education (*e.g.,* Pianta *et al.,* 1995) and Pianta (1999) found these to assist youth in school transitions.

Students who display quality relationships with their teachers also tend to have positive attitudes toward school, experience early adjustment to school, and show improved grades and achievement scores (*e.g.,* Ladd *et al.,* 1999; Ladd, Kochenderfer, & Coleman, 1996). Further, children who have quality relationships with their teachers tend to have higher academic motivation and positive attitudes toward school than those who do not have such relationships (*e.g.,* Anderman & Maehr, 1994; Eccles *et al.,* 1993). Doll and Lyon (1998) found having a quality relationship with at least one adult served as a protective factor against negative outcomes such as school dropout and substance abuse. These findings forecast that students who form trusting, warm, and low-conflict relationships with teachers adapt well to the social environment and achieve academically. It is expected that these protective factors in the relationships with teachers reduce the number of risks faced by children and may alter the trajectory associated with the negative outcomes described above. Therefore, efforts related to teacher training and support could be used more strategically to alter the tendency of poor outcomes for such children (see Hamre & Pianta, 2005).

From a somewhat different perspective, theories of motivation suggest that students who experience sensitive, responsive, and positive interactions with their teachers perceive teachers as more supportive and as a result are more motivated academically (Connell & Wellborn, 1991; Eccles, 1993). Further, one study reported that when teachers provided a child-centered climate, kindergarteners were on-task and engaged in learning activities (Pianta *et al.,* 2002). On the other hand, positive relations among older students and teachers was predictive of gains in student engagement (Furrer & Skinner, 2003), academic motivation (Roeser *et al.,* 2000) and achievement (Crosnoe, Johnson, & Elder, 2004; Gregory & Weinstein, 2004).

INTERVENTIONS TO PROMOTE POSITIVE TEACHER-STUDENT RELATIONSHIPS

As noted previously, conflict in the teacher-student relationship can interfere with students; academic and social-emotional functioning, and negatively affect the teacher. In considering interventions for targeting problematic dyads in the classroom, schools should consider interventions that include (a) a thorough assessment of the relationship, (b) allocating time for the teacher and student to build more positive interactions together, and (c) supportive strategies for the student through consistency in communication in the dyad (Hamre & Pianta, 2006).

Assessing the Relationship Between Students and Teachers: There are numerous complex components of student and teacher behaviors that interact and attribute to the teacher-student relationship. To date, there have been many attempts to acknowledge how characteristics such as teachers' attentiveness, supportiveness, patterns of interactions and time spent with the student reflect on the teacher-student relationship(*e.g.,* Howes & Hamilton, 1992; Toth & Cicchetti, 1996; Wentzel, 1996). Pianta (1999) described the necessity of utilizing multiple informants, methods, contexts and occasions when assessing and describing teacher-student relationships. Even though previous research has primarily focused on teachers' perspectives when assessing teacher-student relationships (*e.g.,* Kesner, 2000; Hughes, Gleason, & Zhang, 2005; Pianta, 1994; Pianta & Steinberg, 1992), recent attention has been brought to the importance of assessing this dyadic relationship from both the student and teacher perspectives (*e.g.,* Saft & Pianta, 2001; Pianta, 1999). Further, both teacher and student characteristics appear to be contributing features of the teacher-student relationships (Saft & Pianta, 2001). It's important to assess for both positive and negative characteristics and features of the relationship in order to collect informative data for designing or selecting an intervention. For instance, identifying positive contexts or resources in the relationship may be useful for teachers during particularly challenging conflicts.

Interventions to Address Problematic Teacher-Student Dyads: Given that teachers' report of relationship quality and student behaviors have been found to influence each other in a reciprocal manner (Hughes *et al.,* 2005), interventions to improve the dyad must address both student and teacher influences on the relationship. Many interventions have been designed specifically to build positive interactions between teachers and students among those who have difficulty with conflict. These interventions include Students, Teachers, and Relationship Support (STARS; Pianta & Hamre, 2001), Teacher Child Interaction Therapy (TCIT; McIntosh, Rizza, & Bliss, 2000), and Primetime (Hughes & Cavell, 1999). Each of the following interventions emphasizes the importance of helping teachers and students to develop supportive ways to interact.

Students, Teachers, and Relationship Support: *(STARS;* Pianta & Hamre, 2001). This intervention program implements a primary procedure called "Banking Time" where a teacher and student spend one-on-one time together to "bank" positive experiences together from the school day (Pianta, 1999; Pianta & Hamre, 2001). "Banking Time" is not necessarily used to complete a goal or specific activity, but rather is time for the teacher and student to interact and develop a positive relationship together during an activity that the student has chosen. This intervention is designed to create a positive teacher-student relationship that the teacher can subsequently apply to future classroom interactions.

Teacher Child Interaction Therapy: (*TCIT;* McIntosh *et al.,* 2000). TCIT is an adaptation of PCIT (Eyberg & Boggs, 1998) for the use in the classroom setting. McIntosh and colleagues (2000) presented a single case study design of TCIT in a preschool setting and reported an increase in the number of positive interactions between a child and teacher. It was also found effective in decreasing disruptive behaviors in students and the need for commands from teachers, as well as increasing compliance from students (McIntosh *et al.,* 2000). TCIT focuses on improving the teacher-student relationship by helping teachers identify new way to address behavior problems with their students. Similar to PCIT (Eyberg & Boggs, 1998), TCIT aims to improve the quality of the teacher-student relationship by employing behavioral therapy skills to teachers and helping teachers to strategize and develop problem solving skills for managing behaviors in the classroom. School mental health professionals provide direct coaching to teachers to assist in learning these skills.

Primetime: Hughes and Cavell (1999) developed this school-based secondary prevention program specifically for aggressive children. It focuses on strengthening the teacher-student relationship by utilizing a mentoring style as a support and source of problem-solving skills training. Primetime aims to reduce aggressive behavior in youth by reorganizing their relational skills with parents, peers, and teachers. Cavell and Hughes (2000) and Cavell and colleagues (2009) found that relationships between students and the mentors (*i.e.,* teacher) were associated with reduced externalizing behavior at follow-up assessments using the Child Behavior Checklist, Teacher Report Form (TRF, Achenbach, 1991).

CONCLUSIONS

Throughout this chapter is has been argued that the teacher-student relationship is important for predicting a number of student outcomes. Teachers have the ability to promote competent functioning for all students and resilience for students contending with conditions of risk. Prevention and early intervention efforts increasingly target the social and emotional climate of the classroom in order to promote health development across academic, behavioral and social domains (Greenberg *et al.,* 1995). Further research on these processes would inform school mental health preventions and interventions at the individual, classroom and school levels. For instance, interventions targeted towards youth should emphasis the quality of teachers' interactions with students (*e.g.,* Ladd *et al.,* 2002; Pianta & Hamre, 2001). When students form strong and supportive relationships with teachers, they feel more competent and secure in their performance in the classroom and form better connections with peers. In contrast, when conflict arises between teachers and students, students often feel disconnected to that academic and social emotional resource.

Teachers differ in their ability to establish quality relationships consisting of low conflict with students (Pianta *et al.,* 2007). In fact, educators receive little training or preparation for promoting students' mental health in the classroom (Burke, 2002; Koller & Svoboda, 2002). Therefore, increasing the availability of effective and ongoing professional development efforts in this area for teachers is a high priority. Teachers could better assist students with mental health problems by promoting positive interpersonal relationships in the classroom (Weist, 2005). While the importance of the teacher-student relationship has been well established, the current empirical base for improving this relationship quality is limited. Recent research suggests that professional development efforts that are sustained over time, embedded in teachers' classrooms and provide mentors or coaches with feedback and emotional support can improve teachers' abilities to provide a positive and emotionally supportive context for their students (Landry, Anthony, Swank, & Monseque-Bailey, 2009; Pianta, Mashburn, Downer, Hamre, & Justice, 2008).

School mental health professionals are critical change agents in schools and can help intervene when relationships between students and teachers become problematic. These SMH staff may work with these students and teachers to improve the quality of the relationship and in return improve students' behavioral and academic outcomes. For example, SMH professionals can help teachers to recognize the critical nature of the relationship and mentor them on ways to interact with students in a way that conveys their support and concern for students.

Most often, when preventive and early intervention efforts are short-term, they are limited to short-lived results. Conversely, SMH initiatives that are multiyear and muilti-component are more likely to foster enduring benefits for students (Weist & Albus, 2004; Anderson & Kincaid, 2005). For instance, when classroom components are combined with efforts to form quality relationships among peers, family members, school personnel, health professionals and other community members, students are more likely to adopt positive social, emotional and behavioral health practices (Osher *et al.,* 2002; Weissberg & Greenberg, 1998). Further, in SMH promotion, programs that provide continuous instruction, encouragement, and reinforcement will also support students' ongoing development of positive behavior.

Few would question the value of quality teacher-student relationships wherein the teacher is sensitive, supportive, and responsive to students. Although many have recognized the importance of quality relationships in their recommendations, little direction has been provided to translate these guidelines into practice in the classroom. Research is continuing to accumulate to support of the efficacy of these endeavors, however further empirical evidence is necessitated.

For example, it is clear that characteristics of teacher-student relationships often change as students develop and mature (Harter, 1996), however little has been done to explain the functional implications of these changes for the teacher-student relationship. Younger children heavily rely on their teachers for a daily structure, controlling their behavior and facilitating communication, which in return profoundly affects their daily classroom experiences (Hamre & Pianta, 2006).

However, as students enter later grade levels, the relationships they form with their teachers are more restricted and teachers provide more indirect guidance to their students. Studies are needed to better understand differences in importance in and key variables in teacher-student relationships at different developmental stages. There is a considerable lack of empirical focus on the quality and impact of the teacher-student relationship for students of varied cultural-ethnic backgrounds (see Decker, Dona, Christenson, 2007). An important direction for future research would be to examine how teachers' cultural competence is associated with the quality of the teacher-student relationship.

This chapter underscores the importance of student-teacher relationships, provides directions for future program development and research and emphasizes a critical need for increased focus on these relationships in the increasingly prominent school mental health field.

ACKNOWLEDGEMENT

Declare none.

CONFLICT OF INTEREST

The author(s) confirm that this chapter content has no conflict of interest.

REFERENCES

Achenbach, T. M. (1991). Manual for the Child Behavior Checklist 4-18 and 1991 profile. Burlington: University of Vermont, Department of Psychiatry.

Anderman, E. M. & Maehr, M. L. (1994). Motivation and schooling in the middle grades. *Review of Educational Research, 64,* 287-309.

Anderson, C. & Kincaid, D. (2005). Applying Behavior Analysis to School Violence and Discipline Problems: School wide Positive Behavior Support. *The Behavior Analyst*, *28*(1), 49-63. Retrieved from Psyc INFO database.

Arnold, D. H. McWilliams, L. & Arnold, E. H. (1998). Teacher discipline and child misbehavior in day care: Untangling causality with correlational data. *Developmental Psychology, 34,* 276-287.

Baker, J. A. (2006). Contributions of teacher–child relationships to positive school adjustment during elementary school. *Journal of School Psychology, 44,* 211–229.

Battistich, V. Solomon, D. Watson, M. & Schaps, E. (1997). Caring school communities. *Educational Psychologist, 32*, 137-151.

Begeny, J. C. & Martens, B. K. (2006). Assessing pre-service teachers' training in empirically-validated behavioral instruction practices. *School Psychology Quarterly, 21,* 262-285.

Birch, S. H. & Ladd, G. W. (1996). Interpersonal relationships in the school environment and children's early school adjustment: The role of teachers and peers. In J. Juvonen, K. R. Wentzel (Eds.) Social Motivation. New York: Cambridge University Press.

Birch, S. H. & Ladd, G. W. (1997). The teacher-child relationship and children's early school adjustment. *Journal of School Psychology, 35,* 61-79.

Birch, S. H. & Ladd, G. W. (1998). Children's interpersonal behaviors and the teacher-child relationship. *Developmental Psychology, 34,* 934-946.

Brendgen, M. Bukowski, W. Wanner, B. Vitaro, F. & Tremblay, R. (2007). Verbal Abuse by the Teacher During Childhood and Academic, Behavioral, and Emotional Adjustment in Young Adulthood. *Journal of Educational Psychology*, *99(1)*, 26-38.

Brendgen, M. Wanner, B. & Vitaro, F. (2006). Verbal Abuse by the Teacher and Child Adjustment From Kindergarten Through Grade 6. *Pediatrics*, *117(5),* 1585-1598.

Brophy, J. E. & Good, T. L. (1986). Teacher behavior and student achievement. In M. L. Wittrock (Ed.), *Handbook of research on teaching* (3rd ed. pp. 328-275). Indianapolis, IN: Macmillan Publishing.

Burchinal, M. R. Peisner-Feinberg, E. Pianta, R. & Howes, C. (2002). Development of academic skills from preschool through second grade: family and classroom predictors of developmental trajectories. *Journal of School Psychology, 40,* 415–436.

Burchinal, M. Howes, C. Pianta, R. C. Bryant, D. Eatly, D. Clifford, R. *et al.,* (2005). Predicting child outcomes at the end of kindergarten from the Quality of pre-kindergarten teaching, instruction, activities, and caregiver sensitivity: Manuscript under review.

Burke, R. W. (2002). Social and emotional education in the classroom. *Kappa Delta Pi Record, 38,* 108–111.

Burke, R. W. & Paternite, C. E. (2007). Teacher engagement in expanded school mental health. In S. Evans, Z. Serpell & M. D. Weist (Eds.), *Advances in school-based mental health, Volume 2* (pp. 21-1 to 21-15). Kingston, NJ: Civic Research Institute, Inc.

Catalano, R. F. Mazza, J. J. Harachi, T. W. Abbott, R. D. Haggerty, K. P. & Flemming, C. B. (2003). Raising healthy children through enhancing social development in elementary school: Results after 1. 5 years. *Journal of School Psychology, 41,* 143-164.

Cavell, T. A. Elledge, L. C. Malcolm, K. T. Faith, M. A. & Hughes, J. N. (2009). Relationship quality and the mentoring of aggressive, high-risk children. *Journal of Clinical Child and Adolescent Psychology, 38(2),* 185-198.

Cavell, T. A. & Hughes, J. N. (2000). Secondary prevention as context for assessing chance processes in aggressive children. *Journal of School Psychology, 38(3),* 199-235.

Cavell, T. A. & Hughes, J. (1999). Secondary prevention a context for assessing change processes in aggressive children. Unpublished manuscript, Texas A&M University, College Station.

Conduct Problems Prevention Research Group (1999). Initial impact of the fast track prevention trial for conduct problems: II. Classroom effects. *Journal of Consulting and Clinical Psychology, 67,* 648-657.

Conduct Problems Prevention Research Group (2004). The effects of the Fast Track program on serious problem outcomes at the end of elementary school. *Journal of Clinical Child and Adolescent Psychology, 33,* 650-661

Connell, J. P. & Wellborn, J. G. (1991). Competence, autonomy, and relatedness: A motivational analysis of self-system processes. In M. Gunnar & L. A. Sroufe (Eds.), *Minnesota Symposium on Child Psychology* (Vol. 22, pp. 43-77). Hillsdale, NJ: Lawrence Erlbaum Associates, Inc.

Costello, E. J. Mustillo, S. Erkanli, A. Keeler, G. & Angold, A. (2003). Prevalence and development of psychiatric disorders in childhood and adolescence. *Archives of General Psychiatry, 60,* 837-844.

Crone, D. A. Horner, R. H. & Hawkin, L. S. (2003). *Responding to problem behavior in schools: The Behavior Education Program.* New York: Guilford.

Crosnoe, R. Johnson, M. K. & Elder, G. H. (2004). Intergenerational bonding in school: The behavioral and contextual correlates of student-teacher relationships. *Sociology of Education, 77,* 60-81.

Decker, D. M. Dona, D. P. & Christenson, S. L. (2007). Behaviorally at-risk African American students: The importance of student–teacher relationships for student outcomes. *Journal of School Psychology, 45,* 83−109.

DePry, R. L. & Sugai, G. (2002). The effect of active supervision and pre-correction on minor behavioral incidents in a sixth grade general education classroom. *Journal of Behavioral Education, 11,* 255 -267.

Doll, B. (1996). Children without friends: Implications for practice and policy. *School Psychology Review, 25,* 165-183.

Doll, B. & Lyon, M. A. (1998). Risk and resilience: Implications for the delivery of educational and mental health services in the schools. *School Psychology Review, 27,* 348-363.

Duncan, G. J., & Brooks-Gunn, J. (1997). Consequences of growing up poor. New York: Russell Sage Foundation.

Eber, L. Breen, K. Rose, J. Unizycki, R. & London, T. (2008). Wraparound. *Teaching Exceptional Children, 40(6),* 16-22.

Eber, L. Sugai, G. Smith, C. & Scott, T. (2002). Wraparound and Positive Behavioral Interventions and Supports in the Schools. *Journal of Emotional & Behavioral Disorders, 10(3),* 171.

Eccles, J. S. (1993). School and family effects on the ontogeny of children's interests, self-perceptions, and activity choices. In J. Jacobs (Ed.), *Nebraska symposium on motivation: Vol. 40. Developmental perspectives on motivation* (pp. 145-208). Lincoln: University of Nebraska Press.

Eccles, J. S. Wigfield, A. Midgley, C. Reuman, D. MacIver, D. & Feldlaufer, H. (1993). Negative effects of traditional middle schools on students' motivation. *The Elementary School Journal, 5,* 553-574.

Eccles, J. & Roeser, R. (1998). School and community influences on human development. In M. H. Bornstein & M. E. Lamb (Eds.), *Developmental psychology: An advanced textbook* (4thEd. pp. 503-554). Mahwah, NJ: Erlbaum.

Evans, S. W. Mullett, E. Weist, M. D. & Franz, K. (2005). Feasibility of the *Mind Matters* school mental health promotion program in American schools. *Journal of Youth and Adolescence, 34,* 51-58.

Evans, S. W. Weist, M. D. & Serpell, Z. N. (2007). *Advances in school-based mental health interventions: Best practices and program models, Vol II.* New Jersey: Civic Research Institute.

Eyeberg, S. M. & Boggs, S. R. (1998). Parent-child interaction therapy for oppositional preschoolers. In C. E. Schaefer & J. M. Briesmeister (Eds.). *Handbook of parent training: Parents as co-therapists for children's behavior problems (2nd Ed.)* (pp. 61-97). New York: Wiley.

Filter, K. J. McKenna,M. K. Benedict, E. Horner, R. H. Todd, A. W. &Watson, J. (2007). Check-in/check-out: A post-hoc evaluation of an efficient, secondary-level targeted intervention for reducing problem behaviors in schools. *Education and Treatment of Children, 30*, 69-84.

Foster S, Rollefson M, Doksum T, Noonan D, Robinson G. (2005). *School Mental Health Services in the United States, 2002–2003.* DHHS Pub. No. (SMA) 05-4068. Rockville, MD: Center for Mental Health Services, Substance Abuse and Mental Health Services Administration.

Fry, P. S.*(*1983*)*.Process measures of problem and non-problem children's classroom behaviour: The influence of teacher behaviour variables. *British Journal of Educational Psychology, 53,* 79–88.

Furrer, C. & Skinner, E. (2003). Sense of relatedness as a factor in children's academic engagement and performance. *Journal of Educational Psychology, 95,* 148−162.

Greenberg, M. T. Domitrovich, C. & Bumbarger, B. (2001). The prevention of mental disorders in school-aged children: Current state of the field. *Prevention and Treatment, 4*(1). Available at: http://content.apa.org.journals/pre/4/1/1.

Greenberg, M. Kusche, C. Cook, E. & Quamma, J. (1995). Promoting emotional competence in school-aged children: The effects of the PATHS curriculum. *Development and Psychopathology, 7,* 117-136.

Gregory, A. & Weinsteinm R. S. (2004). Connection and regulation at home and in school: Predicting growth in achievement for adolescents. *Journal of Adolescent Research, 19,* 405-427.

Hamre, B. K. & Pianta, R. C. (2005). Can instructional and emotional support in the first-grade classroom make a difference for children at risk of school failure? *Child Development, 76(5),* 949-967.

Hamre, B. K. & Pianta, R. C. (2006). Student-teacher relationships. In G. G. Bear & K. M. Minke (Eds.), *Children's needs: Part III. Development, prevention, and intervention* (pp. 59-72). Bethesda, MD: National Association of School Psychologists.

Hamre, B. & Pianta, R. (2001). Early teacher-child relationships and the trajectory of children's school outcomes through eighth grade. *Child Development, 72,* 625-638.

Harter, S. (1996). Teacher and classmate influences on scholastic motivation, self-esteem, and level of voice in adolescents. In J. Juvonen & K. Wentzel (Eds.), *Social motivation: Understanding children's school adjustment* (p. 11-42). New York: Cambridge.

Hazell, T. Vincent, K. Waring, T. & Lewin, T. (2002). The challenges of evaluating national mental health promotion programs in schools: A case study using the evaluation of *MindMatters. International Journal of Mental Health Promotion, 4,* 21-27.

Hill, L. G. Coie, J. D. Lochman, J. E. & Greenberg, M. T. (2004). Effectiveness of early screening for externalizing problems: Issues of screening accuracy and utility. *Journal of Consulting and Clinical Psychology, 72*, 809-820.

Hoagwood, K. Olin, S. Kerker, B. Kratochwill, T. Crowe, M. & Saka, N. (2007). Empirically based school interventions targeted at academic and mental health functioning. *Journal of Emotional and Behavioral Disorders, 15(2),* 66-92.

Horner, R. H. & Sugai, G. (2000). School-wide behavior support: An emerging initiative. *Journal of Positive Behavior Interventions, 2,* 231–232.

Horner, R. H. Sugai, G. Smolkowski, K. Eber, L. Nakasato, J. Todd, A. W. *et al.,* (2009). A randomized, wait-list controlled effectiveness trial assessing school-wide positive behavior support in elementary schools. *Journal of Positive Behavior Interventions, 11*, 133-144.

Howes, C. (2000). Social-emotional classroom climate in child care, child-teacher relationships and children's second grade peer relations. *Social Development, 9,* 191-204.

Howes, C. & Hamiltion, C. E. (1992). Children's relationships with child care teachers: Stability and concordance with parental attachments. *Child Development, 63,* 867-868.

Howes, C. Phillipsen, L. & Peisner-Feinberg, E. (2000). The consistency and predictability of teacher-child relationships during the transition to kindergarten. *Journal of School Psychology, 38(2),* 113-132.

Howes, C. Hamilton, C. E. & Phillipsen,L. C. (1998). Stability and continuity of child-caregiver and child-peer relationships. *Child Development, 69(2),* 418-426.

Howes, C. Burchinal, M. Pianta, R. Bryant, D. Early, D. Clifford, R. & Barbarin, O. (2008). Ready to learn? Children's pre-academic achievement in pre-kindergarten programs. *Early Childhood Research Quarterly, 23(3),* 429-430.

Hughes, J. N. Cavell, T. A. & Jackson, T. (1999). Influence of the teacher-student relationship on childhood conduct problems: A prospective study. *Journal of Clinical Child Psychology, 28,*173-184.

Hughes, J. Gleason, K. A. & Zhang, D. (2005). Relationship influences on teachers' perceptions of academic competence in academically at-risk minority and majority first grade classrooms. *Journal of School Psychology, 43,* 303–320.

Ialongo, N. Poduska, J. Werthamer, L. & Kellam, S. (2001). The distal impact of two first-grade preventive interventions on conduct problems and disorder in early adolescence. *Journal of Emotional and Behavioral Disorders, 9,* 146-160.

Jennings, P. A. & Greenberg, M. T. (2009). The prosocial classroom: Teacher social and emotional competence in relation to student and classroom outcomes. *Review of Educational Research, 79,* 491-525.

Keenan, K. & Wakschlag, L. S. (2000). More than the terrible twos: The nature and severity of behavior problems in clinic-referred preschool children. *Journal of Abnormal Child Psychopathology, 10*, 165-185.

Kellam, S.G. Mayer, L. S. Rebok, G. W. & Hawkins, W. E. (1998). Effects of improving achievement on aggressive behavior and of improving aggressive behavior on achievement through two preventive interventions: An investigationof causal paths. In B. P. Dohrenwend (Ed.), *Adversity, stress, and psychopathology* (pp.486-505). London: Oxford University Press.

Kesner, J. E. (2000). Teacher characteristics and the quality of child-teacher relationships. *Journal of School Psychology, 38(2),* 133-150.

Koller, J. R. & Svoboda, S. K. (2002). The application of a strengths based mental health approach in schools. *Childhood Education:Infancy Through Early Adolescence, 78,* 291–294.

Ladd, G. W. & Burgess, K. B. (2001). Do relational risks and protective factors moderate the linkages between childhood aggression and early psychological and school adjustment? *Child Development, 72,* 1579-1601.

Ladd, G. W. Birch, S. H. & Buhs, E. S. (1999). Children's social and scholastic lives in kindergarten: Related spheres of influence? *Child Development, 70,* 1373-1400.

Ladd, G. W. Buhs, E. S. & Troop, W. (2002). Children's interpersonal skills and relationships in school settings: Adaptive significance and implications for school-based prevention and intervention programs. In P. K. Smith & C. H. Hart (Eds.), *Blackwell handbook of childhood social development. Blackwell handbooks of developmental psychology* (pp. 394 – 415). Malden, MA: Blackwell Publishers.

Ladd, G. W. Kochenderfer, B. J. & Coleman, C. C. (1996). Friendship quality as a predictor of young children's early school adjustment. *Child Development, 67,* 1103-1118.

Landry, S. H. Anthony, J. L. Swank, P. R. & Monseque-Bailey, P. (2009). Effectiveness of comprehensive professional development for teachers of at-risk preschoolers. *Journal of Educational Psychology, 101,* 448-465.

Lane, K. Wehby, J. Robertson, E. & Rogers, L. (2007). How Do Different Types of High School Students Respond to School-wide Positive Behavior Support Programs? Characteristics and Responsiveness of Teacher-Identified Students. *Journal of Emotional & Behavioral Disorders, 15(1),* 3-20.

Lei, C. Hongyun, L. Fung, K. Yan, W. Zhonglin, W. Hongli, L. *et al.,* (2007). The Mediating and Moderating Effects of Teacher Preference on the Relations between Students' Social Behaviors and Peer Acceptance. *Merrill-Palmer Quarterly, 53(4),* 603-630.

Liew, J. Chen, Q. & Hughes, J. N. (in press). Child effortful control and teacher support on achievement: additive and interactive effects. *Early Childhood Research Quarterly.*

Lochman, J. E. & The Conduct Prevention Research Group. (1995). Screening of Child Behavior Problems for Prevention Programs at School Entry. *Journal of Consulting and Clinical Psychology, 63,* 549-559.

Lynn, C. J. McKay, M. M. & Atkins, M. S. (2003). School social work: Meeting the mental health needs of students through collaboration with teachers. *Children & Schools, 25(4),* 197-209.

Marzano, R. J. with J. S. Marzano, & D. Pickering. (2003). *Classroom management that works: Research-based strategies for every teacher.* Alexandria, VA: Association for Supervision and Curriculum Development.

May, S. Ard, W. Todd, A. Horner, R. Glasgow, A. Sugai, G. & Sprague, J. (2000). School-wide Information System [SWIS™(c)], University of Oregon, Educational and Community Supports.

McIntosh, K. Filter, K. Bennett, J. Ryan, C. & Sugai, G. (2010). Principles of sustainable prevention: Designing scale-up of School-wide Positive Behavior Support to promote durable systems. *Psychology in the Schools, 47(1),* 5-21.

McIntosh, D. E. Rizza, M. G. & Bliss, L. (2000). Implementing empirically supported interventions: Teacher-child interaction therapy. *Psychology in the Schools, 37,* 453-462.

McIntosh, K. Campbell, A. L. Carter, D. R. & Dickey, C. R. (2009). Differential effects of a tier two behavior interventionbased on function of problem behavior. *Journal of Positive Behavior Interventions, 11,* 82-93.

Metlife. (2002). *The Metlife Survey of the American Teacher 2002-Student life: School, home, and community.* New York: Author.

Mullett, E. K. Evans, S. & Weist, M. D. (2004). A whole school approach to mental health promotion: The Australian *Mind Matters* program. In Clauss-Ehlers, C. & Weist, M. D. (Eds.), *Community Planning to Foster Resilience in Children.* Kluwer Academic/Plenum Publishers, New York, pp. 297-310.

Netzel, D. M. & Eber, L. (2003). Shifting from reactive to proactive discipline in an urban school district: A change of focus through PBIS implementation. *Journal of Positive Behavior Interventions, 5(2),* 71-79.

Noam, G. G. & Hermann, C. A. (2002). Where education and mental health meet: Developmental prevention and early intervention in schools. *Development and Psychopathology, 14,* 861–875.

Noam, G. G. Warner, L. A. & Van Dyken, L. (2001). Beyond the rhetoric of zero tolerance: Long-term solutions for at-risk youth. *New Directions for Youth Development, 92,* 155-182.

Offord, D. R. (2000). Selection levels of prevention. *Addictive Behaviors, 25,* 833-842.

Osher, D. Dwyer, K. & Jackson, S. (2002). *Safe, supportive, and successful schools, step by step.* Rockville, MD: U. S. Department of Health and Human Services, Substance Abuse and Mental Health Services Administration, Center for Mental Health Services.

Parker, J. G. & Asher, S. R. (1987). Peer relations and later personal adjustment: Are low-accepted children at risk? *Psychological Bulletin, 102*, 357-389.

Paternite, C. E. (2004). Involving educators in school-based mental health programs. In Evans, S. W. Weist, M. D. & Serpell, Z. (Eds.). *Advances in school-based mental health interventions: Best practices and program models.* Civic Research Institute, New Jersey, pp. 1-21.

Pederson, E. Faucher J. A. & Eaton, W. W. (1978). A new perspective on the effects of first grade teachers on children's subsequent adult status. *Harvard Educational Review, 48,* 1-31.

Pianta, R. C. (1994). Patterns of relationships between children and kindergarten teachers. *Journal of School Psychology, 32,* 15-31.

Pianta, R. C. (1999). *Enhancing relationships between children and teachers.* Washington, DC: American Psychological Association.

Pianta, R. C. (2001). *Student – teacher relationship scale.* Lutz, FL: Psychological Assessment Resources Inc.

Pianta, R. C. & Hamre, B. (2001). *Students, teachers, and relationship support [STARS]: User's guide.* Lutz, FL: Psychological Assessment Resources, Inc.

Pianta, R. C. & McCoy, S. J. (1997). The first day of school: The predictive validity of early school screening. *Journal of Applied Developmental Psychology, 18,* 1-22.

Pianta, R. C. & Steinberg, M. S. (1992). Teacher-child relationships and the process of adjusting to school. In R. C. Pianta (Ed.), *Beyond the parent: The role of other adults in children's lives.* (pp. 61-80). San Francisco: Jossey-Bass Publishers.

Pianta, R. C. Belsky, J. Houts, R. Morrison, F. Early, The N. I. C. H. D. & Network, Child Care Research (2007). Opportunities to learn in America's elementary classrooms. *Science, 315,* 1795-1796.

Pianta, R. C. Hamre, B. & Stuhlman, M. (2003). Relationships between teachers and children. In W. M. Reynolds & G. E. Miller (Eds.), *Handbook of child psychology: Vol. 7 educational psychology.* (pp. 199–234). Hoboken, NJ: John Wiley & Sons.

Pianta, R. C. Mashburn, A. J. Downer, J. T. Hamre, B. K. & Justice, L. (2008). Effects of web-mediated professional development resources on teacher-child interactions in pre-kindergarten classrooms. *Early Childhood Research Quarterly, 23,* 431-451.

Pianta, R. C. Nimetz, S. L. & Bennett, E. (1997). Mother-child relationships, teacher-child relationships, and school outcomes in preschool and kindergarten. *Early Childhood Research Quarterly, 12,* 263-280.

Pianta, R. C. Steinberg, M. S. & Rollins, K. B. (1995). The first two years of school: Teacher-child relationships and deflections in children's classroom adjustment. *Developmental and Psychopathology, 7, 295*-312.

Pianta, R. La Paro, K. Payne, C. Cox, M. & Bradley, R. (2002). Observed quality of the kindergarten classroom environment: Description and relations with teacher, family, and school characteristics and child outcomes. *Elementary School Journal, 102,* 225-238.

Positive Behavior Intervention and Support Network (2010). *Enhanced phases of implementation.* Eugene, OR: University of Oregon, Educational and Community Supports.

Poulou, M. & Norwich, B. (2000). Teachers' causal attributions, cognitive, emotional and behavioral responses to students with emotional and behavioral difficulties. *The British Journal of Educational Psychology, 70,* 559-581.

President's New Freedom Commission on Mental Health. (2003). *Achieving the promise: Transforming mental health care in America. Final report* (DHHS Pub. No. SMA-03-3832). Rockville, MD: U. S. Department of Health and Human Services.

Ransford, C. Greenberg, M. Domitrovich, C. Small, M. & Jacobson, L. (2009). The Role of Teachers' Psychological Experiences and Perceptions of Curriculum Supports on the Implementation of a Social and Emotional Learning Curriculum. *School Psychology Review, 38(4),* 510-532.

Raver, C. C. & Knitzer, J. (2002). *Ready to enter: What research tells policymakers about strategies to promote social and emotional school readiness among three and four year olds.* New York: National Center for Children in Poverty.

Rimm-Kaufman, S. E. Early, D. M. Cox, M. J. Saluja, G. Pianta, R. C. Bradley, R. H. *et al.,* (2002). Early behavioral attributes and teachers' sensitivity as predictors of competent behavior in the kindergarten classroom. *Journal of Applied Developmental Psychology, 23,* 451 – 470.

Rimm-Kaufman, S. E. Voorhees, M. D. Snell, M. E. & La Paro, K. M. (2003). Improving the sensitivity and responsivity of preservice teachers toward young children with disabilities. *Topics in Early Childhood Special Educations, 23(3),* 151-163.

Ritchie, S. & Howes, C. (2003). Program practices, caregiver stability, and child-caregiver relationships. *Journal of Applied Developmental Psychology, 24,* 497–516.

Roberts, M. C. (1996). *Model programs in child and family mental health.* Hillsdale, NJ: Erlbaum.

Roberts, R. E. Attkisson, C. C. & Rosenblatt, A. (1998). Prevalence of psychopathology among children and adolescents. *American Journal of Psychiatry, 155,* 715-725.

Roeser R. Eccles, J. & Sameroff, A. (1998). Academic and emotional functioning in early adolescence: Longitudinal relations, patterns, and prediction by experience in middle school. *Development and Psychopathology, 10,* 321-352.

Roeser, R. W. Eccles, J. S. & Sameroff, A. J. (2000). School as a context of early adolescents' academic and social-emotional development: A summary of research findings. *The Elementary School Journal, 100,* 443-471.

Roeser, R. W. Midgley, C. & Urdan, T. C. (1996). Perceptions of the school psychological environment and early adolescents' psychological and behavioral functioning in school: The mediating role of goals and belonging. *Journal of Educational Psychology, 88,* 408-422.

Roff, M. Sells, S. B. & Golden, M. M. (Eds.). (1972). *Social adjustment and personality development in children.* University of Minnesota Press, Oxford.

Rollin, S. Subotnik, R. Bassford, M. & Smulson, J. (2008). Bringing psychological science tothe forefront of educational policy: Collaborative efforts of the American Psychological Association's Coalition for Psychology in the Schools and Education. *Psychology in the Schools*, *45(3),* 194-205.

Rose, L. C. & Gallup, A. M. (2000). *The 32nd Annual Phi Delta Kappa. Gallup poll of the public's attitudes towards the public schools.* Retrieved July 7, 2002, from http://www.pdkintl.org/kappan/kpol0009.htm

Saft, E. W. & Pianta, R. C. (2001). Teachers' perceptions of their relationships with students: Effects of child age, gender and ethnicity of teachers and children. *School Psychology Quarterly, 16,* 125-141.

Shonkoff, J. P. & Phillips, D. A. (2000). *From Neurons to Neighborhoods: The Science of Early Childhood Development.* Washington, D. C: National Academy Press.

Silver, R. Measelle, J. Armstrong, J. & Essex, M. (2005). Trajectories of classroom externalizing behavior: Contributions of child characteristics, family characteristics, and the teacher – child relationship during the school transition. *Journal of School Psychology, 43,* 39 – 60.

Skinner, E. A. Zimmer-Gembeck, M. J. & Connell, J. P. (1998). Individual differences and the development of perceived control. *Monographs of the Society for Research in Child Development, 63(2/3),* i-231.

Sugai, G. Horner, R. Dunlap, G. Hieneman, M. Nelson, C. Scott, T. *et al.,* (2000). Applying Positive Behavior Support and Functional Behavioral Assessment in Schools. *Journal of Positive Behavior Interventions*, *2(3),* 131-141.

Thompson, R. A. (1994). Emotion regulation: A theme in search of definition. In N. A. Fox (Ed.), *The development of emotion regulation: Biological and behavioral considerations. (Monographs of the Society for Research in Child Development, 59 [2-3],* Serial No. 240, pp. 25-52.

Toth, S. & Cicchetti, D. (1996). The impact of relatedness with mother on school functioning. *Journal of School Psychology, 34,* 247-266.

U. S. Department of Education, Office of Special Education Programs (2010). Implementation blueprint and self-assessment: School-Wide positive behavior interventions and supports. Technical Assistance Center on Positive Behavioral Interventions and Supports. Available online: http://www.pbis.org/pbis resourcedetailpage.aspx?Type=3&PBISResourceID=216

U. S. Department of Health and Human Services (1999). *Mental Health: A Report of the Surgeon General.* Substance Abuse and Mental Health Services Administration, Center for Mental Health Services, National Institutes of Health, National Institute of Mental Health, Rockville, MD.

U. S. Department of Health and Human Services. (November 2000). *Healthy People 2010,* 2nd ed. With Understanding and Improving Health and Objectives for Improving Health, 2 vols.U. S. Government Printing Office, Washington DC.

Van Acker, R. & Grant, S. (1996). Teacher and student behavior as a function of risk for aggression. *Education & Treatment of Children, 19(3),* 316-334.

Walker, H. M. Stiller, B. Severson, H. H. Feil, *E.G.,*& Golly, A. (1998). First step to success: Intervening at the point of school entry to prevent antisocial behavior patterns. *Psychology in the Schools, 35,* 259-269.

Weissberg, R. P. & Greenberg, M. T. (1998). School and community competence-enhancement and prevention programs. In *I.E.,* Siegel & K. A. Renninger (Eds.), *Handbook of child psychology: Child psychology in practice* (Vol.4.5th ed. pp. 877-954). New York: John Wiley.

Weist, M. D. (2005). Fulfilling the promise of school-based mental health: Moving toward a public mental health promotion approach. *Journal of Abnormal Child Psychology, 33,* 735-741.

Weist, M. D. & Albus, K. E. (2004) Expanded school mental health: exploring program details and developing the research base. *Behavior Modification, 28,* 463–71.

Weist, M. D. Evans, S. W. & Lever, N. A. (Eds.). (2003). *Handbook of school mental health: Advancing practice and research.* New York: Kluwer Academic/Plenum Press.

Wentzel, K. (1996). *Effective teachers are like good parents: Understanding motivation and classroom behavior.* Paper presented at the annual meeting of the American Educational Research Association, New York.

Wentzel, K. (2002). Are effective teachers like good parents? Teacher styles and student adjustment in early adolescence. *Child Development, 73,* 287-301.

Werner, E. & Smith, R. (1980). *Vulnerable but invincible.* New York: Wiley.

Wyn, J. Cahill, H. Holdsworth, R. Rowling, L. & Carson, S. (2000). *MindMatters,* a whole-school approach promoting mental health and wellbeing. *Aust. N. Z. J. Psychiatry, 34,* 594-601.

Zelli, A. Dodge, K. A. Lochman, J. E. Laird, R. D. & Conduct Problems Prevention Research Group. (1999). The distinction between beliefs legitimizing aggression and deviant processing of social cues: Testing measurement validity and the hypothesis that biased processing mediates the effects of beliefs of aggression. *Journal of Personality and Social Psychology, 77*, 150-166.

CHAPTER 5

Response to Intervention: A Proactive Approach Addressing a Spectrum of Student Need

Allison Nealy*

Department of Communication Sciences and Special Education, 516 Aderhold Hall, University of Georgia, USA

Abstract: Response to intervention is a proactive approach addressing the needs of students who do not progress at the expected pace or at a rate commensurate with peers. With this approach, students receive additional needed assistance through the ongoing collection and analysis of data, progress monitoring, and implementation of evidence based practices across all levels of student needs. Intervention without exclusion is emphasized. Avoidance of failure is a paramount concern, and early, intense assistance is an additional focus. Response to intervention was outlined in the newest authorization of the Individuals with Disabilities Education Act, and has been adopted in several states. Though the approach began in the area of learning disabilities, it has been expanded to other domains. Many scholars and practitioners have likewise conceptualized response to intervention to address students'behavioral concerns. This chapter describes response to intervention and proposes that it may be a model for meeting student needs that promotes student mental health in the school setting.

Keywords: Response to intervention, mental health, public schools, mental health professionals, educators, special education, strengths-based approach, universal screening, progress monitoring, models of RtI, standard protocol models, problem solving models, tiers of support, research-based interventions, fidelity.

INTRODUCTION

The topic of mental health in the schools is one that should be of great interest to all professionals working with children. According to the *Surgeon Generals' Report on Mental Health* (1999), an estimated 21% of U.S. students ages 9 to 17 will experience some type of mental health problem during their school years, with 11% experiencing a significant mental health impairment that will adversely impact their educational performance. According to this report, this translates into

***Address correspondence to Allison Nealy:** Department of Communication Sciences and Special Education, 516 Aderhold Hall, University of Georgia, USA; Tel: 706-542-4595; E-mail: anealy@uga.edu

four million children who will suffer from a mental illness that will impact home, school, and relationships with peers.

For many students and their families, school provides a point of entry into mental health services that may otherwise not be available to them (Kutash, Duchnowski, & Lynn, 2006). Although schools have a long history of providing access to mental health services for children, it is critical-as evidenced by the level of need-that newer and more focused model of seeking, finding, and supporting students at-risk for academic, developmental, mental health, and behavioral issues is adopted by educators. The traditional approach of attempting to help students once they are identified as having deficiencies in some functional area is no longer appropriate or viable; we must embrace a more prevention-based and proactive model of addressing student needs.

Response to Intervention (RtI) is a model of service delivery that can serve this purpose. Outlined in the reauthorization of the Individuals with Disabilities Education Act (IDEA) in 2004, this model emphasizes early intervention for students at-risk by employing research-based practices across several tiers of intensity. It also emphasizes collaborative problem solving across general and special education.

This chapter will first discuss mental health conditions often observed in the school setting and relate these to RtI in public education. It will then outline the history and definition of the RtI delivery model. Within this outline, common terms and essential components of RtI will be described. The application of the RtI model to mental health and behavioral conditions will be discussed, as well as how the RtI model might be used to promote mental health in the schools.

MENTAL HEALTH

Mental health in childhood can be defined as the achievement of typical developmental milestones in the areas of cognition, socialization, emotionality, and effective coping strategies (Hoagwood, Jensen, Petti, & Burns, 1996). Mentally healthy children function well both at home and at school, and are successful in establishing long-term relationships with people in their communities. Mental *disorders*, in contrast to mental *health*, are considered deviations from expected cognitive, social, and emotional development. It is important to view children in the context of their physical, social, and cultural surroundings when investigating and considering the identification and labeling of potential developmental abnormalities.

For school personnel, this means being considerate of home and community environments when discussing a student's mental health. School personnel should also be aware that the discussion of 'mental disorders', 'developmental abnormalities', and similar terminology is contrary to the approach favored by many clinicians—the *strengths-based* approach. The terminology in this chapter reflects much of the traditional thought associated with student needs in the school setting—terminology that may be familiar to many professionals in the education field. Other chapters in this text will include more terminology and discussion of the strengths-based perspective of mental health.

There are several concepts of children's mental health that are based on the premise that psychopathology arises from complex interactions of the child, his or her environment, and the child's past experiences (Cicchetti & Cohen, 1995). Characteristics of a child, including temperament, biological factors, and genetic make-up, interact with how the child lives (*e.g.,* parenting style, peer interactions, neighborhood settings, and cultural expectations). Defining and describing mental health, therefore, can be a daunting task. In fact, defining mental health may be more difficult than defining abnormalities, which might partially explain a historical predilection for deficits-based mental health conceptualization. For the purpose of this chapter, discussion is limited to how mental health issues are identified and addressed within the context of a school and support structures that can and should be put into place to promote mental health.

MENTAL HEALTH AND SCHOOL

School and educators play a critical role in the developmental of a child's mental health. School is one of many contexts that shape a child's development. Starting at a young age, many children spend more time at school with teachers and peers than they do with their own families. Educators play important roles in identifying children with mental health issues, making referrals to appropriate personnel, collaborating with professionals, and participating in school-wide efforts to promote and support good mental health for all children. Selecting a child as one that needs additional, supplemental support in the area of mental health does not necessarily put them on a fast-track into accessing special education services but rather recognizes the need for more intense and frequent interventions.

In fact, what is often misunderstood is that not *all* students with diagnosed mental health disorders are eligible for supplemental school-based interventions and/or special education services of any kind. As described in further detail in the following section, many students with diagnosed mental health disorders experience academic and social success at school and therefore do not require intense tiers of interventions or special education services. Eligibility requirements set forth by federal guidelines mandate that a condition must adversely affect a child's school performance in order to warrant services (IDEA, 1997). Of those who do qualify for special education services based on a mental health disorder, most fall under the category of Other Health Impaired.

OTHER HEALTH IMPAIRMENT

Other Health Impaired (OHI) is one of 14 federal categories of eligibility and encompasses students that have medical conditions that warrant special education services. According to the federal regulations:

Other Health Impairment means having limited strength, vitality or alertness, including a heightened alertness to environmental stimuli, that results in limitedalertness with respect to the educational environment, that (i) is due to chronic or acute health problems such as asthma, attention deficit disorder or attention deficit hyperactivity disorder, diabetes, epilepsy, a heart condition, hemophilia, lead poisoning, leukemia, nephritis, rheumatic fever, and sickle cell anemia; and (ii) adversely affects a child's educational performance (34 Code of Federal Regulations, section 300.7(c)(9)).

The conditions mentioned in this definition are not meant to be exclusive. Other conditions can also fall under the umbrella of OHI. The United States Department of Education (2006) specifically mentions fetal alcohol syndrome, bipolar disorders, and other organic neurological disorders as further conditions that may qualify a child for services under IDEA. According to Grice (2002), a child must meet four conditions to be eligible for services under OHI.

- First, he or she must suffer from a chronic or acute health condition,
- Second, the condition must cause limited alertness to the educational environment,
- Third, the child's educational performance must be adversely affected by the disability,
- Fourth, the condition must create a need for special education services.

The U.S. Department of Education is careful to state that health conditions *may* make a child eligible for interventions and/or special education services, but simply having a diagnosis is not enough. This is an important distinction. The finding of a health disorder, including a mental health disorder, does not alone qualify a child for special education services. The condition or disorder must also *adversely affect educational performance*. Health conditions are intentionally not defined by either IDEA or the Office of Special Education Programs (OSEP) in the U.S. Department of Education. Rather, OSEP contends that the meaning of this term must be established in a case-by-case basis in consideration of circumstances.

For example, consider an adolescent girl with a diagnosis of bipolar disorder. If she is able to receive medical attention outside of school, exhibits functional social skills, and is performing at a passing level in all of her classes, she may not require special education services. However, if the same girl began to exhibit anti-social behaviors such as aggression or withdrawal and began failing her classes, it could be said that the disorder is adversely affecting her educational performance. She may then benefit from supplemental academic and behavioral interventions and perhaps eventually special education services.

Other mental health conditions that may qualify a child for IDEA services include anxiety disorders, eating disorders, anti-social behaviors, attachment disorder, and complications from Attention Deficit Hyperactivity Disorder. Again, having a formal diagnosis in any one of these areas is not sufficient to require interventions or supplemental services in school. It is how these disorders manifest themselves in social, emotional, and academic functioning that determines a need for intervention. As previously stated in this chapter, it is critical that we move towards a more proactive-and strengths-based-model of identifying and serving students. Response to Intervention can serve this purpose.

RESPONSE TO INTERVENTION

Response to Intervention is at the most fundamental level, the practice of providing high-quality instruction and research-based interventions across multiple tiers of intensity, monitoring student progress frequently, and allowing child response data to inform and guide important educational decisions (Fuchs & Deshler, 2007). It is a multi-tiered approach to providing instruction, services, and interventions at increasing levels of intensity to students struggling academically or behaviorally. Based on a problem-solving model, the RtI approach takes into consideration environmental factors that may impact a student's performance in school and provides intervention as soon as possible (Sandomierski, Kincaid, & Algozzine, 2007).

The principle behind RtI is that if a child is not responding typically to current instruction and strategies, then supplemental interventions should be introduced and monitored across multiple levels or tiers of intensity, culminating in consideration of evaluation for special education services. Unlike historically employed school intervention models, RtI places more responsibility on general educators to determine the need for more intense interventions based on academic and behavioral data collected in the general education classroom (Richards, Pavri, Golez, Canges, & Murphy, 2007). Following are discussions of the history and development of RtI, its components and terminology, and the two common models used to implement it.

THE HISTORY OF RESPONSE TO INTERVENTION

RtI evolved out of the field of learning disabilities. Since 1977, the number of students in this country identified as having a learning disability has increased by

200 percent (McCook, 2006). Traditionally, a student has been identified as having a learning disability when a severe discrepancy existed between his or her cognitive abilities as measured by standardized intelligence tests, and the student's achievement in an academic area. This model looked at expected achievement based on cognitive potential and compared it to actual achievement. Identification of students varied across states as each state had its own formula for determining when a discrepancy would be considered "severe" (Fuchs & Fuchs, 2006).

From its inception, there were criticisms of the discrepancy model. First and foremost, use of the discrepancy model made early identification and intervention difficult. Among young children, those in kindergarten through grade three, many do not demonstrate the cognitive ability-achievement discrepancy required to meet eligibility because intelligence and achievement testing is generally not considered accurate or reliable at early ages (Speece, 2002). As a result, identification of students with learning disabilities peaks in grades three and four (Lyon, Fletcher, Fuchs, & Chhabra, 2006). Critics argue that the discrepancy model represents a "wait-to-fail" approach which results in a loss of valuable instructional time in the early grades that most likely would have made a significant impact on educational performance of those students affected (Bradley, Danielson, & Doolittle, 2007). The model is reactive rather than proactive in its approach to struggling students.

A second major criticism of the discrepancy model is that many students do not qualify for special education services because of a low intellectual ability that fails to establish a severe discrepancy. For example, if a child has a cognitive ability test score of 80 (below average) and academic scores in the 70s (below average) they will not qualify for special education services under Specific Learning Disability because the discrepancy is not "severe" enough. However, this same child will also not qualify for services under Mild Intellectual Disability (Mild Mental Retardation) because their cognitive ability is too high. Although it is clear that a child with lower than average cognitive ability and academic scores in the 70 to 80 range needs support, school systems have historically been unable to provide this student any type of special education services. Consequently, labels such as "slow learner" have been applied (Restori, Katz, & Lee, 2009).

A final prominent criticism is that there is little scientific basis or empirical evidence in favor of using the discrepancy model (Francis, Fletcher, & Stuebing, 2005). There is, however, a substantial body of research that the cognitive ability--achievement discrepancy model may not accurately and consistently identify students with specific learning disabilities. Critics argue that making a decision for whether a student qualifies for services based on a single test score, at a single point in time, with an instrument that has measurement error, is not a reliable or psychometrically sound practice (Fletcher *et al.,* 2002).

Out of these criticisms, RtI rose as a movement toward a responsive and proactive method of identifying struggling students early in school and providing interventions *before* they demonstrate school failure. In contrast with the discrepancy model, RtI focuses on the context in which a child receives instruction and how well the he or she responds to instruction rather than on deficits within the child. The assumption that a child cannot learn only because he or she has a neurological deficit fails to account for the possibility that interacting variables such as a lack of good instruction, language barriers, and a limited number of opportunities to learn may account for the lack of academic or behavioral progress.

RtI AND FEDERAL REGULATIONS

Although the components have been around for more than 40 years (Bender & Shores, 2007), RtI was first mentioned in federal law in IDEA 2004:

> Notwithstanding section 607(b), when determining whether a child has a specific learning disability as defined in section 602, a local educational agency shall not be required to take into consideration whether a child has a severe discrepancy between achievement and intellectual ability….In determining whether a child has a specific learning disability, a local educational agency may use a process that determines if the child responds to a scientific, research-based intervention as part of the evaluation procedures…(H.R. 1350, 2005, Section 614 (b) (6) (A&B)).

This statement indicates that state agencies can no longer require local school districts to use the discrepancy formula to determine eligibility. Also included in

IDEA 2004 is language that provides local school districts the opportunity to use up to 15% of their special education monies to fund early intervention strategies, and specifically distinguishes RtI as one of these approaches. While the law stops short of requiring RtI, the federal implementation regulations published in 2005 clearly endorse its use:

Models that incorporate response to research-based intervention should be given priority in an effort to identify students with learning disabilities. Identification models that incorporate response to intervention represent a shift in special education toward the goals of better achievement and behavioral outcomes forstudents....[Federal Register: June 21, 2005 (Volume 70, Number 118) [Proposed Rules] (Page 35781-35892)].

Furthermore, the No Child Left Behind Act of 2002 mandated that scientifically validated curricula be used for all students (NCLB, 2002). The purpose of this mandate was to ensure that every child has an opportunity to learn the general education curriculum. RtI is a model that supports this mandate by exposing each and every child to best practices while providing access to the general curriculum.

COMPONENTS OF RtI

RtI provides a framework for prevention of learning and behavioral difficulties, early intervention for those students not making expected gains, and identification of students who need intensive, supplemental interventions. RtI is a function of the general education classroom and should be considered a system of instruction that is available to every student (Rudebusch, 2007). No current legislation actually defines RtI; however, national organizations have created definitions commonly used in the literature. The National Center on Research for Learning Disabilities (NCRLD) provides a framework for the essential components of RtI:

1) Students receive high-quality, research-based instruction from qualified staff in their general education setting;

2) General education staff members assume an active role in students' assessment in the curriculum;

3) School staff conducts universal screening of academics and behavior;

4) School staff implements specific, research-based interventions to address the students difficulties;

5) School staff conducts continuous progress monitoring of student performance (*i.e.,* weekly or biweekly) for secondary and tertiary interventions and less frequently in general education;

6) School staff uses progress monitoring data and explicit decision rules to determine interventions effectiveness and necessary modification;

7) Systematic assessment is made regarding the fidelity or integrity with which instruction and interventions are implemented; and

8) The RtI model includes, as required, provisions for referral for comprehensive evaluation, free appropriate public education, and due process protections ("Core concepts," 2006).

The RtI model employs a team of individuals to implement the components presented by NCRLD. As evident by these statements, the emphasis of RtI is on helping every student be successful in the general education classroom. The foundation of the RtI model is standards-based instruction delivered by a qualified teacher in a general education setting. Supplemental supports are provided as needed, but the students remain in the general education setting until instructional options are exhausted across the tiers of intensity.

KEY TERMS

There are several key terms central to the RtI model mentioned above that need defining. These terms appear frequently in not only the description of RtI as a concept, but also within the implementation guidelines embedded within the context of the tiered system.

Universal screening is an outcome measure administered to all students early in the school year to identify which students may be at risk for not meeting grade level standards or those who have behavioral or emotional difficulties that may interfere with their learning (Klotz & Canter, 2007). A screener is designed to assess all students several times per year with the express purpose of identifying as early as possible students not making expected gains in the core curriculum. For a screener to be useful, it should be practical and simple to implement by all teachers in the general education setting (McCook, 2006). Screeners can use either criterion referenced (compare scores to a set criterion) or normative (compare scores to other peers) comparison standards. The National Center on Response to Intervention (NCRTI) provides examples of screeners that will assess oral reading fluency, early math skills including number identification, and reading comprehension (www.rti4success.org).

Progress monitoring is a scientifically-based practice of assessing students' academic and behavioral performance on a regular basis to determine the extent to which each student is responding to instruction within each tier of support. Progress monitoring procedures can be used with individual students, in small groups, or with an entire class depending on the assessment needs. Progress monitoring becomes critical and more frequent in Tiers 2 and 3 to accurately determine a child's response to supplemental interventions beyond the core curriculum of Tier 1. It is used to not only determine an intervention's effectiveness, but to determine whether instructional modifications are necessary and provide critical information needed for placement purposes. The National Center of Student Progress Monitoring identifies several commonly used tools to monitor student progress (www.studentprogress.org). Descriptions of these are beyond the scope of this chapter but it is important to note that many progress monitoring tools are curriculum-based measures designed for the purpose of assessing students' progress in academic areas and provide alternate forms of equivalent difficulty over time.

Research-based interventions are those that have been verified as effective. They have been scientifically researched and reported in peer-reviewed journals. These interventions are also referred to as evidence-based practices in the literature and are described as "teaching practices that have been proven to work" (U.S. Department of Education, 2003). It is worth noting that, as was previously noted of RtI, exactly what criteria determine or define 'research-based interventions' has not been universally adopted.

Fidelity means that an intervention is implemented in the manner in which it was researched and validated. NCRTI defines it as, "the accurate and consistent provision or delivery of instruction in the manner in which it was designed or prescribed according to research findings and/or developers' specifications" (www.rti4success.org). For example, if an intervention requires four, 30-minute sessions a week and it is only conducted twice a week for 20 minutes, it is not being done with fidelity. Materials and directions may not be altered from their original state if one hopes to implement a strategy with fidelity.

THE THREE-TIERED SYSTEM

RtI is often visually depicted as a pyramid with three tiers of educational interventions through which students may advance as their individual needs necessitate such as is represented in Fig. **1**. The premise behind the pyramid is that 80% of students will demonstrate academic and behavioral success at Tier 1, generally considered a universal level available to every student. Of the 20% of students needing additional support, 15% will respond to Tier 2 level of interventions. The remaining 5% of students, those not responsive to Tier 1 and Tier 2 interventions, will need to be moved into Tier 3. While a three-tiered model is the most common, some states use additional tiers to indicate referral for evaluation into special education (Stepanek & Peixotto, 2009). It is recommended, however, that schools use a three-tier model with only one tier separating general and special education (Fuchs & Fuchs, 2007). This recommendation is made because it is difficult to design more than one tier of preventative intervention that can be easily distinguished from both general and special education services. An overview of each tier follows.

Tier 1 should consist of quality, research-supported classroom instruction by a qualified teacher in general education. Instruction is based on your state curriculum and includes all students. It should incorporate practices such as differentiation of instruction, flexible grouping, and other best practices scientifically determined to be good for all students. At Tier 1, interventions are done within the framework of the general classroom. The focus of Tier 1 is on the quality of instruction that all students receive (McCook, 2006). Universal screeners are administered and data are collected to identify students that are not performing on grade level. Adjustments to instruction in Tier 1 focus on targeted students needing additional support are made in a whole-group setting. If a teacher identifies a student that is not making expected gains, the number of probes on his or her progress (through a progress monitoring tool) should increase in order to collect baseline data in the area of concern. Once a data-based decision has been made that a student is not positively responding to the instruction in Tier 1, it is recommended that the student advance to Tier 2 interventions. Using the pyramid model, it is estimated that 15-20% of students will need additional support provided in Tier 2 (Bender & Shores, 2007).

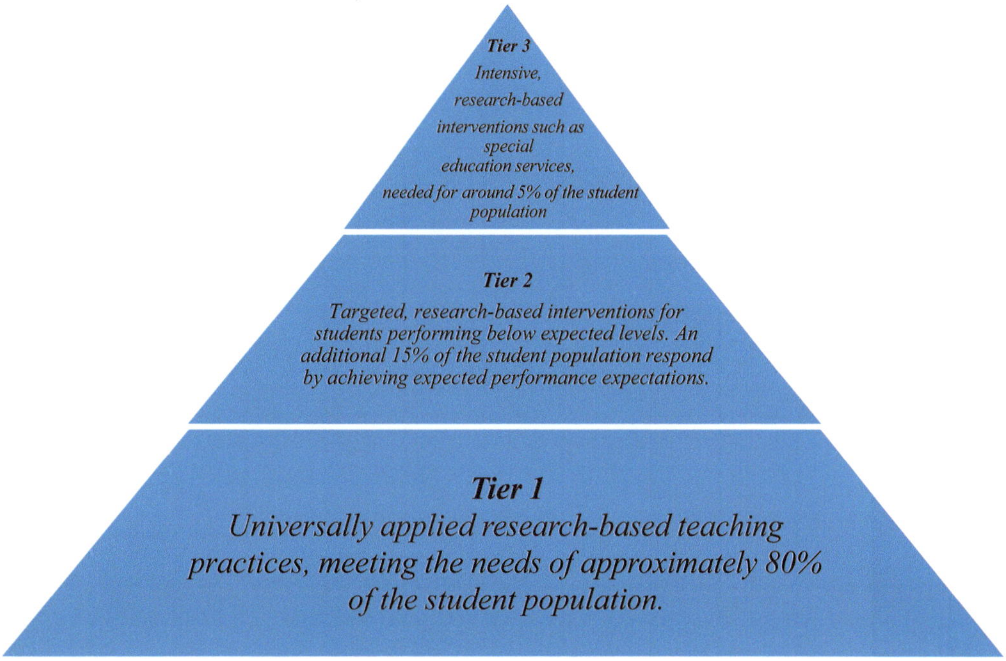

Figure 1: Visual Representation of the RtI Tiers of Intervention.

Tier 2 is designed to provide *supplemental instruction in addition to* the standard classroom curriculum. The interventions in this tier are not designed to replace classroom instruction but rather supplement the curriculum. The idea here is that more of the same will not make a difference. Consider the example of a patient going to see her physician. If a patient was diagnosed with strep throat and prescribed an antibiotic, she would take it for 10 days. If after that time, the patient was still sick with strep throat and returned to the doctor, he or she would expect a *different* prescription. If the patient took medication for the proper amount of time and it did not work, why would he take it again? It is the same idea for students and instruction. If a student is not responding to the instruction provided in Tier 1, it is senseless to continue on the same path and allow valuable time to slip away. Tier 2 is targeted to students who exhibit performance below expected levels in academic or behavioral issues, and students who are not learning at an anticipated rate and are, therefore, falling behind their peers.

According to McCook (2006), services in Tier 2 should include the following:

1. Flexible scheduling to allocate sufficient time for small group instruction;
2. Create use of personnel;
3. 30 minutes of additional instruction at least three times per week;
4. Prescribed supplemental instruction with assigned timelines;
5. Documented progress monitoring at least bi-weekly, if not weekly.

Fuchs and Fuchs (2007) provide a sample RtI model that includes 15- to 20-week sessions at Tier 2, which they refer to as "secondary prevention" (p.15). Interventions at this level need to be scientifically based and delivered with fidelity either one-on-one or in small groups.

Progress monitoring for students in Tier 2 continues for a specific period of time, such as 10 weeks, and data are used to determine whether:

- The student has made accelerated progress and her rate of progress places her on a trajectory to be on grade-level. If so, she returns to Tier 1. If, alternatively,
- Progress is occurring but is slower than expected; the student will remain in Tier 2. If
- No progress has been demonstrated, the student will be moved to Tier 3. Approximately 5% of all students will require this final level of support.

Tier 3 is for students who continue to have difficulty reaching grade level benchmarks despite the supplemental supports provided in Tier 2. These students have demonstrated the need for individualized, explicit instruction designed specifically for their individual learning needs (Stecker, 2007). The frequency, intensity, and duration of interventions at this level are higher than in Tier 2, and progress monitoring becomes a weekly requirement. The purpose of Tier 3 becomes ensuring that all possible supports, interventions, and scientifically-based instructional methods have been exhausted in the general education setting prior to referring a child for an evaluation for special education services. By the time a student reaches Tier 3, the school has had enough time to gather data to demonstrate that academic or behavioral difficulties are not due to a lack of good instruction. A school must be able to say with confidence that all instruction and interventions in Tiers 1 and 2 were both research-based and implemented with fidelity.

After another specified period of time, such as 6 weeks, if the student continues to be unresponsive to the intensified instruction, then the child is considered to potentially have a disability. While the lack of success at Tier 3 does not automatically identify a child as needing special education services, the child is referred for a full evaluation and therefore protected under the procedural safeguards of IDEA (McCook, 2006).

TWO MODELS OF RtI

Two models of RtI have emerged over time: the problem-solving model and the standard protocol model. Both approaches have similar structure and require the use of research based interventions, progress monitoring, and data based decision making. However, they differ in their evaluation of an intervention's effectiveness.

Problem Solving Model: Within this model, the interventions are designed to specifically meet the needs of an individual student or small group of students (Grimes & Kurns, 2003). Data are used to continually evaluate a student's progress, determine length of time an intervention should be used and whether further instructional supports needed. Teams convene regularly to evaluate progress and set/reset timelines. The advantage of this model is that it is personalized to the needs of each student. Potential disadvantages are the amount of time required to meet on a regular basis and the absence of a defined time period for each level or tier.

Standard Protocol Model: The protocol model identifies specific interventions that struggling students will receive and defines a fixed time period for which the interventions will be implemented (Pierangelo & Giuliani, 2008). These interventions are research based, and personnel are trained on their implementation and progress monitoring components. Students are grouped according to deficit (*e.g.,* reading fluency) and then they all receive the same intervention. One advantage to this model includes being able to better track accuracy of implementation by training personnel to conduct one intervention and control for quality (Fuchs, Mock, Morgan, & Young, 2003). Logistically, schools find this model more practical. A disadvantage of this model is that no one intervention is going to be a perfect match to every student. Unlike the problem solving model, the protocol model is not specifically designed for individual students but rather casts a broad net across students exhibiting similar difficulties. Another profound disadvantage is that, as is inherently obvious, the standard protocol model is deficiency focused.

COMMON MYTHS ABOUT RtI

RtI represents a new way of conceptualizing how to respond to struggling students, and has, therefore, been vulnerable to misinterpretation. The National Association of State Directors of Special Education (NASDSE) has identified some common myths about RtI. Three common myths about RtI are as follows:

1. *The purpose of RtI is to identify students who need special education.* The purpose of RtI is to provide scientifically-based instruction and interventions to every student and use student data to guide the type, frequency, and duration of further instruction. Identification may or may not occur as a result of using the tiered system. Early identification of struggling students and subsequent immediate intervention is critical.

2. *Tier 3 is only special education.* Tier 3 is most intensive level provided to students in general education. A student that does not respond to the intervention in Tier 3 may qualify for special education, but only after data have demonstrated that the intensity of the Tier 3 intervention is ineffective. It must be determined that there are no more viable options in the general education setting prior to referral to special education.

3. *Tier 2 should be short in duration, not the 10-weeks suggested in most RtI models.* There is no formula for how long any given intervention should last. Even in the protocol model, enough time must be provided to allow for student response. Six weeks is generally not enough time to make a data-driven decision.

These and other common myths about RtI must be addressed across the profession. It is important for all schools to realize that RtI is a general education initiative and requires collaboration across personnel (Richards, *et al.,* 2007). As NASDSE states, "RtI is a dramatic redesign of general and special education; both need to change and the entire system needs to reform if schools are going to make AYP [annual yearly progress] targets and meet the needs of all students. Tweaking the traditional model will not be sufficient" (www.nasdse.org). Much work remains to be done, as the most recent survey of state laws reveals that only 12 states have adopted the RtI approach as the required approach (Zirkel, 2010). Other states are making the use of RtI optional.

RtI AND MENTAL HEALTH

Although RtI was developed in the field of learning disabilities, its application to other domains of performance is emerging. It is the position of the Council for Exceptional Children that, "positive and appropriate educational interventions, as well as mental health supports, should be provided routinely to all children and youth that need them" (CEC, 2010). There is a need for a proactive approach to behavioral and mental health issues in the schools just as there is with academic ones (Morrisey, Bohanon, & Fenning, 2010). IDEA 2004 mandates that students with special needs have access to the general education curriculum in the least restrictive environment (U.S Department of Education, 2006). As a result, general education teachers with little to no training in how best to support students with disabilities are now responsible for students with increased social, emotional, and behavioral needs which may include mental health diagnoses (Couvillon, Peterson, Ryan, Scheuermann, & Stegall, 2010). Most RtI discussions revolve around prevention of academic failure but it is critical to explore how the RtI process can also be applied to behavioral and emotional needs.

Positive Behavior Supports (PBS) is a problem-solving model that applies the principles of RtI to behavior. As is true of academics, RtI as applied to behavior is often conceptualized as a three-tiered system intended to prevent inappropriate behavior through teaching and reinforcing appropriate behaviors. PBS presents a range of interventions that are selected and systematically applied to students based on behavioral data (Sandomierski, *et al.,* 2007). Research-based curricula for behavior promotes social skills that all students are expected to display. PBS is preventative by design, reinforcing students for displaying the school-wide and classroom-wide behavioral expectations. IDEA specifically requires the IEP team to consider the use of Positive Behavioral Interventions and Supports for any student whose behavior impedes his or her own learning or the learning of others (IDEA, 2004).

Commonly, mental health conditions can manifest themselves in behavioral symptoms that transcend settings to include school. It is appropriate to consider that the application of RtI to behavior is comprehensive enough to include students with potential mental health disorders. Pearce (2009) successfully applied the RtI model to nine students with diagnoses that included depression, attachment disorder, oppositional defiant disorder, bipolar disorder, and attention deficit disorder. Inappropriate behaviors exhibited by these students were identified and defined in the study, and all nine students went through a tiered system of behavioral interventions over two years. Seven of the nine students responded positively to the interventions while two were eventually referred to and found eligible for special education services.

Similarly, Bond and colleagues (2004) found that a multilevel school based intervention had positive effects on the emotional well-being and health risk behaviors of adolescents. The authors conducted a three year study with 2678 adolescent students and found that the implementation of a multi-tiered intervention program had positive outcomes on measures such as self-reported anxiety, depressive symptoms, school engagement, and substance abuse. Such findings are encouraging for the potential use of an RtI model for the purposes of both prevention and intervention.

As previously mentioned in this chapter, being diagnosed with a mental disorder in and of itself does not warrant the need for special education services. However, if exhibited behavior is documented and addressed across three tiers of intervention, data may indicate that a student is in need of support through special education services. Undesirable school behaviors that warrant movement across tiers can include aggression, non-compliance, crying, ritualistic behaviors, theft, and self-injurious behaviors (Morrisey, *et al.,* 2010). Potential Tier 2 and Tier 3 interventions for these behaviors include social skills training (McGinnis & Goldstein, 1997), cognitive behavioral intervention (Bloomquist, 1996), differentiated instruction (Tomlison, 1999), and group counseling.

CONCLUSIONS

The landscape of our general education classrooms continues to change. With recent legislation instructing that 90% of children with disabilities be included in the general education classroom for 80% of the school day, general educators are now held accountable for the success of not only more students, but students with a wider range of abilities and needs (NCLB, 2002). A student's success at school now largely depends on the general education teacher's ability to provide quality instruction to *all* students (Jenkins & Yoshimura, 2010). Response to Intervention was designed as a tool to support teachers in their efforts of delivering, monitoring, and adjusting instruction to best fit the needs of all learners. For students with mental health issues, this process of screening and implementing tiers of intervention provides a safety net. While there is a call out for more applied research to identify scientifically validated research in the areas of emotional and behavioral supports (Sandomierski, *et al.,* 2007), steps are being made to validate application of the RtI process to domains beyond academics, thus ensuring a greater likelihood of success for all students and expanding the traditional mission of public schools to the promotion of mental health.

ACKNOWLEDGEMENT

Declare none.

CONFLICT OF INTEREST

The author(s) confirm that this chapter content has no conflict of interest.

REFERENCES

Bender, W. N. , & Shores, C. (2007). *Response to intervention: A practical guide for every teacher.* Thousand Oaks, CA: Corwin Press.

Bloomquist, M. L. (1996). *Skills training for children with behavioral disorders.* New York: The Guilford Press.

Bond, L. , Patton, G. , Glover, S. , Carlin, J. B. , Butler, H. , Thomas, L. , & Bowes, G. (2004). The Gatehouse Project: Can a multilevel school intervention affect emotional wellbeing and health risk behaviors? *Journal of Epidemiology Community Health, 58,* 997-1003.

Bradley, R. , Danielson, L. , & Doolittle, J. (2007). Responsiveness to intervention: 1997 to 2007. *Teaching Exceptional Children, 39(5),* 8-12.

Brown-Chisdey, R. , & Steege, M. W. (2005). *Response to intervention: Principles and strategies for effective practice.* New York: Guilford Press.

Cicchetti, D. , & Cohen, D. J. (1995). *Developmental psychopathology.* New York: John Wiley.

Council for Exceptional Children's Policy on Physical Restraint and Seclusions Procedures in School Settings (2010). *Teaching Exceptional Children, 42(5),* 24- 25.

Couvillon, M. , Peterson, R. L. , Ryan, J. B. , & Scheuermann, B. , & Stegall, J. (2010). A review of crisis intervention training programs for schools. *Teaching Exceptional Children, 42(5),* 6-16.

Davis, N. G. , Lindo, E. J. , & Compton, D. L. (2007). Children at risk for reading failure: Constructing an early screening measure. *Teaching Exceptional Children, 39(5),* 32-37.

Fletcher, J. M. , Coulter, W. A. , Reschly, D. J. , & Vaughn, S. (2004). Alternative approaches to the definition and identification of learning disabilities: Some questions and answers. *Annals of Dyslexia, 54,* 304-331.

Fletcher, J. M. , Lyon, G. R. , Barnes, M. , Stuebing, K. K. , Francis, D. J. , Olson, R. K. , Shaywitz, S. E. , & Shaywitz, B. A. (2002). Classification of learning disabilities; An evidence-based evaluation. In R. Bradley, L. Danielson, & D. Hallahan (Eds.). *Identification of learning disabilities: Research to practice* (pp. 467-519). Mahwah, NJ: Erlbaum.

Francis, D. J. , Flectcher, J. M. , & Stuebing, K. K. (2005). Psychometric approaches to the identification of LD: IQ and achievement scores are not sufficient. *Journal of Learning Disabilities, 38,* 98-108.

Fuchs, D. , & Fuchs, L. S. (2005). Responsiveness to intervention: A blueprint for practitioners, policy makers, and parents. *Teaching Exceptional Children, 38(1),* 57-61.

Fuchs, D. , & Fuchs, L. S. (2006) Introduction to response to intervention: What, why and how valid is it? *Reading Research Quarterly, 41(1),* 93-99.

Fuchs, D. , & Deshler, D. D. (2007). What we need to know about responsiveness to intervention (and shouldn't be afraid to ask). *Learning Disabilities Research & Practice, 22,* 129-136.

Fuchs, L. S. , & Fuchs, D. (2007). A model for implementing responsiveness to intervention. *Teaching Exceptional Children, 39(5),* 14-20.

Fuchs, D. , Mock, D. , Morgan, P. L. , & Young, C. L. (2003). Responsiveness-to- intervention: Implications for the learning disabilities construct. *Learning Disabilities Research & Practice, 18(3),* 157-171.

Grice, K. (2002). Eligibility under IDEA for Other Health Impaired Children. *School Law Bulletin, 33(3),* 7-12.

Grimes, J. , & Kurns, S. (2003, December). *An intervention-based system for addressing NCLB and IDEA expectations: A multiple tiered model to ensure every child learns.* Paper presented at the National Research Center on Learning Disabilities Responsiveness-to-Intervention Symposium, Kansas City: MO.

Hoagwood, K. , Jensen, P. S. , Petti, T. , & Burns, B. J. (1996). Outcomes of mental health care for children and adolescents: A comprehensive conceptual model. *Journal of the American Academy of Child and Adolescent Psychiatry, 35*, 1055–1063.

Individuals with Disabilities Act of 1990, Pub. L. 101-476.

Individuals with Disabilities Improvement Act of 2004, Pub. L. 108-446.

Jenkins, A. A. , & Yoshimura, J. (2010). Not another inservice: Meeting the special education professional development needs of elementary general educators. *Teaching Exceptional Children, 42(5),* 36-43.

Klotz, M. B. , & Canter, A. (2007). *Response to intervention: A primer for parents.* National Association of School Psychologists. Retrieved from www. nasponline. org.

Kutash, K. , Duchnowski, A. J. , & Lynn, N. (2006, April). *School based mental health: A guide for decision makers.* Tampa, FL: University of South Florida, Department of Child & Family Studies, Research and Training Centre for Children's Mental Health.

Lyon, G. R. , Fletcher, J. M. , Fuchs, L. S. , & Chhabra, V. (2006). Learning disabilities. In E. J. Mash & R. Barkley (Eds.). *Treatment of childhood disorders* (pp. 512-594). Hillsdale, NJ: Erlbaum.

McCook, J. E. (2006). *The RtI Guide: Developing and implementing a model in your schools.* Horsham, PA: LRP Publications.

McGinnis, E. , & Goldstein, A. P. (1997). Skill *streaming the elementary school child: New strategies and perspectives for teaching prosocial skills.* Champaign, IL: Research Press.

Morrisey, K. L. , Bohanon, H. , & Fenning, P. (2010). Teaching and acknowledging expected behaviors in an urban high school. *Teaching Exceptional Children, 42(5),* 26-35.

National Association of State Directors of Special Education (2005). *Response to intervention: Policy considerations and implementation.* Alexandria, VA: Author.

National Association of State Directors of Special Education (2006). *Myths about response to intervention.* Alexandria, VA: Author.

NationalResearchCenter on Learning Disabilities, (2006). *Core Concepts of RtI.* Retrieved from http://www. nrcld. org/about/research/rti/concepts. html

No Child Left Behind Act of 2002, Pub. L. 107-110.

Pearce, L. R. (2009). Helping children with emotional difficulties: A response to intervention investigation. *The Rural Educator, 30(2),* 34-46.

Pierangelo, R. , & Giuliani, G. (2008). *Frequently asked questions about response to intervention.* Thousand Oaks, CA: Corwin Press.

Restori, A. F. , Gresham, F. M. , & Cook, C. R. (2008). *Old habits die hard: Past and current issues pertaining to response to intervention.* The Free Library. Retrieved from http://www. thefreelibrary. com

Restori, A. F. , & Katz, G. S. , & Lee, H. N. (2009). A critique of the IQ/achievement discrepancy model for identifying specific learning disabilities. *Europe's Journal of Psychology, 4,* 128-145.

Richards, C. , Pavri, S. , Golez. , F. , Canges, R. , & Murphy, J. (2007). Response to intervention: Building the capacity of teachers to serve students with learning disabilities. *Issues in Teacher Education, 16(2),* 55-64.

Rudebusch, J. (2007). Lingui *Systems' Guide to Response to Intervention.* East Moline, IL: Lingui Systems.

Sandomierski, T. , Kincaid, D. , & Algozzine, B. , (2007). Response to intervention and positive behavior support: Brothers from different mothers or sisters with different misters? *PBIS Newsletter, 4(2).* Retrieved from http://www. pbis. org/pbis_newsletter/volume_4/issue2. aspx.

Speece, D. (2002). Classification of learning disabilities: Convergence, expansion, and caution. In R. Bradley, L. Danielson, & D. Hallahan (Eds.). *Identification of Learning Disabilities: Research to Practice* (pp. 467-519.)Mawwah, NJ: Erlbaum.

Stecker, P. M. (2007). Tertiary intervention: using progress monitoring with intensive services. *Teaching Exceptional Children, 39(5),* 50-57.

Stepanek, J. , & Peixotto, K. (2009). Models of response to intervention in the Northwest region states. *Regional Educational Laboratory Northwest.* ED506348.

Tomlison, C. A. (1999). *The differentiated classroom: Responding to the needs of all learners.* Alexandria, VA: Association for Supervision and Curriculum Development.

U. S. Department of Education (2003). *Proven methods: Questions and answers on No Child Left Behind.* Washington, D. C: Author. Retrieved from http://www.ed.gov. nclb/methods/whatworks/doing. html

U. S. Department of Education (2006). *Special education & rehabilitative services: IDEA 2004 news, information, and resources.* Retrieved from http://www.ed.gov/policy/speced/guid/idea/idea2004. html

U. S. Department of Health & Human Services, Office of the Surgeon General (1999). *Mental Health: A Report of the Surgeon General.* Retrieved from http://www. surgeongeneral. gov/library/mentalhealth/home. html

Zirkel, P. A. (2007). Responsiveness to Intervention: What does the law say? *Teaching Exceptional Children, 39(5),* 65-67.

Zirkel, P. A. (2010). The legal meaning of specific learning disability for special education eligibility. *Teaching Exceptional Children, 42(5),* 62-67.

CHAPTER 6

The Contribution of Extracurricular Activities to School Priorities and Student Success

Aidyn L. Iachini[1,*] and Dawn Anderson-Butcher[2]

[1]University of South Carolina, College of Social Work, 123 DeSaussure, Columbia, SC 29208, USA and [2]College of Social Work, The Ohio State University, Columbus, OH 43210, USA

Abstract: In response to the momentous challenges schools face in meeting the diverse and growing needs of students, many schools have expanded their school improvement priorities beyond academic learning. Health and social services, youth development, parent/family engagement, and community partnership development are four additional school improvement pathways of growing importance. Many schools also are focusing on how these priorities are addressed in the out-of-school time hours, particularly as a way to complement and extend learning and development that occurs during the hours of the school day. Extracurricular activities are examples of out-of-school time opportunities provided by many schools that can have an important impact on school priorities and student success. The purpose of this chapter is to highlight how extracurricular activities can contribute to these five school improvement pathways. Data collected from 21st Century Community Learning Centers from Ohio are provided as an example. Implications for school leaders and practitioners in relationship to maximizing the impact of extracurricular activities on school priorities and student success also are shared.

Keywords: School improvement, student success, academic learning, mental health, extracurricular activities, non-academic barriers, parent/family engagement, community partnerships, 21st century community learning centers, youth development, out-of-school time, resource assessment, leadership, referral systems, School-family-community partnership coordinator, single point of contact, school-based strategies, school-linked strategies, community-based strategies, design strategies.

INTRODUCTION

As increasing accountability has been placed on schools through the No Child Left Behind (NCLB) Act, schools have expanded their priorities beyond traditional

***Address correspondence to Aidyn L. Iachini:** Assistant Professor, University of South Carolina, College of Social Work, 123 DeSaussure, Columbia, SC 29208, USA; Tel: 803-777-2373; E-mail: iachini@mailbox.sc.edu

Raymond J. Waller (Ed)

standards-based reforms. Schools are now focusing on other important strategies contributing to students' success and healthy development. School improvement pathways involving academic intervention and acceleration, youth development, health and social services, parent/family engagement, and community partnerships are of growing importance (Brener, Weist, Adelman, Taylor, & Vernon-Smiley, 2007; Anderson-Butcher, Lawson, Iachini, Wade-Mdivanian, & Bean, 2008; Anderson-Butcher *et al.,* 2010; Anderson-Butcher, Lawson, *et al.,* in press; Hawkins, Catalano, & Miller, 1992). Many of the programs and activities addressing these multiple pathways to student success are offered during the school day. Increasing attention, however, has been directed towards the importance of programs and services offered during the out-of-school time hours.

This chapter explores the contributions of extracurricular activities specific to these five school improvement pathways. In addition, the chapter offers key mechanisms and processes essential for coordinating all of the in-school and extracurricular activities designed to maximize student learning and healthy development.

THE CHALLENGE OF TIME, RESOURCES, AND EXPERTISE

Since the passage of NCLB, schools across the country have focused on standards-based accountabilities, curriculum alignment, and high quality instruction in classrooms. Traditional school improvement models incorporating these strategies have multiple strengths and create positive academic outcomes for students (Borman, Hewes, Overman, & Brown, 2002). Research shows, however, that many students are still falling behind. New, innovative strategies to ensure all youth succeed are needed, especially given the presence of large achievement gaps among racial, ethnic, and socio-economic groups (Callan, Finney, Kirst, Usdan, & Veneia, 2006; Pipho, 2001).

One challenge for schools today is the issue of time. In essence, there are only so many hours in a traditional school day. As a result, some systems across the country are lengthening the school day or academic year to gain more instructional time. Still, we know the majority of students' time is spent outside of school, in homes and communities. In fact, youth spend upwards of 40% of their lives in discretionary time (Larson, 2001; Larson & Verma, 1999). The question remains: *How do schools gain more influence over students' learning time in these other social settings during the non-school hours?*

An additional challenge for schools involves the multiple barriers to learning that often impede student success. Many students come to school with unmet needs that must be addressed before learning occurs in classrooms (Adelman & Taylor, 1999; 2000). Risk factors such as unaddressed mental health problems, conflicts in the home, and family/community instabilities are everyday realities for many youth, especially those coming from disadvantaged circumstances and those of color. *How do schools leverage in school and out-of-school time resources to address these multiple barriers to learning that exist in the individual, peer, school, family, and community systems?*

Still other students crave positive youth development experiences, ones that prepare them with 21st century skills and foster student engagement in learning and life. Schools do not necessarily have the resources (or enough time in the school day) to fully strengthen these protective factors and assets. Many teachers, as well, were not prepared to embed these strategies into their instruction (Weston, Anderson-Butcher, & Burke, 2008), begging the following question: *How do schools build competencies and social reinforcements to support student achievement and other healthy youth outcomes, while also staying focused on critical academic priorities?*

Given these multiple challenges, schools are expanding their school improvement priorities by focusing on academic intervention and acceleration, youth development, health and social services, parent/family engagement, and community partnership strategies (Brener, Weist, Adelman, Taylor, & Vernon-Smiley, 2007; Anderson-Butcher *et al.,* 2008; Anderson-Butcher *et al.,* 2010; Anderson-Butcher, Lawson, *et al.,* in press; Hawkins, Catalano, & Miller, 1992). For example, some schools are employing school-based mental health professionals in order to address students' non-academic barriers to learning (Iachini, Dorr, & Anderson-Butcher, 2008; Weist, 1999). Other schools are implementing school climate approaches focused on increasing students' engagement in learning and sense of connectedness to the school. Additionally, others are cultivating new community partnerships that support student learning by bringing valuable private sector resources and expertise to bear on student learning in classrooms.

Most strategies implemented by schools, however, are implemented during the school day. Extracurricular activities offered in the non-school hours also are critical to overall school success (Anderson-Butcher, 2010; Eccles, Barber, Stone, & Hunt, 2003). The importance of these social settings is the focus of this chapter.

THE CONTRIBUTION OF EXTRACURRICULAR ACTIVITIES TO SCHOOL IMPROVEMENT PATHWAYS

Extracurricular activities include the myriad of programs, services, and strategies happening before and/or after school, during the summer, and on weekends. Examples include sports teams, faith-based programs, mentoring and tutoring programs, job training opportunities, school councils, service clubs, and afterschool enrichment programs. Other examples include summer camps, arts and technology programs, and youth development programs such as Boys & Girls Clubs, Scouts, and 4-H.

These extracurricular activities are operated by many different providers and offered in a variety of locations. For example, some programs are operated by the school and located on school grounds. Examples of such *school-based* extracurricular activities are sports and student clubs. Other extracurricular activities might be located at the school, but operated by a community agency. For instance, an afterschool program may be co-located at the school but operated by a community youth development organization. *School-linked* strategies involve the connection of a *community-based* program to the school. Here, extracurricular offerings are operated by community agencies in the local community but strategically connected to the school. An example is a local church offering a mentoring program in the local neighborhood that targets youth identified by the school as in need of additional supports.

In the end, a multitude of extracurricular activities are regularly implemented by schools and community partners. These opportunities make important contributions to students' learning and positive development. The key, however, is the maximization of these extracurricular strategies in parallel with in-school strategies. Together they comprehensively address important school priorities and ultimately enhance overall student success.

The next section of this chapter demonstrates the contributions of extracurricular activities to each of the five school improvement pathways mentioned previously, including academic learning, youth development, parent/family engagement, health and social services, and community partnerships. Specifically, each pathway will be defined and then relevant research will be synthesized. Key design strategies helpful for maximizing these extracurricular activities in support of school priorities also are shared.

ACADEMIC LEARNING AND EXTRACURRICULAR ACTIVITIES

Extracurricular activities serve as valuable opportunities to extend the academic learning that happens during the school day. Academic learning refers to students' mastery of grade-level content standards, development of transferable knowledge and skills important for learning (*e.g.,* goal-setting, reflection, study skills, *etc.*), and ability to be motivated from within and persist in the face of challenges and barriers to learning (Anderson-Butcher *et al.,* 2004). Maximizing students' time for academic learning is important for academic achievement and graduation, as well as for preparation to enter the workforce and/or postsecondary opportunities.

Research evidence suggests that youth participation in extracurricular programs, especially those connected to classroom curricula, correlates with increased academic achievement as measured by grades and standardized test scores (Broh, 2002; Durlak, Weissberg, & Pachan, 2010; Eccles, Barber, Stone, & Hunt, 2003; Fredericks & Eccles, 2006; Lauer *et al.,* 2006). Extracurricular opportunities also strengthen students' feelings of school connectedness and promote youth engagement, important predictors of students' academic success in school (Anderson-Butcher, 2010; Brown & Evans, 2005; Faulkner, Adlaf, Irving, Allison, & Dwyer, 2009).

To maximize the impact of these social settings on students' academic learning, there are several key design strategies to consider. Formal communication mechanisms between teachers/school staff and extracurricular program leaders need to be developed to ensure that extracurricular activities are reinforcing the learning that happens in the classroom. For example, extracurricular program staff may work with teachers to identify key academic priorities and then emphasize these components of the classroom curricula during the non-school hours. Some schools use short-cycle assessment data to identify students falling behind academically and then connect with extracurricular program staff so that these students are targeted for instruction in the program (Anderson-Butcher, Lawson, *et al.,* in press). In fact, Anderson-Butcher (2010) suggests that when afterschool programs integrally connect teachers and classroom learning to program activities, students also experience a more seamless transition between the school day and the out-of-school time and ultimately feel a stronger sense of connectedness to their school.

Parent/family engagement also is a key design strategy to support students' learning. For example, some afterschool programs offer parent/family educational opportunities that share strategies to facilitate learning in the home. Other parent/family classes focus on outlining the core content standards that students are expected to master at each grade level.

Extracurricular activities also may be designed to maximize student-to-student connections in support of academic learning. For example, high school students might serve as mentors and tutors to younger students. Discussions might focus on study habits, along with students' future goals and aspirations. High school students also might lead specific activities for younger peers, developing their own leadership skills. Implementing these peer-mentoring approaches often further facilitates the development of transferable learning skills.

Regardless of the strategy, prioritizing academic learning during the out-of-school time is an important school improvement strategy that improves student outcomes. If schools maximize both school and community resources in this area, there is no doubt that student learning will be enhanced.

YOUTH DEVELOPMENT AND EXTRACURRICULAR ACTIVITIES

In many ways, the contribution of extracurricular activities to positive youth development seems the most obvious. When individuals think of extracurricular activities, they most often view them as pro-social opportunities for youth to learn skills and competencies valuable for navigating their social world. Specifically, youth development refers to a dual focus on maximizing students' strengths and assets, while simultaneously reducing students' exposure to risk factors that are predictive of poor behaviors and outcomes. Afterschool programs are good examples. These social settings serve students during the hours of 3pm-7pm, providing supervision during a time that might otherwise be spent engaging in risky behaviors, such as substance use and sexual activity. Beyond supervised time, many afterschool programs also explicitly focus on building students' strengths, oftentimes incorporating social skill development activities within their programmatic designs.

Research supports the commonly held notion that students' participation in extracurricular activities enhances youth development. For example, Larson, Hansen, and Moneta (2006) found that participation in faith-based programs relates to enhanced social and teamwork skills. Participation in sports relates to increased initiative, along with enhanced social competence and interpersonal skills (Larson *et al.,* 2006; McHale, Vinden, Bush, Richer, Shaw, & Smith, 2005).

To maximize the impact of extracurricular activities on social skill development, there are several important strategies programs can adopt. Extracurricular programs should identify a core list of social competencies that they aim to target (Durlak *et al.,* 2010). These skills should be selected based on their ability to generalize to other important social settings, such as at school, at home, and in the community (Sheridan, Maughan, & Huungelmann, 1999). Activities should then be selected based on existing curricula or designed to ensure targeted efforts toward the development of these important social skills (Durlak *et al*., 2010). These programs also should inform and involve parents and teachers, as they can help with the transfer and maintenance of social skills into these other important settings (*e.g.,* home, school, *etc.*; Nation *et al.,* 2003).

Beyond the development of social competence, extracurricular activities also provide opportunities for youth to develop meaningful connections to adult leaders and a sense of belonging to a program, team, or organization. For example, Larson and colleagues (2006) found that youth participation in faith-based programs was related to stronger connections to adults. Anderson-Butcher and Fink (2006) found in a study of youth development programs that students' feelings of belonging were an important predictor of risk factors, protective factors, and school-related problem behaviors.

There are a host of strategies that extracurricular activities may implement that facilitate the development of adult-student connections and broader connections with a program, prosocial group, or organization. For example, programs should hire staff reflecting the diversity of their program participants. Once hired, staff should take the time to know each student's name and provide individualized attention and feedback where feasible to student participants. Professional development opportunities also should be offered for staff, highlighting additional strategies they might implement in their practice with youth to further facilitate this connection.

Obviously, extracurricular activities contribute to much more than just these three aforementioned positive developmental outcomes. To describe them all, however, is beyond the scope of this chapter. For a comprehensive review of the contribution of sport to positive youth development, see Anderson-Butcher, Riley and colleagues (in press). For a review of afterschool programs, see Durlak (2010). Nonetheless, schools should prioritize this school improvement pathway and maximize these important developmental experiences during the in-school and out-of-school time to ensure overall student success and healthy development.

PARENT/FAMILY ENGAGEMENT AND EXTRACURRICULAR ACTIVITIES

Parent/family engagement is another important school improvement pathway, and refers to the variety of ways that parents or other caring adults (*e.g.,* grandparents, step-parents, guardians, *etc.*), and families, support and are involved with students' learning. It also refers to the strategies and activities that schools implement to support parents and families. This mutual and reciprocal relationship between parents/families and schools is essential for maximizing the impact of parent/family engagement on student learning and success (Ward, Anderson-Butcher, & Kwiatkowski, 2006).

Extracurricular activities serve as valuable opportunities to strengthen parent and family engagement. For example, extracurricular activities can facilitate cultivation of parent-child bonds. Dorsch, Smith, and McDonough (2009) documented sports' contribution to these relationships, finding that both the overall relationship between parent and child and parent-child communication were enhanced through sport. Anderson-Butcher, Riley, and others (in press) also suggest extracurricular programs promote family-to-family bonds and mutual family support networks. Specific outcomes may include parents connecting with other parents around transportation and other program-related activities and challenges.

In addition to helping promote and strengthen bonds between students and parents/families, some extracurricular opportunities also provide specific programming for parents to help meet identified needs. For example, some afterschool programs offer literacy programs for parents. Many faith-based programs provide baby-sitting services and supports for parents/families. And yet others link and refer parents to community supports to help meet identified needs.

To maximize the impact of parent/family engagement, though, one key design strategy is to incorporate parents into extracurricular activities in meaningful ways (Anderson-Butcher *et al.,* 2004). Parents and families should have opportunities to provide leadership in relationship to areas in which they feel comfortable. Therefore, it is important to assess and understand the range of parents' strengths and competencies. For example, some parents might feel more comfortable supporting specific activities with student participants. Others might want to serve on a team focused on engaging other parents and families. Regardless, ensuring parents have meaningful roles will not only benefit students in the program but will empower the parents as well.

In the end, focusing on the meaningful engagement of parents/families during the non-school hours complements and strengthens parent/family engagement strategies implemented during the school day. Obviously, maximizing parent/family engagement in this way contributes to school priorities and ultimately to overall student success.

HEALTH AND SOCIAL SERVICES AND EXTRACURRICULAR ACTIVITIES

Extracurricular programs also serve as important resources for addressing the host of non-academic barriers students face to learning. Example non-academic barriers include mental health needs, health-related challenges, and family conflict. Oftentimes, students face multiple non-academic barriers simultaneously, and thus schools have focused on the provision of health and social services and supports to address these barriers to learning and healthy development. For example, many schools implement important comprehensive systems of learning supports and response to intervention (RtI) strategies. These systems prioritize prevention and early intervention strategies along with treatment approaches, and maximize both in-school and out-of-school time resources and supports. In addition, schools connect with community partners to provide both school-based and/or school-linked services to address these needs. For example, mental health services are provided by a community organization and co-located in a school building (Weist, 1999). Other examples of critical health and social service providers include child welfare services, community clinics, hospitals, shelters, family support and preservation services, and workforce development services.

The contribution of extracurricular activities to these efforts is well documented. As discussed previously, not only do extracurricular activities contribute to the development of important social skills, these activities also contribute to overall positive mental and physical health (Martinsen, 1990; Steiner *et al.,* 2000). Specifically, youth participation in these programs is related to enhanced self-esteem and self-perceptions, along with reduced feelings of depression (Daley, 2002; McHale *et al.,* 2005; Pedersen & Seidman, 2004; Piko & Keresztes, 2006). Participation in extracurricular activities also builds skills students can use to manage stress and emotions during the school day (Rostad & Long, 1996; Larson *et al.,* 2006). Physical health-related outcomes from extracurricular activity involvement include improvements in dietary habits (Baumert, Henderson, & Thompson, 1998; Delisle, Werch, Wong, Bian, & Weiler, 2010) and reduced body mass indices (Agbuga, Xiang, & McBride, 2007; Weintraub *et al.,* 2008).

Strategically designing extracurricular programs to further maximize their impact on physical and mental health related outcomes is important. For example, afterschool programs must ensure they allocate a specified amount of time (*e.g.,* 30-60 minutes) to physical activity each day. This time also may be used as an opportunity to teach and discuss healthy eating habits, body image, and lifelong physical activity with student participants. Other extracurricular activities, such as faith-based programs or mentoring programs, might ensure adequate attention is devoted to teaching students stress management skills and positive coping strategies to deal with emotions. Yet other programs might utilize or adapt existing curricula designed to help teach health and mental health promotion strategies.

Obviously, we know many students come to school facing multiple challenges that impede their ability to learn and succeed. Maximizing both in-school and out-of-school time health and social service strategies often helps students overcome these non-academic barriers, and ensure their success and healthy development. School improvement models must include this important pathway to student achievement, or we will continue to leave many students behind.

COMMUNITY PARTNERSHIPS AND EXTRACURRICULAR ACTIVITIES

Schools cannot expect to address all of the needs and challenges of their students, families, and communities alone. Forming relationships with community partners around identified needs is vital. A community partnership is defined as "every formal arrangement a school can make with an individual, association, private sector organization or public institution to provide a program, service or resource that will help support student achievement" (Anderson-Butcher *et al.,* 2004, p. 249). For example, schools might partner with a local business to create service learning opportunities for students. Another school might develop a partnership with a local church to provide space for community events and afterschool program activities.

The development of community partnerships is beneficial for many reasons. First and foremost, community partnerships provide another critical support mechanism to address students' and families' needs. They may complement the resources already in place, or provide new resources that are needed in the community. Partnerships also provide community reinforcement for student success, and often help leverage additional dollars and resources, such as grant funding.

The role of extracurricular activities in helping schools cultivate these partnerships should not go unnoticed. For example, sporting events often bring local community members to the school setting and provide an opportunity for these members to develop feelings of connectedness with the school community (Anderson-Butcher *et al.,* in press). Science fairs and other culminating extracurricular activities also can spark this same sense of identification with the school. In turn, these feelings may translate into volunteer hours for the classroom and other school-related events, resource contributions to support school-related priorities, and social networking avenues to disseminate information about upcoming events and priorities. Additionally, many individuals working in extracurricular programs often have strong ties to the local business sector or other public institutions or associations. As such, these individuals may be critical linkage agents and facilitate the development of new partnerships.

To help facilitate partnership development, there are several important strategies and principles to remember. First, both partners should benefit from the collaboration. For instance, if a school partners with a business for service learning opportunities, then the business also benefits from cultivating potential employees or serving the family members of its employees. Norms and goals for the partnership should be established to ensure that all partners are focused on the same priorities and outcomes. Communication and problem-solving mechanisms also should be in place if challenges arise. Forming partnerships using these principles is a great beginning to a potentially long-lasting and sustainable relationship in support of student success.

Again, schools cannot possibly provide all of the programs and services needed to support the multitude of pathways leading to student success without involvement of collaborative partnerships. Community partnerships are central to schools, especially as schools expand their traditional school improvement priorities and maximize both in-school and out-of-school resources and supports available to students and families.

MAXIMIZING THE CONTRIBUTIONS OF EXTRACURRICULAR PROGRAMS AND ACTIVITIES

To summarize, traditional school improvement models that emphasize school-based strategies to support students' learning and healthy development are important. Beyond this, though, schools also need to expand their school improvement pathways to prioritize other key areas linked to student success. Extended and accelerated academic learning opportunities, youth development, parent/family engagement, health and social services, and community partnerships also need to be explicit priorities. Schools, however, cannot be expected to address all of these multiple priorities solely within the hours of the school day. Maximizing these pathways during the non-school hours through extracurricular activities is one approach to address this reality.

Given this, the question remains as to how school leaders and others coordinate and manage all of the in-school and out-of-school time activities centered around these multiple school improvement pathways. The next section provides guidance to school leaders and others related to key mechanisms and processes needed for coordinating the myriad of in-school and out-of-school time strategies designed to maximize student learning and healthy development.

IMPLICATIONS FOR SCHOOLS: KEY MECHANISMS AND PROCESSES TO COORDINATE THE MULTIPLE PATHWAYS TO STUDENT SUCCESS

Because schools oftentimes have many programs and services being implemented simultaneously to support students' learning and healthy development, attention must be focused on how to coordinate and manage these multiple in-school and extracurricular activities in a systematic and effective manner. The authors of this chapter have been involved in several initiatives designed to understand and document "how" this complex work happens in practice. For example, the two authors were involved in the implementation and research of an expanded school improvement model, the Ohio Community Collaboration Model for School Improvement (OCCMSI), in twelve pilot schools and districts throughout Ohio (Anderson-Butcher, Lawson, Iachini, Wade-Mdivanian, & Bean, 2008). The two authors also were involved in an initiative in two pilot districts that specifically prioritized the health and social services pathway. For a case study in relationship to this work, please see Iachini and colleagues (2008).

From this research, several key mechanisms and processes for schools trying to coordinate and manage these multiple pathways to student success have been identified. These include the following:

Data-Driven Decision Making: Schools benefit from data-driven decision making processes involving needs and resources assessments, gap analyses, and strategic planning. These are common steps within effective school improvement planning, and also have relevance to partnership-building agendas. More specifically, a thorough assessment of academic and non-academic barriers to learning allows for the determination of top priorities and needs. This needs assessment includes not only an examination of existing academic and behavioral data (*e.g.,* grades, attendance, discipline and behavioral data), but also requires new types of data collection in relationship to students' perceptions of school connectedness and climate, opportunities for pro-social involvement in school and in the community, and family/engagement and support.

Resource assessments examining school and community assets and programming help systems identify what is currently in place to support student learning and top priority needs, as well as determine if these school and community resources are implemented both effectively and efficiently. Engaging in this resource assessment also allows a school to determine all of the available programs and services to support student learning and development, including community- and school-based, community-owned and operated, and school-owned and operated. Fig. **1** is a sample tool that the authors found helpful for schools engaging in this process.

Resource Assessment Tool	
Pathway 1: Academic Learning	
In-School Activities	Extracurricular Activities
Pathway 2: Youth Development	
In-School Activities	Extracurricular Activities
Pathway 3: Parent/Family Engagement	
In-School Activities	Extracurricular Activities
Pathway 4: Health and Social Services	
In-School Activities	Extracurricular Activities
Pathway 5: Community Partnerships	
In-School Activities	Extracurricular Activities

Figure 1: Resource Inventory of In-School and Extracurricular Activities to Support Student Success.

Once a needs and resources assessment is complete, gap analyses allow schools and their community partners to examine their programmatic inventory and top priority needs, and determine if there are gaps in programs/services, if there are duplication in programs/services, or if existing programs/services might be strengthened to support the top emergent priority areas (*i.e.,* an afterschool program might be re-designed to not only support academic learning and youth development, but also to engage and support parents/families). In turn, schools and their partners make better and more informed determinations about all of the in-school and extracurricular activities they offer and for whom.

Collaborative Leadership Structures: As previously mentioned, schools may identify many emergent priorities and implement a variety of in-school and extracurricular activities to meet these needs. Because of this, many things are happening simultaneously and oftentimes one person cannot keep track of it all. As such, development of a collaborative leadership structure is important. Collaborative leadership refers to the distribution of power and leadership across various teams all working towards a common purpose. For example, schools might develop partnership teams around top priority needs or systems (such as a youth development team, parent/family engagement team, *etc.*). Those teams would then be responsible for the leadership in relation to their respective pathway. By organizing and mobilizing individuals in this way, it removes the overwhelming responsibility of having one person responsible for everything that happens in the school. It also harnesses the unique perspective and solutions of many individuals, as opposed to one person's perspective on how to address a challenge or need.

Linkage and Referral System: The development of a linkage and referral system also is helpful. That is, schools should develop a system that allows students and families identified with specific needs to be referred to the most appropriate services and supports to meet those needs. Critical to developing this system is determining how students are identified as having a need, and then how this information is shared and with whom, in order to ensure the timely delivery of service to meet that need. See Anderson-Butcher, Iachini, and Wade-Mdivanian (2007) for a comprehensive technical assistance guide to developing a linkage and referral system.

Clarity in Roles and Responsibilities: In addition to the development of collaborative leadership structures and referral systems, specific roles and responsibilities of people also are important. For example, the role of a school-family-community partnership coordinator has been found critical (Anderson-Butcher, 2008). This person can serve as the broker and linkage agent between what happens during the school day and what happens during the after school hours in extracurricular activities. This person also helps facilitate the collaborative planning process that happens among the school and its community partners, helps ensure the coordination of all of the services and supports across the multiple pathways, and assists with the development of the aforementioned collaborative leadership structures responsible for implementation of identified programs and services (Anderson-Butcher, 2009). An additional role that is important to fill is a single point of contact for student and family referrals. Oftentimes, both of these roles are filled by school social workers, guidance counselors, school psychologists, or other student support staff.

Together, these practical strategies are ways that schools can begin to coordinate, manage, and maximize the myriad of in-school and extracurricular activities to support school priorities and ultimately student success. For additional tools to support implementation of these strategies, please visit the Community and Youth Collaborative Institute website: http://csw.osu.edu/cayci/. A case example from Ohio is shared next to demonstrate the long-term outcomes that can result from implementation of many of these strategies.

A CASE EXAMPLE: 21ST CENTURY COMMUNITY LEARNING CENTERS IN OHIO

Over the past six years in Ohio, comprehensive efforts have been implemented to support schools as they work to integrate and connect all of the multiple programs and strategies aimed at maximizing academic achievement and healthy development. Particular attention has been focused on those schools that operate 21st Century Community Learning Centers (CCLCs).

21st CCLCs are school-based or community-based programs offered in the non-school hours designed to maximize students' academic achievement and overall healthy development. In addition, these programs are designed to support parent and family engagement outcomes and prioritize community partnership development. Schools operating 21st CCLCs have been a special priority because they allow for examination of how schools maximize extracurricular activities in support of school priorities and student achievement. (For additional detail regarding 21st CCLCs, please see Anderson-Butcher, 2004).

Perceptual data document the impact of these extracurricular programs (*i.e.*, 21st CCLCs in Ohio) on school-related priorities. During the 2009-2010 school year, perceptual data were collected from 3,724 stakeholders of 21st CCLCs, including principals, teachers/staff, program staff, community partners, and parents using the Ohio-Quality Assessment Rubric (O-QAR; Anderson-Butcher, Iachini, Wade-Mdivanian, & Gezinski, 2007). Each scale consists of six items asking respondents about the extent to which their program influences that outcome. Respondents respond to each of these items on a 5-point Likert scale, 1=Strongly Disagree and 5=Strongly Agree. Percent agreement was calculated by adding the number of respondents who agreed or strongly agreed with each statement, and then dividing by the total number of respondents for that item. Table **1** synthesizes these perceptual outcome data[1]. Clearly these multiple stakeholders overwhelmingly support the role of extracurricular activities in supporting academic, positive youth development, and parent/family outcomes.

Table 1: Percentage of Stakeholder Agreement regarding 21st Century Community Learning Center Outcomes

Perceptions of Youth Development Outcomes	
Outcome Item	**% Agree**
Increase social and life skills among youth participants	93.1
Increase self-esteem among youth participants	92.7
Increase self-confidence among youth participants	93.5
Enhance leadership skills among youth participants	87.3
Enhance self-control among youth participants	89.5
Reduce exposure to risk among youth participants	91.9
Perceptions of Academic Learning Outcomes	
Outcome Item	**% Agree**
Increase reading skills among youth participants	91.1
Increase math skills among youth participants	91.4
Decrease school absenteeism among youth participants	77.5
Enhance performance on proficiency tests among youth participants	87.2
Increase school climate among youth participants	88.4
Increase engagement in school among youth participants	90.2

[1]Please note that while health and social service- and community partnership- related outcomes are not explicitly identified here, several items within the three scales do relate to these two priorities. For example, self-esteem and self-control are two valuable concepts related to mental health prevention and promotion strategies. Additionally, one item asks about developing relationships with community members along with parents/families.

Table 1: cont….

Perceptions of Parent/Family Engagement Outcomes	
Outcome Item	**% Agree**
Develop effective parenting skills among participants	64.9
Enhance relationships among parents/guardians and their children	80.2
Increase parent/guardian abilities to support their children's learning	82.8
Develop positive relationships among parents/guardians and other adults in the community	81.9
Develop new skills and capacities among parent/guardian participants	73.1
Enhance feelings of support among parent/guardian participants	84.2

Overall, the 21st CCLC initiative serves as one example of how others can begin to simultaneously prioritize and maximize multiple in-school and extracurricular strategies in support of student success. The key strategies shared previously, which build from this work, can hopefully help others as they engage in these complex processes and maximize in-school and extracurricular activities to support school priorities and student success.

CONCLUSIONS

Ultimately, students spend most of their time out of school. Given this reality, it is important for schools to not only strengthen in-school programs and resources, but also leverage and maximize extracurricular activities in support of student success. By doing this, schools are able to address three main challenges – time, resources, and expertise. Schools are able to capitalize on the hours students spend outside of the school day so that it is more focused on learning and development. Schools are able to address non-academic barriers that often impede student learning through school-based and school-linked health and social services and other partnerships. And, through maximizing extracurricular activities, schools can further provide social reinforcements that contribute to positive youth development and overall child well-being. In the end, extracurricular activities become central school improvement strategies that support school-related priorities and student success.

This complex work, however, is challenging. It requires school leaders to engage in new and innovative practices. The key design strategies, along with specific mechanisms and processes (*i.e.,* data-based decision making, collaborative leadership structures, linkage and referral systems, and clarity in roles and responsibilities) discussed in this chapter, all may be helpful to school leaders and others as they mobilize and maximize the contributions of extracurricular activities and in-school services and supports around extended and accelerated academic learning, youth development, parent/family engagement and support, health and social services, and community partnerships. As schools implement these more expanded school improvement strategies, there is no doubt that improved outcomes will result for students, families, schools, and communities.

ACKNOWLEDGEMENT

Declare none.

CONFLICT OF INTEREST

The author(s) confirm that this chapter content has no conflict of interest.

REFERENCES

Adelman, H., & Taylor, L. (1999). Mental health in schools and system restructuring. *Clinical Psychology Review, 19(2),* 137-163.

Adelman, H., & Taylor, L. (2000). Moving prevention from the fringes into the fabric of school improvement. *Journal of Educational and Psychological Consultation, 11(1),* 7-36.

Agbuga, B., Xiang, P., & McBride, R. E. (2007). Pedometer-assessed physical activity level and body composition among minority children in an after-school physical education program. *Research Quarterly for Exercise and Sport, 1*, 88.

Anderson-Butcher, D. (2004). Transforming schools into 21st Century Community Learning Centers. *Children & Schools*, 26*(4),* 248-252.

Anderson-Butcher, D. (2008). School-family-community coordination functions: The missing piece in partnership development and maintenance. *The* Community *Psychologist, 41(3/4),* 28-33.

Anderson-Butcher, D. (2010). The promise of afterschool programs for promoting school connectedness. *The Prevention Researcher, 17*(3), 12-18.

Anderson-Butcher, D. (in press). Sport as a context for building community and supporting families. In R. J. R. Levesque (Ed.), *Encyclopedia of Adolescence.* New York: Springer.

Anderson-Butcher, D., & Fink, J. (2006). The importance of a sense of belonging to youth service agencies: A risk and protective factor analysis. *Journal of Child and Youth Care Work, 20*, 11-21.

Anderson-Butcher, D., Iachini, A., & Wade-Mdivanian, R. (2007). *School linkage protocol technical assistance guide: Expanded school improvement through the enhancement of the learning support continuum.* Columbus, OH: College of Social Work, Ohio State University.

Anderson-Butcher, D., Iachini, A., & Wade-Mdivanian, R. & Gezinski, L. (2007). *Ohio quality assessment rubric*. Columbus, OH: College of Social Work, Ohio State University.

Anderson-Butcher, D., Lawson, H. A., Bean, J., Boone, B., Kwiatkowski, A., Cash, S., *et al.,* (2004). *Implementation guide: The Ohio Community Collaboration Model for School Improvement.* Columbus, OH: Ohio Department of Education.

Anderson-Butcher, D., Lawson, H. A., Bean, J., Flaspohler, P., Boone, B., & Kwiatkowski, A. (2008). Community collaboration to improve schools: Introducing a new model from Ohio. *Children & Schools, 30(3),* 161-172.

Anderson-Butcher, D., Lawson, H. A., Iachini, A., Bean, J., Flaspohler, P., & Zullig, K. (in press). Capacity-related innovations resulting from pilot school and district implementation of a community collaboration model for school improvement. *Journal of Educational and Psychological Consultation.*

Anderson-Butcher, A., Lawson, H., Iachini, A. L., Flaspohler, P., Bean, J. & Wade-Mdivanian, R. (2010). Emergent evidence in support of a community collaboration model for school improvement. *Children & Schools, 32(3),* 160-171.

Anderson-Butcher. D, Lawson, H. A., Iachini, A., Wade-Mdivanian, R., & Bean, J. (2008). *The Ohio Community Collaboration Model for School Improvement.* Columbus, OH: College of Social Work, Ohio State University.

Anderson-Butcher, D., Riley, A., Iachini, A., Wade-Mdivanian, R., & Davis, J. (in press). Using sport to enhance adolescent development. In R.J.R. Levesque (Ed.), *Encyclopedia of Adolescence.* New York: Springer.

Baumert, P. W., Henderson, J. M., & Thompson, N. J. (1998). Health risk behaviors of adolescent participants in organized sports. *Journal of Adolescent Health, 22,* 460-465.

Borman, G. D., Hewes, G. M., Overman, L. T., & Brown, S. (2002). *Comprehensive school reform and student achievement: A meta-analysis.* Baltimore: Johns Hopkins University and Howard University: Center for Research on the Education of Students Placed At Risk.

Brener, N. D, Weist, M., Adelman, H., Taylor, L., & Vernon-Smiley, M. (2007). Mental health and social services: Results from the school health policies and programs study 2006. *Journal of School Health, 77(8),* 486-499.

Broh, B. A. (2002). Linking extracurricular programming to academic achievement: Who benefits and why? *Sociology of Education, 75(1),* 69-95.

Brown, R. & Evans, W. P. (2005). Developing school connectedness among diverse youth through extracurricular programming. *The Prevention Researcher, 12(2),* 14-17.

Callan, P. M., Finney, J. E., Kirst, M. W., Usdan, M. D., & Veneia, A. (2006). *Claiming common ground: State policymaking for improving college readiness and success.* Stanford, CA: National Center for Public Policy and Higher Education.

Daley, A. J. (2002). Extra-curricular physical activities and physical self-perceptions in British 14-15-year-old male and female adolescents. *European Physical Education Review, 8(1),* 37-49.

Delisle, T. T., Werch, C. E., Wong, A. H., Bian, H., Weiler, R. (2010). Relationship between frequency and intensity of physical activity and health behaviors in adolescents. Journal of School Health, *80(3),* 134-140.

Dorsch, T. E., Smith, A. L., & McDonough, M. H. (2009). Parents' perceptions of child-to-parent socialization in organized youth sport. *Journal of Sport and Exercise Psychology, 31,* 444-469.

Durlak, J. A., Weissberg, R. P., & Pachan, M. (2010). A meta-analysis of after-school programs that seek to promote personal and social skills in children and adolescents. *American Journal of Community Psychology, 45,* 294-309.

Eccles, J. S., Barber, B. L., Stone, M., & Hunt, J. (2003). Extracurricular activities and adolescent development. *Journal of Social Issues, 59(4), 865*-889.

Faulkner, G. E. J., Adlaf, E. M., Irving, H. M., Allison, K. R., & Dwyer, J. (2009). School disconnectedness: Identifying adolescents at risk in Ontario, Canada. *Journal of School Health, 79(7),* 312-318.

Fredricks, J. A., & Eccles, J. S. (2006a). Is extracurricular participation associated with beneficial outcomes? Concurrent and longitudinal relations. *Developmental Psychology*, *42(4),* 698-713.

Hawkins, D., Catalano, R., Miller, J. (1992). Risk and protective factors for alcohol and other drug problems in adolescence and early adulthood: Implications for substance abuse prevention. *Psychological Bulletin*, *112(1),* 64-105.

Iachini, A. L., Dorr, C., & Anderson-Butcher, D. (2008). Fostoria Community Schools' innovative approach to refining and coordinating their school-based mental health service delivery system. *Report on Emotional and Behavioral Disorders in Youth*, *8(3),* 69-75.

Larson, R. (2001). How U.S. children and adolescents spend time: What it does (and doesn't) tell us about their development. *Current Directions in Psychological Science, 10(5),* 160-164.

Larson, R. W., Hansen, D. M., & Moneta, G. (2006). Differing profiles of developmental experiences across types of organized youth activities. *Developmental Psychology, 42(5),* 849-863.

Larson, R. & Verma, S. (1999). How children and adolescents around the world spent time: Work, play, and developmental opportunities. *Psychological Bulletin, 125*, 701-736.

Lauer, P. A., Akiba, M., Wilkerson, S. B., Apthorp, H. S., Snow, D., & Martin-Glenn, M. L. (2006). Out-of-school time programs: A meta-analysis of effects for at-risk students. *Review of Educational Research, 76(2), 275*-313.

Martinsen, J. (1990). Benefits of exercise for the treatment of depression. *Sports Medicine, 96,* 380-389.

McHale, J. P., Vinden, P. G., Bush, L., Richer, D., Shaw, D., & Smith, B. (2005). Patterns of personal and social adjustment among sport-involved and noninvolved urban middle school children. *Sociology of Sport Journal, 22*, 119-136.

Nation, M., Crusto, C., Wandersman, A., Kumpfer, K., Seybolt, D., Morrisey-Kane, E., & Davino, K. (2003). What works in prevention: Principles of effective prevention programs. *American Psychologist, 58*, 449-456.

Pedersen, S. & Seidman, E. (2004). Team sports achievement and self-esteem development among urban adolescent girls. *Psychology of Women Quarterly, 28*, 412-422.

Piko, B. F. & Keresztes, N. (2006). Physical activity, psychosocial health, and life goals among youth. *Journal of Community Health, 31(2),* 136-145.

Pipho, C. (2001). *State policy options to support a P-16 system of public education: Preschool through postsecondary.* Philadelphia, PA: Pew Charitable Trusts.

Rostad, F. G. & Long, B. C. (1996). Exercise as a coping strategy for stress: A review. *International Journal of Sport Psychology, 27*, 197-222.

Sheridan, S. M., Maughan, D. P., & Hungelmann, A. (1999). A contextualized framework for social skills assessment, intervention, and generalization. *School Psychology Review, 28(1),* 84-104.

Steiner, H., McQuivey, R. W., Pavelski, R., Pitts, T., & Kraemer, H. (2000). Adolescents and sports: Risk or benefit? *Clinical Pediatrics, 39(3),* 161-166.

Ward, H., Anderson-Butcher, D., & Kwiatkowski, A. (2006). Effective strategies for involving parents in schools. In C. Franklin, M. Harris, & P. Allen-Meares (Eds.), *The school services sourcebook: A guide for school-based professionals* (pp. 641-649). Oxford, UK: Oxford University Press.

Weintraub, D. L., Tirumalai, E.C., Haydel, K. F., Fujimoto, M., Fulton, J. E., & Robinson, T. N. (2008). Team sports for overweight children. *Archives of Pediatric and Adolescent Medicine, 162(3),* 232-237.

Weist, M. (1999). Challenges and opportunities in expanded school mental health. *Clinical Psychology Review, 19(2),* 131-135.

Weston, K., Anderson-Butcher, D., & Burke, R. (2008). Developing a comprehensive curricular framework for teacher preparation in expanded school mental health. *Advances in School Mental Health Promotion, 1(4),* 25-41.

CHAPTER 7

Positive Approaches to Behavior Management: Friend or Beast of Burden for Professional Educators?

Kim Sheffield[1] and Raymond J. Waller[2,*]

[1]Kim Sheffield, Lilburn Middle School, 4994 Lawrenceville Highway, Lilburn, GA, USA and [2]College of Health and Human Services, PO Box 8368, Troy University-Dothan, Dothan, AL 36304, USA

Abstract: An opportunity to affect entire student populations in the effort to promote mental health but that resists being universally applied is the use of positive behavior management approaches. In many schools, behavior management based on variables that tend to negatively impact school engagement and functioning still predominates in some locations. Such behavior management approaches are based on interventions emphasizing factors such as punishment for rule violations rather than teaching and reinforcing rule adherence. The continued use of negative approaches to behavior management is puzzling, since substantial data supports numerous positive behavior management methodologies and techniques. One approach thus described is functional behavior assessment and function-based intervention planning. Though sometimes criticized as too difficult or impractical for the typical classroom teacher, we propose that, given certain caveats, educators can employ the techniques effectively and with positive results. This review summarizes a sample of the literature on function-based interventions utilized by teachers to reduce disruptive behaviors of students. This review was included in 20 articles published between 2001 and 2009 across 9 peer-reviewed journals. Studies included in the review met the following criteria: teachers implemented the interventions utilized as well as participated in the intervention development process; students displayed disruptive behavior that interfered with their own or others academic success; and each intervention was function-based, meaning it was created from data collected and analyzed from a functional behavioral assessment. The reviewed studies support the contention that teachers can implement function-based interventions and participate in the process of creating the interventions utilized to reduce disruptive behavior of students.

Keywords: Evidence based, functional analysis, functional behavior assessment (FBA), functional behavior intervention (FBI), positive behavior supports.

INTRODUCTION

The Individuals with Disabilities Education Act of 1997 (IDEA) required that a

***Address correspondence to Raymond J. Waller:** College of Health and Human Services, PO Box 8368, Troy University-Dothan, Dothan, AL 36304, USA; Tel: 334-983-6556; Email: rjwaller@troy.edu

functional behavioral assessment be completed for a child who was at risk of being removed from the general education setting due to a behavior problem (IDEA, 1997), and the current reauthorization encourages continued use of these methodologies as evidence-based tools for effectively resolving classroom behavior challenges (IDEA, 2004). Functional behavioral assessment (FBA) has been described as a process of gathering information to help develop a hypothesis about the function of a problem behavior (*e.g.,* Waller, 2009). From such hypotheses, function-based interventions can be developed. IDEA also stipulated that teachers may receive training in developing and implementing positive behavioral interventions, referred to in this review as function-based interventions (FBI).

Lane and colleagues (2006) defined function-based interventions as approaches created based on *why* behavioral problems occur. It has been asserted by many researchers and practitioners that clinical practice application and research shows that the majority of behavior problems serve one or more of the following functions: to receive or avoid attention, to escape undesirable stimuli, to receive tangibles, or to acquire or avoid sensory stimulation (*e.g.,* Waller, 2009). If the function of a disruptive behavior can be accurately hypothesized through the FBA process, then an FBI can be created to effectively address it. This FBI can be used to guide interventions focused on replacing undesirable behavior with more appropriate replacement behaviors that serves as a functional equivalent to that of the disruptive behavior (Lane *et al.,* 2007). These researchers continued by reporting that an FBI can also be used to alter the classroom environment to include more effective practices and to adjust the consequences of disruptive behavior if needed, and finally proposed that more effective FBIs addressat least three outcomes:

1) The antecedent condition that prompted the disruptive behavior is modified,

2) Positive reinforcement for a functionally equivalent replacement behavior, and

3) Consequences of the disruptive behavior are altered so that the behavior is no longer reinforced.

There are techniques associated with a positive behavior management approach that are both evidence-based and extremely nonintrusive and undemanding to implement. An example includes self-monitoring, which places the onus for implementation on students and can be used to facilitate numerous classroom outcomes (Sheffield & Waller, 2010). FBA is typically used with moderate to severe classroom behavior challenges and is more time and effort intensive than some other viable intervention approaches at the disposal of professional educators effective with minor classroom behavior challenges, and Waller (2008) reported that some educators were skeptical regarding classroom implantation due to training and time related concerns. If, however, evidence supports the contention that classroom teachers can take an active role in planning, developing, and implementing function-based interventions despite the mentioned challenges, then it stands to reason that FBA and FBI (as well as other positive behavior management approaches) are within the purview of consideration and implementation in school settings. Substantial evidence already exists that supports the use of these methods of behavior intervention planning. The majority of the remainder of this chapter, therefore, is devoted to a review of these techniques within the classroom setting by educators. It is worth noting that the benefits of FBA and FBI (and other evidence-based, positive approaches to behavior management) in promoting student mental health are numerous and significant and include:

- Advancing positive classroom social interactions between teachers and peers (Baker, Grant, &Morlock, 2009),

- Improving classroom climate by accentuating positive rather than punitive intervention (Barth, Dunlap, Dane, Lochman, & Wells, 2004),

- Focusing on teachable, remedial behavior rather than more negative, stigmatizing, and ostracizing explanations of undesirable student behavior (Waller, 2008), and

- Fostering an internal locus of control (Adelman & Taylor, 2005).

METHODS

Three criteria were used as inclusionary for articles in this review.

1) Teachers were the interventionists and also participated at least partially in the intervention development process,

2) The studies'participants were students with disruptive behaviors that interfered with their own or others' academic success, and

3) Each intervention was function-based, meaning it involved implementation of an FBI based on FBA.

RESULTS

Participants: The articles were analyzed according to several participant subcategories including age, gender, and disability, if any was identified. There were a total of 37 students in the studies reviewed. Their ages ranged from 5 to 18 years; 25 were males and 12 were females. Ten diagnostic or label categories were used: no identified disability, at-risk for emotional and behavioral disorders (EBD), attention-deficit/hyperactivity disorder (ADHD), developmental delay, learning disability, behavioral disorder, EBD, other health impaired (OHI), mild mental impairments (MMI), and co-morbid (to include two or more of the following: mental retardation, autism, and Down syndrome).

Settings: All studies occurred in a school setting, with only four settings outside a traditional public school. One study took place in an alternative school; one in a private school and two in charter schools. Fifteen studies occurred in a general education setting. Four studies took place in any one or a combination of the following classrooms: resource, self-contained special education, alternative school, special education resource and general education. One study participant's interventions areas were the playground and the cafeteria. This participant is included to maintain continuity in the studies as well as to provide evidence that FBIs can be implemented in a variety of school settings beyond the classroom.

Target Behaviors: Wide variations in disruptive behaviors were targeted for assessment and intervention. In all instances, more than one undesirable behavior was identified for the same participant. Most participants had disruptive behavior, operationally defined at least in part as talking out, out-of-seat behavior, or both. Table **1** presents information regarding target behaviors.

Table 1: Target Behaviors of 37 participants.

	# out of 37	**% of 37**
Physical aggression	13	(35%)
Verbal aggression	6	(16.2%)
Talking out/interrupting	18	(48.6%)
Out-of-seat	15	(40.5%)
Not following directions	3	(8%)
Refusing to work	3	(8%)
Playing with objects/inappropriate use of	3	(8%)
Not engaged	2	(5.4%)
Non-compliance	5	(13.5%)
Property destruction	2	(5.4%)
Yelling	5	(13.5%)
Off-task	9	(24.3%)
Withdrawn	1	(2.7%)
Inappropriate verbalizations cursing/disrespectful	10	(27%)
Making noises	4	(10.8%)
Not completing/incomplete tasks	6	(16.2%)
Task avoidance	1	(2.7%)
Obscene hand gestures	2	(5.4%)
Distracting facials	2	(5.4%)
Throwing spitballs	1	(2.7%)
Insubordination	1	(2.7%)
Teasing/taunting	4	(10.8%)
Attending to others	1	(2.7%)

Note: Multiple behaviors were targeted for the participants so totals exceed 100%.

Functional Behavioral Assessment Procedures: As stated previously, a requirement for inclusion in this review was that a teacher had to implement the FBA as well as at least partially participate in developing the intervention.A variety of FBA techniques were used in data collection and in formulating a hypothesis of the function of the target behavior. Eleven of 20 studies completed a functional analysis to test their hypotheses. "Functional analysis is a strategy of manipulating the student's environment and observing the effect on his behavior. Changes in the student's behavior lead to a hypothesis" (Alberto & Troutman, 2009, p. 178). Functional analysis is the most sophisticated of FBA methods, and should be limited to experienced and trained personnel (Waller, 2008). Table **2** shows what procedures were utilized during the FBA process, as well as interventions employed, and whether or not social validity and treatment integrity were assessed during and after the intervention process.

Function-Based Intervention Strategies: Function-based interventions have been shown to help reduce or eliminate a variety of disruptive behaviors. Eight out of 20 studies reported decreases in the target behavior almost immediately after implementing the intervention (Blair, Umbreit, Dunlap, & Jung, 2007; Ingram, Lewis-Palmer, & Sugai, 2005; Lane, Weisenbach, Phillips, & Wehby, 2007; Liaupsin, Umbreit, Ferro, Urso, & Upreti, 2006; Packenham, Shute, & Reid, 2004; Payne, Scott, & Conroy, 2007; Preciado, Horner, & Baker, 2009; Wright-Gallo, Higbee, Reagon, & Davey, 2006). TheFBI strategy used frequentlyacross the studies included in this review was a multi-component intervention consisting of;

- Making antecedent adjustments,
- Providing positive reinforcement for replacement behaviors, and
- Employing extinction procedures by not reinforcing the target behavior.

Ten participants across six studies showed decreases in disruptive behavior after this multi-component intervention was implemented (Lane *et al.,* 2007; Lane *et al.,* 2006; Lane *et al.,* 2007; Liaupsin *et al.,* 2006; Newcomer & Lewis, 2004; Wood, Umbreit, Liaupsin, & Gresham, 2007).

Self-monitoring, self-management, or self-recording comprised the entire or constituent components of interventions utilized in 4 studies reviewed (Brooks, Todd, Tofflemoyer, & Horner, 2003; Ingram *et al.,* 2005; Kamps *et al.,* 2006; Sterling-Turner, Robinson, & Wilczynski, 2001). A token economy was part of or the sole intervention utilized with five participants across multiple studies (Ingram *et al.,* 2005; Kamps *et al.,* 2006; Packenham *et al.,* 2004; Payne *et al.,* 2007). Instructional strategies were part of 9 interventions utilized (Bessette & Wills, 2007; Biniker & Pindiprolu, 2008; Blair *et al.,* 2007; Burke, Hagan-Burke, & Sugai, 2003; Ingram *et al.,* 2005; Kern, Gallagher, Starosta, Hickman, & George,

2006; Preciado *et al.,* 2009; Stage *et al.,* 2006; Wright-Gallo *et al.,* 2006). Function-based interventions worked with all but one participant in the studies reviewed. The explanation proposed for the unsuccessful intervention was a lack of treatment fidelity. Specifically, the general education teacher in this study reported having a difficult time implementing the intervention, asserting that having 29 other students made it hard to monitor the stipulated 5 minute intervals for data collection (Stage *et al.,* 2006).

In three studies comprising a total of 9 participants, function-based intervention outcomes were compared to non-function-based intervention outcomes (Ingram *et al.,* 2005; Newcomer & Lewis, 2004; Payne *et al.,* 2007). With a majority of participants, the FBI worked to reduce inappropriate behavior while the alternatively selected intervention strategies increased the inappropriate target behavior. Only one participant showed a decrease in the target behavior after such an alternative was implemented (Newcomer & Lewis, 2004).

Follow up: Packenham and colleagues (2004) collected follow-up data on two participants and at 4-5 weeks post-treatment, finding that the interventions utilized continued to show treatment effects on the disruptive behaviors targeted. Kern and colleagues (2006) followed a participant for three years, dramatically extending the previous follow-up period, to see if the interventions utilized would continue to maintain the target behaviors at acceptable levels. They reported that, even with inconsistent intervention implementation, the participant's target behaviors showed ongoing stability with maintenance of behavioral improvements.

Research Designs: Single case research designs were employed in each study. Single case studies were used in this review because they more accurately reflect how interventions are applied in the classroom setting when conducted by a teacher. The studies included reversal designs, alternating treatment designs, multiple baseline designs across participants and settings, and changing criterion designs. Teaching designs, more often referred to as AB designs, were employed in 4 studies reviewed (Bessette & Wills, 2007; Biniker&Pindiprolu, 2008; Kamps *et al.,* 2006; Packenham *et al.,* 2004). In two of these, a functional analysis—the most sophisticated FBA approach—was conducted to test the hypothesized function of the target behaviors and strengthen the evidence upon which the FBI was developed (Bessette & Wills, 2007; Kamps *et al.,* 2006).

Reliability Data. Interobserver agreement was calculated and reported in 19 of 20 studies reviewed. Three frequently used methods of determining inter observer agreement were employed. One method was taking the number of observer agreements, dividing by the number of agreements plus disagreements, and then multiplying by 100 to reach the percentage of agreement (Lane *et al.,* 2006). A second method utilized was to divide the number of interval sessions in agreement by the total number of interval sessions (Brooks *et al.,* 2003). The final commonly reported method employed was taking the smaller number of occurrences divided by the larger number of occurrences and then multiplying by 100 to reach the percentage of agreement (Lane *et al.,* 2007).

DISCUSSION

The evidence reviewed in this chapter supports the contention FBIs worked better for the majority of participants and supports a large body of evidence that determining the function of a target behavior and then using function-based interventions increases the likelihood of a more successful intervention for school related undesirable behaviors.

This review provides supportive evidence that researcher and practitioner attention is increasing regarding the use of function-based interventions by teachers to reduce disruptive behaviors in their classrooms with their students. There is a large and expanding body of evidence that indicates that FBA and FBI work for resolution of many undesirable school behaviors. The studies included in this review reflect evidence that teachers and other school personnel can participate or conduct entirely the FBA and can assist or design effective function-based interventions. This review seems to refute concerns that, depending on the methodology used, FBA requires too much time and specialized training for practical classroom consideration. While training is needed before use, a growing body of evidence supports the contention that teachers can take a more substantial role in the FBA process. With proper training in a robust behavior management methodology that has noted effectiveness even when applied to more challenging behavioral issues-such as the FBA process and FBI- teachers can become masters of behavior change in their classrooms.

It should be noted that the training needed to use FBA and FBI is not prohibitive. Bessette and colleagues (2007) conducted a study in which a paraprofessional was trained to conduct a functional analysis and implement the FBI. The paraprofessional gave positive feedback in regards to the ease of learning and performing the functional analysis process and implementing the FBI. Wright-Gallo and colleagues (2006) also sought feedback in a study in which the classroom teacher conducted an FBA. The classroom teacher reported that "it was not a time-consuming process and that she would continue to use it when aberrant behavior could not be decreased through existing classroom behavior management routines" (Wright-Gallo *et al.,* 2006, p. 431).

In fact, of the eleven studies in this review involving a completed functional analysis [again the most sophisticated approach to FBA] as part of their assessment, eight were accomplished by a teacher who had access to assistance or were conducted solely by the teacher of record (Bessette & Wills, 2007; Blair *et al.,* 2007; Kamps *et al.,* 2006; Kern *et al.,* 2006; Newcomer & Lewis, 2004; Payne *et al.,* 2007; Sterling-Turner *et al.,* 2001; Wright-Gallo *et al.,* 2006). It is worth noting further that, even though only 55% of the studies included completing a functional analysis as part of an FBA process, all of the FBIs implemented with fidelity reduced or eliminated the target behavior.

Nearly half of the effective interventions were developed with supporting evidence of an FBA methodology that excluded functional analysis. This is not to say that a functional analysis is not an integral part of the FBA process, but gives reason to believe that a curtailed FBA process can yield positive results in many situations involving undesirable classroom behavior. More pointedly, while many scholars advocate the inclusion of functional analysis as a tool for any FBA, this level of sophistication may well be unnecessary for practicing teachers in the classroom setting addressing the most common undesirable school behaviors (Waller, 2008).

Additional voices supporting this contention were provided by Packenham and colleagues (2004), who completed a study involving a classroom teacher who completed a simplified FBA procedure to identify the function of the disruptive behavior of two students. The teacher and researcher designed intervention options, and ultimately the teacher chose an FBI to employ in the classroom. The intervention chosen succeeded at decreasing the disruptive behavior of both students in the study. The teacher rated the simplified FBA approach as socially valid and "rated the process as 'taking up hardly any time' and as 'worth the time'" (p. 20). These researchers suggested that a teacher's knowledge of and experience with a student can assist her in quickly identifying the function of the problem behavior, thus increasing the efficiency of developing an appropriate intervention for the student. They concluded that advantages such as these may reduce the level of complexity required for FBA, though research addressing this question is lacking.

These points are significant for school mental health promotion efforts of all sorts: It is really not relevant how much data exists supporting the effectiveness of a particular intervention if the teacher addressing the behavior challenge in her classroom lacks confidence in the strategy, the teacher has not had sufficient training to successfully implement the strategy, the teacher lacks confidence in the technique or her skill in implementation, or the teacher simply cannotpractically apply the intervention due to other classroom obligations or logistical constraints (Waller, 2008). When students actively engage with the school community, positive student outcomes tend to ensue and become synergistic. When teachers actively engage good teaching and behavior management strategies, positive student outcomes tend to ensue. Practice of forceful mandates and coercion at all levels of school use risks negative student outcomes. These points encourage more use of these methodologies.

Table 2: Summary of the Studies.

Authors/ Year of Publication	**# in Study; Age(s); Disabilities**	**FBA Procedures Used**	**Intervention**	**Function of the behavior**	**Social Validity**	**Treatment Integrity**
Bessette& Wills (2007)	1; age 8; no identified disability	FAI, DO, FA	Functional Communication Training, Extinction	Teacher attention/escape tasks	No	Yes
Biniker&Pindiprolu (2008)	1; age 18; BD	FAI, SDFAI, DO CBM	Behavior support card; DRA	Teacher attention/escape tasks	No	No
Blair, Unbreit, Dunlap, & Jung (2007)	1; age 6; MR, Autism	PFAS, DO, FA DA	Physical & verbal prompts thinned to no prompts	Teacher attention/escape tasks	Yes	Yes

Table 2: cont….

Brooks, Todd, Tofflemoyer& Horner (2003)	1; age 10; Downs Syndrome and MR	DA, CBM	Self-management	Peer/adult attention	No	Yes
Burke, Hagan-Burke, &Sugai (2003)	1; age 8; LD	Review school history Curriculum based Measures, DO, Student/teacher interviews, FA	Preteaching vocabulary concepts	Escape tasks	No	Yes
Ingram, Palmer, &Sugai(2005)	2; 6th grade (ages not given); Bryce: ADHD Carter: no identified disability	FAI, SDFAI, DO BIP	Bryce: Token reinforcement system, earned breaks, self-management Carter: Token reinforcement system; self-management	Both: escape tasks	Yes	Yes
Kamps, Wendland, &Culpepper (2006)	2; both age 7; no identified disabilities	FAI, DO, SSBD DA, FA	Patricia: DRA; self-recording, limited reminders of class rules, modeling, help tickets to allow brief escape Michael: Self-monitoring; praise/points during group instruction; limited attention to inappropriate behaviors; lottery reinforcement system	Patricia: attention and escape from tasks Michael: attention, escape, & sensory stimulation	No	Yes
Kern, Gallagher, Starosta, Hickman, & George (2006)	1; age 10; Developmental Disability, ADHD, & ODD	Review school history Medial history 2 school-based questionnaires FAOF, DO, FA	Multi-component support plan	Attention & escape	No	Yes
Lane, Weisenbach, Little, Phillips, &Wehby (2006)	2; 2nd grade (ages not given); at risk for EBD	PFAS, SDFAI, FBIDM SSRS, Function Matrix	Antecedent adjustments, Positive reinforcement, Extinction	Marcus: teacher attention Julie: peer attention and escape tasks	Yes	Yes
Lane, Weisenbach, Phillips, &Wehby (2007)	2; both age 7; at risk for EBD	PFAS, SDFAI, SSRS, DO Function Matrix, FBIDM	Margaret: antecedent adjustments; positive reinforcement; and extinction	Margaret: attention from teacher/peers Charlie: teacher/peer attention &	Yes	Yes

Table 2: cont….

			Charlie: adjusting consequences; positive reinforcement; programming for extinction	escape tasks		
Lane, Rogers, Parks, Weisenbach, Mau, Merwin, & Bergman (2007)	2; Claire-age 7; no identified disability Aaron-age 14; LD in written expression/special education	PFAS, SDFAI, DO, SSRS Function Matrix FBIDM	Antecedent adjustments, reinforcement for replacement behaviors, extinction	Claire: escape teacher/peer attention Aaron: teacher attention & escape tasks	Yes	Yes
Liaupsin, Umbreit, Ferro, Urso, &Upreti (2006)	1; age 14; no identified disability	PFAS, SDFAI, DO, Function Matrix, FBIDM	Antecedent adjustments, positive reinforcement of replacement behavior, extinction	Escape tasks	No	Yes
Newcomer & Lewis (2004)	3; Matthew-age 9; OHI Jerrod-age 11; no identified disability Emma-age 11; no identified disability	DA, SDFAI, FAI, PBQ, DO, Scatter plot, FA	Antecedent adjustments, positive reinforcement for replacement behaviors, minimize positive reinforcement after problem behavior AND behavior support plan for each	Matthew: escape peers Jerrod: escape tasks Emma: teacher attention	Yes	Yes
Packenham, Shute, & Reid (2004)	2; Michelle-age 8; no identified disability Jack-age 9; no identified disability	Truncated FBA: Teacher interview Behavior function guidelines Hypothesis formulation Intervention design	Michelle: Attention contingent on appropriate behavior Jack: Antecedent adjustments/Token economy	Michelle: teacher attention Jack: escape tasks	Yes	Yes
Payne, Scott, & Conroy (2007)	4; Julie-age 11; LD Amy-age 10; LD Brian-age 9; no identified disability Barry-age 11; MMI	Structured interviews, DO, DA, FA	Julie: Access by earned breaks Amy: Access by earned breaks Brian: Verbal Teacher attention/DRI/Token economy Barry: Escape by earned passes	Julie/Amy: peer attention Brian: teacher attention Barry: escape tasks	No	Yes

Table 2: cont….

Preciado, Horner, & Baker (2009)	4; Juan-2nd grade Jose-2nd grade; Sp. Ed. & LD Javier-4th grade Julia-3rd grade Others: no identified disability	FACTS A&B, DO, FA, Skills assessments	Language-matched instructional priming	All: escape tasks	Yes	Yes
Stage, Jackson, Moscovitz, Erickson, Thurman, Jessee, & Olson (2006)	3; Will-age 5; ADHD Joshua-age 6; Dev. Disability Gale-9th grade; ADHD	FACTS A&B, SDFAI, FBA Checklist for students/teachers, FAI-parent version, DO, FA	Will: Communication training/Popcorn party Joshua: DRA Gale: DRA	Will: teacher attention/escape tasks Joshua: teacher attention/escape tasks Gale: escape tasks/peer attention	Yes	Yes
Sterling-Turner, Robinson, &Wilczynski (2001)	1; James-age 13; LD in math and reading	Teacher interviews, CBA, DO, DA FA	Self-monitoring of appropriate behavior with reinforcement of peer tutoring	Peer attention	No	No
Wood, Umbreit, Liaupsin, & Gresham (2007)	1; age 8; no disability	PFAS, SDFAI, DO, Function Matrix, FBIDM	Antecedent adjustments, positive reinforcement and extinction	Teacher attention/escape tasks	Yes	Yes
Wright-Gallo, Higbee, Reagon, & Davey (2006)	2; age 12 Age 14 Both EBD	FA, Data collection	DRA-raise hand & verbal request for a break or interaction with teacher/peer	Both: attention & escape tasks	No	Yes

Notes: BIP=behavior intervention plan; CBA=curriculum-based assessment; CBM=competing behavior model; DA=descriptive assessment; DO=direct observation; FA=functional analysis; FACTS=functional assessment checklist for teachers & staff; FAI=functional assessment interview; FAOF=functional assessment observation form; FBIDM=function-based intervention decision model; MAS=motivation assessment scale; PBQ=problem behavior questionnaire; PFAS=preliminary functional assessment survey; SDFAI=student directed functional assessment interview; SFA=student functional assessment; SSBD=systematic screening for behavior disorders; SSRS=social skills rating system.

CONCLUSIONS

Widespread adoption of evidence-based behavior management practices is essential if mild to moderate occurrences of undesirable classroom behavior are to be redressed *in the classroom* so that students:

- Do not loose instructional time,

- Avoid negative labels that often become quite recalcitrant to coercive control,
- Circumvent inadvertent reinforcement *via* ineffective attempts to punish, and
- So that school engagement is fostered and positive relationships and outcomes are maximized.

It may be wise to stress that advocating for classroom use of effective behavior management approaches such as FBA that promote student mental health is *not* tantamount to:

- Legerdemain insinuating that teachers do not currently have sufficient job responsibilities to fill a work day, or
- That an infinite quantity of straw can be piled on the proverbial pachyderm without something breaking.

Selecting the right evidence-based approaches for the right faculty and the right student body is a less than enviable responsibility and requires the highest level of competence on behalf of school leaders tasked with making, guiding, or mediating such decisions. Part of obtaining faculty acceptance and engendering engagement of unknown though evidence-based interventions of any kind includes helping personnel understand:

some initial work invested in learning and implementing good management techniques will be offset by time and effort saved and frustration sidestepped for everyone, with ultimately far less time being squandered in executing mediocre or ineffective behavioral strategies.

Ultimately, of course, it is the needs of the student body which should guide policy and practice decisions. Nonetheless, it is shortsighted, perhaps, to forget that improved student performance, engagement, and mental health can ***only improve*** the work environment and professional satisfaction of educators, as well.

ACKNOWLEDGEMENT

Declare none.

CONFLICT OF INTEREST

The author(s) confirm that this chapter content has no conflict of interest.

REFERENCES

Adelman, H.,& Taylor, L. (2005). Classroom climate. In S. W. Lee (Ed.), *Encyclopedia of school psychology*. Thousand Oaks, CA: Sage.

Alberto, P. A., & Troutman, A. C. (2009). *Applied Behavior Analysis for Teachers* (8th Ed.). Upper Saddle River, NJ: Pearson Education.

Baker, J. A., Grant, S., & Morlock, L. (2008). The teacher-student relationship as a developmental context for children with internalizing or externalizing behavior problems. *School Psychology Quarterly*, *23(1),* 3–15.

Barth, J., Dunlap, S., Dane, H., Lochman, J., & Wells, K. (2004). Classroom environment influences on aggression, peer relations, and academic focus. *Journal ofSchool Psychology, 42,* 115–133.

Bessette, K. K., & Wills, H. P. (2007). An example of an elementary school paraprofessional-implemented functional analysis and intervention. *Behavioral Disorders*, *32(3),* 192-210.

Biniker, K. L., & Pindiprolu, S. S. (2008). Functional assessment based intervention plans in alternative educational settings in the USA: A case study. *The Journal of the International Association of Special Education*, *9(1),* 68-77.

Blair, K. C., Umbreit, J., Dunlap, G., & Jung, G. (2007). Promoting inclusion and peer participation through assessment-based intervention. *Topics in Early Childhood Special Education*, *27(3),* 134-147.

Brooks, A., Todd, A. W., Tofflemoyer, S., & Horner, R. H. (2003). Use of functional assessment and a self-management system to increase academic engagement and work completion. *Journal of Positive Behavior Interventions*, *5(3),* 144-152.

Burke, M. D., Hagan-Burke, S., & Sugai, G. (2003). The efficacy of function-based interventions for students with learning disabilities who exhibit escape-maintained problem behaviors: preliminary results from a single-case experiment. *Learning Disability Quarterly*, *26(Winter),* 15-25.

Individuals with Disabilities Education Act of 1997, P.L. 105-17, (enacted).

Individuals with Disabilities Improvement Act of 2004, P. L. 108-446.

Ingram, K., Lewis-Palmer, T., & Sugai, G. (2005). Function-based intervention planning: Comparing the effectiveness of fba function-based and non-function-based intervention plans. *Journal of Positive Behavior Interventions*, *7(4),* 224-236.

Kamps, D., Wendland, M., & Culpepper, M. (2006). Active teacher participation in functional behavior assessment for students with emotional and behavioral disordersrisks in general education classrooms. *Behavioral Disorders*, *31(2),* 128-146.

Kern, L., Gallagher, P., Starosta, K., Hickman, W., & George, M. (2006). Longitudinal outcomes of functional behavioral assessment-based intervention. *Journal of Positive Behavior Interventions, 8(2),* 67-78.

Lane, K. L., Rogers, L. A., Parks, R. J., Weisenbach, J. L., Mau, A. C., &Merwin, M. T. *et al.,* (2007). Function-based interventions for students who are nonresponsive to primary and secondary prevention efforts: illustrations at the elementary and middle school levels. *Journal of Emotional and Behavioral Disorders, 15(3),* 169-183.

Lane, K. L., Weisenbach, J. L., Little, M. A., Phillips, A., & Wehby, J. (2006). Illustrations of function-based interventions implemented by general education teachers: Building capacity at the school site. *Education and Treatment of Children, 29(4),* 549-571.

Lane, K. L., Weisenbach, J. L., Phillips, A., & Wehby, J. H. (2007). Designing, implementing, and evaluating function-based interventions using a systematic, feasible approach. *Behavioral Disorders, 32*(2), 122-139.

Liaupsin, C. J., Umbreit, J., Ferro, J. B., Urso, A., &Upreti, G. (2006). Improving academic engagement through systematic, function-based intervention. *Education and Treatment of Children, 29(4),* 573-591.

Newcomer, L. L., & Lewis, T. J. (2004). Functional behavioral assessment: An investigation of assessment reliability and effectiveness of function-based interventions. *Journal of Emotional and Behavioral Disorders, 12(3),* 168-181.

Packenham, M., Shute, R., & Reid, R. (2004). A truncated functional behavioral assessment procedure for children with disruptive classroom behaviors. *Education and Treatment of Children, 27(1),* 9-25.

Payne, L. D., Scott, T. M., & Conroy, M. (2007). A school-based examination of the efficacy of function-based intervention. *Behavioral Disorders, 32(3),* 158-174.

Preciado, J. A., Horner, R. H., & Baker, S. K. (2009). Using a function-based approach to decrease problem behaviors and increase academic engagement for LatinoEnglish language learners. *The Journal of Special Education, 42(4),* 227-240.

Sheffield, K. & Waller, R. J. (2010). A review of single-case studies utilizing self-monitoring interventions to reduce problem classroom behaviors. *Beyond Behavior, 19(2),* 7-13.

Stage, S. A., Jackson, H. G., Moscovitz, K., Erickson, M. J., Thurman, S. O., & Jessee, W. *et al.,* (2006). Using multimethod-multisource functional behavioral assessment for students with behavioral disabilities. *School Psychology Review, 35(3),* 451-471.

Sterling-Turner, H. E., Robinson, S. L., & Wilczynski, S. M. (2001). Functional assessment of distracting and disruptive behaviors in the school setting. *School Psychology Review, 30(2),* 211-226.

Waller, R. J. (2008). *The educator's guide to solving common behavior problems.* Thousand Oaks, CA: Corwin Press.

Waller, R. J. (2009). *The teacher's concise guide to functional behavioral assessment.* Thousand Oaks, CA: Corwin Press.

Wood, B. K., Umbreit, J., Liaupsin, C. J., & Gresham, F. M. (2007). A treatment integrity analysis of function-based intervention. *Education and Treatment of Children, 30(4),* 105-120.

Wright-Gallo, G. L., Higbee, T. S., Reagon, K. A., & Davey, B. J. (2006). Classroom-based functional analysis and intervention for students with emotional/behavioral disorders. *Education and Treatment of Children, 29(3),* 421-436.

CHAPTER 8

Risk and Resilience in Middle Childhood: Lessons for School Mental Health Promotion

Daisy R. Jackson[1,*] **and Elise Cappella**[2]

[1]Department of Applied Psychology, Steinhardt School of Culture, Education, and Human Development, Kimball Hall, 246 Greene Street, 8th Floor, New York, NY 10003, USA and [2]Steinhardt School of Culture, Education, and Human Development, 82 Washington Square East, New York University, New York, NY 10003, USA

Abstract: Unresolved mental health issues are associated with numerous negative outcomes, both short and long term, for school-aged children. Although effective interventions exist for many mental health conditions, primary prevention of these maladies, whenever possible, is clearly in a child's best interest. Mental health promotion in schools is a viable medium for nurturing prevention. Among the most potent influences schools can affect in the efforts to promote mental health are risk and resiliency factors in a child's environment. Exposure to risk factors is strongly associated with negative mental health outcomes, while the presence of protective factors is strongly predictive of positive mental health outcomes and ultimately pronounced improvements in quality of life. School performance can ultimately be among the most formidable risk or resilience factors, depending on the qualitative and quantitative experience of the individual student. Further, the school has the ability to exert influence on other risk and resilience factors in a student's environment. This chapter delineates risk and resilience factors that have been found to profoundly affect mental health and quality life, evidence-based practices that have been applied to foster positive outcomes, and provides sufficient foundation on the current knowledge base on risk and resilience to facilitate school planning in programming for maximizing student mental health outcomes.

Keywords: Academic press, ecological perspective, protective factors, resilience, risk, social-emotional functioning.

INTRODUCTION

Children and youth with poor mental health are at increased risk for underachievement, delinquency, and relational problems, both concurrent and

***Address correspondence to Daisy R. Jackson:** Department of Applied Psychology, Steinhardt School of Culture, Education, and Human Development, Kimball Hall, 246 Greene Street, 8th Floor, New York, NY 10003, USA; Tel: 212-992-7685; Email: ec79@nyu.edu

Raymond J. Waller (Ed)

subsequent to their initial difficulties (Masi & Cooper, 2006). Given the extensive evidence that early signs of maladaptation lead to more serious problems later on, efforts have been made to develop and implement strategies to prevent serious problems and promote positive mental health among children and youth (Petras, Chilcoat, Leaf, Ialongo, & Kellman, 2004; Lassen, Steele, & Sailor, 2006, WHO, 2006). Schools have been identified as a valuable point of access on many levels, in part because children spend most of their day in school, and in part because of the documented links between achievement and behavior (*e.g.,* Arnold, 1997; Duncan *et al.,* 2007; Miles & Stipek, 2006). In recent years, schools have been an integral context for research on a range of efforts including health promotion activities (Bond *et al.,* 2001), universal prevention programs (Lowry-Webster *et al.,* 2001), and school-based mental health services (Weist *et al.,* 2002; Waller, 2006).

However, it is not only children with early and identifiable mental health disorders that experience later problems. A significant proportion without identified difficulties, or with only isolated or mild symptoms, require additional adult support to maintain a positive developmental trajectory (Noam & Hermann, 2002). Specifically, studies have documented that substantial numbers of children *without* social, emotional, or academic problems show declines in academic achievement and motivation, along with increases in behavior problems and emotional distress, during middle childhood (Eccles, Lord, & Roeser, 1996). Given that students' academic trajectories are largely stable after the third grade (Entwisle & Alexander, 1999; Rutter & Maughan, 2002), and that the roots of adolescent behavior problems are planted in earlier years (*e.g.,* Barkley, Fischer, Edelbrock, & Smallish, 1990; Weisz, Weiss, & Donenberg, 1992), elementary schools are important contexts for mental health promotion for all children, including those both with and without early difficulties. Moreover, given the overwhelming evidence of the longstanding benefits of educational attainment, there has been a recent effort to integrate supportive practices, such as mental health promotion, into the education system (Bond *et al.,* 2001; President's New Freedom Commission on Mental Health, 2003). These efforts have been seen as particularly crucial for schools in high poverty communities, where resources may be inaccessible, ineffective, or underutilized (U.S. Surgeon General Report on Mental Health, 2001).

Beyond the paucity of mental health resources in high poverty communities, the children in these communities are at heightened risk of negative outcomes across multiple domains of development. When compared to children who are not growing up poor, children exposed to financial hardship show deficits in cognitive and social-emotional development and score lower on tests of academic achievement (Aber, Bennett, Conley, & Li, 1997). There is growing evidence that the experience of poverty early, as opposed to later, in a child's life is most strongly related to negative outcomes, with the effects of early exposure accumulating as the child grows older (see Aber at al., 1997; Brooks-Gunn & Duncan, 1997; Cappella *et al.,* 2008). Despite these links, poor children, who are disproportionately racial and ethnic minorities, face serious barriers to adequate mental health care, including lack of resources, lack of awareness, heightened stigma, and poor quality services (U.S. Department of Health and Human Services, 2001). As a result, schools have increasingly been recognized as a valuable base for mental health promotion for students and families. In addition, recent work suggests that schools can provide an important link between students' home and neighborhood environments, which may be able to moderate the effect of poverty on child outcomes (Cappella, Frazier, & Atkins, 2008).

Despite the recent and general acceptance of mental health promotion in schools (Flaherty & Osher, 2003), particularly in schools where mental health need is high, there remains less consensus among professionals about the theoretical framework upon which these activities are based. School mental health promotion involves a variety of approaches, all aimed at having a positive impact on youth mental health. According to the Surgeon's General's report (1999) and World Health Organization (2007), mental health is an overarching term that encapsulates both positive aspects of well-being and healthy functioning, as well as negative aspects of mental disorder and dysfunction (The Mental Health of Adolescents: A National Profile, 2008).

Given the range of activities that may fit into the umbrella of mental health promotion, one useful framework to organize and guide these activities is the risk and resilience paradigm. The literature examining what enables some children to succeed (*i.e.,* resilience) despite adversity (*i.e.,* risk) helps to provides an integrative concept of mental health as well asan understanding of the role of risk and protective factors in children's development. Although research examining the predictors of resilience can be traced to the early 1970s, the work of Urie Bronfenbrenner (1979) provides a contextual foundation for the empirical work. In his ecological systems theory, Bronfenbrenner (1979) described development as a dynamic process of interactions between the individual and the multiple nested systems (*e.g.,* family, school) in which the individual lives. This theory helps to organize our understanding of the effects of poverty (*i.e.,* risk) on children's mental health, and guides the discussion of the multi-level factors that foster positive outcomes (*i.e.,* resilience) among elementary age children.

Thus, the primary goal of this chapter is to use ecological systems theory to organize the risk and resilience research around understanding what helps youth to overcome risk and develop positive mental health. Given the importance of the early years of schooling, we will focus on risk and resilience research and the promotion of mental health among children in elementary school (ages 5-11). The extensive research on the impact of income on children's mental health leads to a chapter focus on poverty and its related stressors as the most powerful and predictable risk for negative outcomes among children. We will apply the risk and resilience paradigm to uncover the specific protective factors that promote resilience—or positive mental health—for elementary age children exposed to chronic poverty. Finally, we will discuss exemplar practices within schools that impact on these protective factors as a means toward positive mental health and development for all children in their care.

RISK AND RESILIENCE

Rooted in the work of Garmezy (1974) and Anthony (1974), resilience has increasingly been a focus of child development, psychology and education research (Luthar & Zigler, 1991; McCubbin, Thompson, Thompson, & Fromer, 1995; McCubbin, Thompson, Thompson, & Futrell, 1995). This framework provides a valuable basis for a wide range of school-based practices aimed at strengthening protective factors and lessening the impacts of risk factors to promote youth mental health (Bond, Glover, Godfrey, Bulter, & Patron, 2001). Resilience represents a dynamic process inherent to development that identifies positive adaptation despite exposure to risk. However, even as the study of resilience has increasingly prevailed as an area of interest, the current state of knowledge pertaining to the theoretical models of resilience remains under-developed. For clarity in this chapter, the major components of the risk-resilience paradigm as it applies to the promotion of youth mental health will be defined in the following ways:

> **Risk** is the set of characteristics, variables, or hazards that, if present for a given individual, make it more likely that this individual, rather than someone from the general population, will exhibit negative mental health outcomes (Mrazek & Haggerty, 1994, p. 127). Given the prevalence of poverty in U.S. public schools, the emphasis in this chapter will be on youth exposure to chronic economic hardship and related stressors associated with poverty.
>
> **Resilience** is a “dynamic process encompassing positive adaptation within the context of significant adversity” (Luthar, Cicchetti, & Becker, 2000, p. 543). Resilience involves both exposure to risk and positive adaptation to adversity (Berger, 2005). For this chapter, positive mental health and adaptation will include academic, social, and emotional domains of development for elementary age children.
>
> **Protective factors** refer to processes that *moderate* the effect of exposure to poverty and its related stressors (Garmezy, 1985; Rutter, 1979). The protective factors that moderate the relationship between poverty and child mental health do so by enabling youth to adapt to adversity more successfully than they would have without the presence of the protective factor(s) (Conrad & Hammen, 1993).

Risk: Over thirteen million children in the United States are growing up in poor families, with black and Hispanic children approximately two to three times more likely than white children to fall below the official poverty line (Thomas & Sawhill, 2005; Adler Lent & Figueria-McDonough, 2008). Research indicates that children living in single-mother households are more than five times as likely to be living in poverty than children living in households with both parents and are more than twice as likely to experience long spells of poverty (US Census Bureau,

1998). The dual disadvantage of poverty *and* single parenthood can leave families with fewer resources to deal with adversity (Jencks, 1991). Furthermore, an increasing proportion of poor families are living in urban neighborhoods with related environmental stressors such as high unemployment, homelessness, crime, noise, lead exposure, and other health hazards (Evans, 2006; U.S Surgeon General Report on Mental Health, 1999).

The childhood poverty rate is of particular concern given the consistent findings linking health and social problems to childhood poverty (Brooks-Gunn & Duncan, 1997). Poverty has been implicated in physical health problems, such as obesity, lead poisoning, asthma, and injuries (Brooks-Gunn *et al.*, 1993; Bradley & Corwyn, 2002; Evans & Kantrowitz, 2002; Sampson, Morenoff, & Gannon-Rowley, 2002). In terms of mental health, research demonstrates that children exposed to chronic economic disadvantage are at increased risk of internalizing symptoms (*e.g.*, anxiety), externalizing problems (*e.g.*, aggression) (Buckner & Bassuk, 1997; Dornfeld & Kruttschnitt, 1992; Duncan, Brooks-Gunn, & Klebanov, 1994), and peer relational difficulties (Hanson, McLanahan, & Thomson, 1997; Patterson, Kupersmidt, & Vaden, 1990). In the related domain of school achievement, children raised in households with income levels below the poverty line are significantly more likely than their more affluent counterparts to be held back in school, receive lower grades and test scores, and drop out of school early (see Byrd & Weitzman, 1994; Brooks-Gunn & Duncan, 1997).

The proposed pathways of the relationship between poverty and child developmental outcomes include family, school, and neighborhood processes. Researchers have found that limited household resources and poor parent-child interactions account for a significant proportion of the influence of poverty on development (Brooks-Gunn, Duncan, Klebanov, & Sealand, 1993). Schools in high poverty communities are less likely to have adequate physical space and materials (Evans, 2004), high academic expectations or support (Weinstein, 2002), and high quality classroom interactions (Pianta *et al.*, 2007). Poor neighborhoods tend to have inadequate resources, community disorganization, and low collective efficacy (Brooks-Gunn, Klebanov, & Liaw, 1995; Evans & Kantrowitz, 2002).

One research team proposed a "continuum of care" framework to highlight the impact of multiple environmental factors on developmental outcomes (Sameroff & Chandler, 1975). Thus, whereas poverty is a construct measured by household income, it is often a summary measure that reflects a complex and dynamic cumulative set of risk factors that include parent mental health, parental education, minority status, employment status, and neighborhood quality, among others. The idea of cumulative poverty-related risk factors highlights the collective and continued impact that poverty and the related environmental stressors can have on children's mental health. However, even though poverty research often concludes that children are at increased risk for mental health problems (Keyes, 2004), this outcome is not universal. Some children who grow up in poverty do *not* develop mental health problems, and instead display developmental trajectories that look similar to those of children from non-poor households.

Resilience: The process wherein children are able to adapt and adequately function in the face of significant adversity is known as *resilience*. The construct of resilience in this chapter refers to the developmental scenario in which a child who is exposed to poverty and its related stressors exhibits mental health outcomes (*i.e.,* cognitive/academic and social-emotional functioning) that are typical for middle childhood. The goal of *resilience research*, therefore, is to identify and examine the mechanisms that account for the adaptation that some youth exhibit despite exposure to significant risk.

Prior to the introduction of resiliency within the field of psychology, much of the literature and research in the area of child and developmental psychology was focused on "at risk" children. Research studies were designed to examine children's susceptibility to negative developmental outcomes after exposure to various risk factors such as maternal depression or poor nutrition in utero (Werner, 1993). What emerged from this "risk-focused" research was that a significant proportion of individuals managed to avoid negative developmental outcomes despite exposure to adverse conditions. It was this work that prompted the field to look more closely at individual strengths and adaptability and to consider outcomes other than the presence or absence of mental illness.

Much of the work on resilience and child development can be traced to the pioneering work of Emmy Werner and Ruth Smith (1993). In their prospective, longitudinal study, Werner and Smith assessed the impact of biological and psychosocial risk factors on the development of approximately 700 infants from the 1955 birth cohort in Kauai, Hawaii. Thirty percent of the children were exposed to four or more risk factors from birth, including chronic poverty and parental psychopathology (Werner, 2005). Although many of the risk-exposed children experienced significant problems later in life, one third of the high-risk children grew into well-adapted adults (Werner & Smith, 1993). Resilience research over the past four decades has sought to identify and understand the factors that contribute to the variance in developmental outcomes after chronic risk exposure.

THEORETICAL FRAMEWORK

The recent research on child resilience and mental health draws from three major theoretical and empirical perspectives. The first is **developmental psychopathology** (Masten, 2006), a body of research that sought to identify predictors (*i.e.,* risk factors) of psychopathology by examining developmental trajectories of "high risk" children (Mrazek & Haggerty, 1994). Developmental psychopathology research offers an integrative framework for understanding the *processes* through which children's emotional and behavioral problems develop, change, and importantly, may be prevented (Masten, 2003). The second body of work on which resilience research draws is **developmental theory** (Sroufe, 1997), which focuses our discussion of resilience on the factors that may influence children's mental health during particular stages of development. In middle childhood, the influences on positive development include not only attributes of the individual child and his/her family, but also the peer group and non-parental adults. The third, and most comprehensive, theoretical framework that guides our discussion is Bronfenbrenner's **bioecological model of human development** (Bronfenbrenner 1979, 1986), described in detail below.

Bronfenbrenner's bioecological systems theory (Bronfenbrenner & Morris, 1998) provides a model for considering the interacting and reciprocal influences of person, process, context, and time on children's mental health (Rudasill, Gallagher, & White,

2010). "Person" characteristics influence children's mental health by impacting everyday interactions between children and their environment. "Process" involves the regular interactions that occur within the child's immediate environment; it is through *proximal processes* that occur over *time* that children develop cognitive, social, and emotional competence (Bronfenbrenner & Morris, 1998). "Context" is the environment in (and with) which the interactions take place that can either activate or inhibit positive processes (Bronfenbrenner, 1999). The environment includes four interrelated systems that directly or indirectly involve the child and influence outcomes.

1) The microsystem involves the immediate relationships with the child and the specific contexts within which the child interacts (*e.g.,* family and classroom).

2) The next level is the mesosystem which includes interrelations between two or more structures of the microsystem (*e.g.,* teacher-parent communication).

3) The third level in the ecological system of human development is the exosystem, which consists of the external relationships and contexts that *indirectly* impact child development (*e.g.,* mother's place of work).

4) The macrosystem refers to the broader ideologies and institutional patterns that define a culture or subculture (*e.g.,* educational or mental health policy) and is the system in which the other three systems are nested.

Bronfenbrenner's bioecological model is a useful framework from which to investigate resilience because it highlights the dynamic relationship between individual and context (Bernat & Resnick, 2006). Applications of this model to school-based mental health promotion underscore the importance of internal and external factors that are "protective" and have the potential to minimize the effect of poverty on child mental health (Anthony *et al.,* 2009). From a bioecological perspective, the process of resilience is dependent on the characteristics of the child (*i.e.,* behavioral dispositions, temperament), characteristics and conditions of the multiple contexts in which development occurs (*e.g.,* quality of relationship), and the interplay between these factors (*e.g.,* child's emotional regulation skills and classroom climate).

RESEARCH AND PRACTICE

In the following section, we will use the ecological perspective to organize an overview of the empirically-derived factors that protect elementary age children from the negative impact of poverty and related stressors. The discussion will focus on the individual, micro-, and mesosystems, which have been the focus of risk-resilience research and may be most immediately relevant to school mental health promotion. In addition, the significant developmental milestones in middle childhood—entering formal schooling, gaining a foundation in academic skills, getting along with peers and adults—are most directly related to the individual and his/her immediate contexts of development (*i.e.,* microsystems). Thus, although important, the under-developed research on the role of the exo- and macro-systems on child mental health will not be the focus of the subsequent discussion. Lastly, we will describe school practices and programs that have been shown to be effective in targeting protective factors across ecological systems and promoting positive mental health for children in poverty.

THE INDIVIDUAL CHILD: PROTECTIVE FACTORS AND SCHOOL PRACTICES TO ENHANCE MENTAL HEALTH

What do we know about child-level protective factors? Educators and mental health professionals alike recognize the significant changes that occur across the cognitive and social-emotional domains of development in elementary school children. Researchers have identified a number of individual-level predictors of positive mental health within these domains (Hartman, Turner, Daigle, Exum, & Cullen, 2008). For example, early cognitive abilities (*e.g.,* attention, logical reasoning, complex thought), self-efficacy, and locus of control have been demonstrated to predict **academic competence**, a critical component of mental health in middle childhood (Adelman & Taylor, 2005; Kumpfer & Hopkins, 1993; Masten *et al.,* 1995). In addition, social skills, emotional regulation, and self-concept relate to positive **social-emotional functioning** among elementary age children (Masten, 2001). Given that academic and social-emotional functioning are strongly interrelated (*e.g.,* Luthar, 1995; Reyes *et al.,* 2000; Welsh *et al.,* 2001), we will discuss the most robust protective factors that impact *both domains* and may be most amenable to prevention and promotion in schools.[1]

Social skills, problem-solving abilities, and emotional regulation facilitate intellectual functioning, even among the most disadvantaged groups (Masten, 1994). Social skills, such as knowing how to enter a group, using reasonable and effective communication, and having a repertoire of prosocial responses to social situations, are components of positive mental health. Children with social skills are likely to seek out and receive support from the individuals around them, which serves to facilitate the development of protective relationships for children growing up in stressful environments (Werner, 1993). Similarly, children who use appropriate and effective problem-solving strategies are better able to prevent and resolve social conflicts, which may grow increasingly complex as children progress through elementary school. Problem-solving abilities also facilitate the completion of academic tasks that are growing increasingly multifaceted across the grades. Finally, emotion regulation, or the ability to control one's emotions, builds through the years and is critical for both social functioning (Izard *et al.,* 2001; Shields *et al.,* 2001) and academic achievement (Gumora & Arsenio, 2002; Trentacosta & Izard, 2007). Research over the past decade suggests that emotion regulation may be especially important for children who are coping with the negative consequences of economic adversity (Shields & Cicchetti, 2001).

Beyond social and emotional skills and abilities, an expanding body of research has focused on the psychological experiences of self-efficacy and locus of control as protective against the negative impact of poverty. Self efficacy, or a child's beliefs about his or her own "capacity to organize and execute" (Bandura, 1977, p. 3), predicts a child's ability to adjust to and cope with adverse environments (Magnusson & Stattin, 2006). In particular, self-efficacy refers to what a child believes he/she can do under certain circumstances and relates to the confidence a child feels when approaching a task. Finally, locus of control, or a child's perceptions of where the underlying responsibilities for life events reside (Battle

[1] It is important to note that although these factors are assessed *within* the individual child, they develop in *interaction* with other individuals across the multiple micro-systems in which the child spends time.

& Rotter 1963), has been identified as a robust protective factor for poor children and has been associated with feelings of empowerment and initiation of problem-solving. Children with a strong *internal* locus of control (*i.e.,* belief that they exert influence over situations) actively respond to risk and are better able to adapt to a range of stressors within their environment (Juby & Rycraft, 2004).

What do we know about school practices to enhance child knowledge and abilities? Given these identified protective factors within the individual child, school-based prevention and promotion programs have been developed to promote child understanding and skills within these areas. One of the more well-studied and efficacious programs is called, Promoting Alternative Thinking Strategies or PATHS (Kam, Greenberg, & Kusche, 2004). Integrated into regular classroom instruction, the PATHS program includes teacher-led curricula with developmentally-based lessons targeting children's emotion regulation, emotional awareness, and problem-solving. The aim is to increase social-emotional competence, decrease aggression and behavior problems, and enhance educational processes in the classroom. Although it is primarily a practice implemented by the classroom teacher, additional information and activities are provided for parents and schools in order to facilitate generalize ability of students' skills beyond the classroom (Greenberg & Kusche, 2006).

In the largest PATHS study to date, Pennsylvania State's Conduct Problems Prevention Research Group randomly assigned 198 first grade classrooms from high-crime neighborhoods to be PATHS classrooms (*i.e.,* implement PATHS curriculum) and 180 first grade classrooms from the same neighborhoods served as control classrooms (*i.e.,* business as usual) (Conduct Problems Prevention Research Group, 1999). Whereas control teachers pursued their usual lesson plans, the PATHS teachers delivered 57 lessons that used a variety of modalities (*e.g.,* hypothetical scenarios, role plays)to help children understand their own and others' emotions, control their behavioral impulses, and use prosocial problem-solving. Results revealed students in the PATHS classrooms performed significantly better than their counterparts on peer reports of aggression and hyperactivity–disruptive behavior. Long term effects include continued reduction in boys' aggression through the fourth grade.

A related program designed to promote children's academic and social-emotional functioning is the 4Rs Program (Reading, Writing, Respect, and Resolution). This universal, school-based intervention trains and supports teachers in kindergarten through fifth grade to integrate social and emotional learning into the school language arts curriculum (Brown, Jones, La Russo, & Aber, 2010). Although the 4Rs Program targets multiple aspects of the school context that have been identified as crucial for the promotion of positive youth development (Brown *et al.,* 2010), the primary component of 4Rs is a literacy-based curriculum in social-emotional learning and conflict resolution skills. Results from a recent randomized controlled trial indicated positive effects on overall classroom quality for 3rd grade classrooms, as well as teacher-reported increases in student literacy and language skills following 4Rs implementation. Thus, teacher-implemented curricula that includes high-quality book reading about "real-life" scenarios that are applicable to students' lives, in combination with interactive classroom discussions and opportunities to practice skills through role play can be effective practices for the development and enhancement of individual (*e.g.,* problem solving) and context level protective factors (*e.g.,* positive classroom interactions).

THE MICROSYSTEMS: FAMILY, PEER, CLASSROOM, AND SCHOOL IN CHILD MENTAL HEALTH

Beyond the individual child, the microsystems within which the child participates have an impact on the child's mental health, and play a critical role in fostering resilience (Fraser, 1997). What have emerged as critical to children's development are the family, peer group, classroom, and school, each of which is discussed in turn below.

Family-Level: Protective Factors. When a child living in poverty exhibits positive mental health, it is often the family system that first emerges as a potential explanation (Condly, 2006). Whereas some of the research findings on the direct effects of poverty on children's functioning are mixed, it is clear that the *indirect effects* of poverty on development occur, in part, through the family context (McLeod & Shanahan, 1993). Researchers have identified two areas of the family context that protect elementary age children growing up in poverty:

(a) Parent-child interactions; and

(b) Parenting practices (Gregory & Cappella, 2008; Jenkins & Smith, 1990).

High quality interactions in the home, which involve parent-child communication and involvement characterized by *warmth, closeness,* and *support*, buffer children from the consequences of economic hardship (Luthar, 2006; Mistry, Vandewater, Huston, & McLoyd, 2002).

In one longitudinal study, children in homes with warm and cohesive family interactions performed better in elementary and middle school and were more likely to attend post-secondary education and improve their life opportunities (Orthner, Jones-Sanpei, & Williamson, 2004). Studies using both observational and experimental data have found that high quality care (*i.e.,* warmth, sensitivity, responsiveness and consistency) promotes cognitive abilities and social competence for children from economically disadvantaged homes (Lee, 2005). Similarly, findings reveal that supportive parenting moderates the relationship between economic disadvantage and child behavior problems (Pettit, Bates, & Dodge, 1997). Thus, the availability of stable and high quality interactions with at least one primary caregiver has been consistently identified as a protective factor that promotes resilience in children exposed to poverty (Gregory & Cappella, 2009; Vanderbilt-Adriance & Shaw, 2008).

In addition to high quality interactions, there is a growing body of literature dedicated to the protective qualities of particular parenting practices. Within this literature, parenting practices linked to mental health in middle childhood include monitoring, discipline, and educational stimulation (Rankin & Quane, 2002; Sampson & Laub 1994). Numerous studies document that high levels of parental monitoring in late middle childhood and early adolescence are associated with fewer externalizing behaviors for children growing up in low-income neighborhoods (*e.g.,* Frick, Christian, & Wootton, 1999; Leve, Kim, & Pears, 2005; Petit, Bates, Dodge, & Meece, 1999). Quality disciplinary practices also predict children's behavior and social-emotional functioning (Stormshak, McMahon, & Lengua, 2000). These include:

(a) Exertion of appropriate control over child behavior;

(b) Instruction about the rationale for punishment; and

(c) Discussion of alternative behaviors to use. Finally, the presence and amount of cognitive and academic simulation in the home enhances child development across developmental domains (Bradley & Corwyn, 2002).

Stimulation such as reading and conversing with children, helping children learn their numbers, and taking children on educational outings (*e.g.,* to the library) promotes academic achievement and reduces behavior problems, particularly for families with limited financial resources (Magnuson & Duncan, 2002).

Family-level: Practices. Research on school efforts to target family-level factors associated with childhood resilience is lacking in both abundance and rigor. However, emerging research points toward promising school practices that provide support to families to increase the academic and mental health opportunities for their children. In Links to Learning, a mental health model in high poverty schools, parent advocates and mental health professionals linked with schools are trained to support home-based learning activities for students with disruptive behavior problems (Cappella *et al.,* 2008). INSIGHTS, a program promoting temperament-responsive parenting (and teaching) practices, improved parenting competence and decreased child disruptive behaviors across the eight-week intervention (O'Connor, Rodriguez, Cappella, Morris, & McClowry, 2010). The 4Rs program includes a parent component with suggestions for related social-emotional and literacy activities for the parent and child to complete together at home (Aber *et al,* 2009). Other effective school outreach to parents includes encouragement of interactive homework and family-child reading (*e.g.,* Epstein & Van Voorhis, 2001; Hoover-Dempsey *et al.,* 2001), strategies that are especially important for parents unable to attend school events due to work or childcare responsibilities, or more subtle barriers related to empowerment or perceptions of school climate (Chavkin & Williams, 1989; McKay *et al.,* 2003).

Peer group level: Protective factors. Although the family context remains important throughout development, the peer context becomes increasingly influential as children grow. From the early work of Piaget and beyond, peer relationships have been identified as critical to child development, with studies pointing to the importance of peer interactions for children's cognitive and social-emotional skills (*e.g.,* perspective-taking and empathy) (Parker, Rubin, Erath, Wojslawowicz, & Buskirk, 2006). The transition to schooling brings exposure to myriad peer interactions that provide opportunities for social learning and development (Hartup, 1984; Oden, 1987). Through building and sustaining different types of peer relationships, children acquire knowledge about themselves and others. In addition, social interactions with peers offer opportunities for children to refine social skills, such as perspective taking, that have been identified as individual-level protective factors.

Friendship in middle childhood represents a "mutually agreed on relationship" in which children like each other's personal qualities, enjoy spending time together, and find ways to support each other (Berndt, 1996). A longitudinal study of fifth graders' peer relationships found that although multiple aspects of peer relationships predicted social and emotional indicators twelve years later, close friendships were most important to positive outcomes (see Bagwell, Schmidt, Newcomb, & Bukowski, 2001). Close friends have been found to protect children from loneliness, isolation, victimization, and rejection (Hodges, Boivin, Vitaro, & Bukowski, 1999; McCloskey & Stuewig, 2001). For children exposed to environmental stressors, the presence of close, supportive, and positive relationships with well-adjusted peers may help to compensate for a lack of protection and resources in other contexts.

Peer group level: Practices. Research indicates that schools can implement practices that promote positive peer relationships and improve children's school functioning. One empirically-based method is peer-assisted learning or peer tutoring in which students help one another to learn new skills or concepts (Thomas, 1993). There has been a considerable amount of research on the positive effects of peer tutoring on children's acquisition of academic skills (Cohen, Kulik, & Kulik, 1982), improved classroom behavior (Fuchs, Fuchs, Phillips, Hamlett, & Karns, 1995), and enhancement of peer relations (Greenwood, Carta, Kamps, & Hall, 1988). Peer tutoring increases the time that children are academically engaged (Delquadri, Greenwood, Whorton, Carta, & Hall, 1986), provides opportunities for practice in self-monitoring (Topping, 2005; Greenwood *et al.,* 1988), and predicts improvements in children's self-esteem (Cardenas, Harris, del Refugio, & Supik, 1991), self-efficacy (Robinson, Schofield, & Steers-Wentzell,

2005) and attitudes toward school (Cardenas *et al.,* 1991). In two meta-analyses, researchers found the positive effects to be strongest for urban low-income children in early elementary grades (Rohrbeck *et al.,* 2003; Ginsburg-Block *et al.,* 2006). Taken together, these findings suggest drawing upon students, particularly students in under-resourced schools, as potential delivery agents of support and instruction (Menesses & Gresham, 2009).

Aside from peer support with academic work, school-based practices that foster peer-support for interpersonal relationships and social interactions can enhance mental health. One school practice that has gained popularity is peer mediation. Rooted in applied conflict resolution, peer mediation empowers students to take an active role in the creation and establishment of positive peer relationships through peer-peer problem-solving and student-initiated decision-making in "real-school" settings (Burrell, Zirbel, & Allen, 2003). As mediators, students are taught skills such as active listening and paraphrasing and receive practice in reframing conflict and using appropriate problem-solving (Jones & Brinkman, 1994). Although research on peer mediation has been variable, studies have shown reductions in disruptive behavior (*e.g.,* fighting, verbal abuse, and arguments), and reductions in suspensions after implementation of peer mediation programs. Mediator trainings also produce gains in student knowledge of effective and positive strategies for conflict response and management (*e.g.,* Bell *et al.,* 2000; Graham & Pulvino, 2000; Johnson & Johnson, 2001).

Classroom-level: Protective factors. Peer interactions occur across multiple school settings but particularly in classrooms. As children transition from preschool to kindergarten and later grades, developmental theories highlight the increasingly important impact of classroom interactions—with peers and with the teacher—on child adjustment (Baker, 1999; Esposito, 1999; Schaps & Solomon, 2003). In particular, considerable attention has been paid to the *type*s of social interactions and the *quality* of interactions as predicting developmental milestones. Although the empirical research on classrooms and child mental health is limited (Eamon, 2001), classroom relationships (teacher-student and peer) and classroom climate have been linked to children's academic and social-emotional functioning and identified as protective factors for children facing risk

(Eamon, 2001; Pianta & Walsh, 1998; Rees & Bailey, 2003; Rutter, 1990; Werner & Smith, 1988).

The quality of the relationship that children have with teachers is critical to academic and social-emotional functioning (Goodenow, 1992). Close and supportive relationships have the potential to mitigate the risk of negative outcomes for children who may otherwise struggle. Given that middle childhood is the primary period when children develop and consolidate academic skills and achievement-related beliefs and attitudes (Alexander & Entwisle, 1988), children who display emotional, social, and behavioral problems in elementary school are at risk for poor adjustment overall. In a study of low-income students, degree of closeness in the teacher-student relationship predicted school adjustment, with warm and trusting relationships predicting positive school outcomes (Baker, Grant, & Morlock, 2009). Hymel and Ford (2003) found associations between early influences of teacher-child relationships and later school performance, even after controlling for cognitive ability. Importantly, teacher-student relationships in kindergarten predict *both* academic and behavioral outcomes (Hamre & Pianta, 2001; Pianta & Stuhlman, 2004)—which are both critical contributors to student mental health.

The overall atmosphere or climate of the classroom also matters for child outcomes (Jones, Brown, & Aber, 2008). Although the definition varies, classroom climate has been assessed through teacher-student interactions, classroom rules, routines, and expectations, and participant experiences of the environment (Creemers & Reezigt, 1999). Positive classroom climate has been associated with greater self-esteem, cognitive competence, self-efficacy, school satisfaction, and academic performance, whereas classrooms with poor climate have worse peer relations and academic focus, and more behavior problems (*e.g.*, Barth, Dunlap, Dane, Lochman, & Wells, 2004). Classrooms with responsive teachers, warm and enjoyable interactions, proactive and positive behavior management, clear and consistent rules and routines, and high quality feedback have been found to promote children's behavioral engagement in learning (*e.g.*, La Paro, Pianta, & Stuhlman, 2004; Pianta, La Paro, Payne, Cox, and Bradley, 2002). Finally, classroom emotional support can serve as a protective factor for children's academic and social functioning, especially for children with adjustment problems (Hamre & Pianta, 2005; Morrison & Connor, 2002). In their study of fifth grade students' perception of the classroom, Patrick and colleagues (2007) found evidence that the relational aspects of classroom climate matter for student engagement, with students who felt emotional support from their teacher and academic support from their peers more likely to use self-regulatory strategies and engage in task-related interaction (Patrick *et al.,* 2007).

Classroom-level: Practices. Behavior management and emotional support can be enhanced through such practices as the Good Behavior Game (GBG; Barrish, Saunders, & Wolf, 1969). A widely-used, group contingency, classroom management practices, the Good Behavior Game promotes behavioral regulation and reduces disruptive behavior in children both concurrently and over time (Embry, 2002). Longitudinal studies examining the impact of the GBG on children identified as "at risk" for disruptive behavior problems have found a positive effect on the aggressive behaviors of sixth grade students who were exposed to the GBG early in elementary school (Ialongo, Poduska, Werthamer, & Kellam, 2001). In a randomized controlled trial with 700 first graders from 19 urban elementary schools, Dolan and colleagues (1993) found significant reductions in teacher ratings of aggression for both boys and girls, peer ratings of aggression for boys, and teacher ratings of shy behavior (a strong risk factor for negative outcomes when coupled with early aggression) among the students in classrooms using the GBG.

Classroom climate is also targeted in the Child Development Project (CDP), a school-based program to create "caring communities," as well as positive academic and social-emotional functioning. Rooted in the work on classroom environment and children's socialization, the classroom component of the CDP uses developmental discipline, cooperative learning, and language arts as a means toward student autonomy, competence, and relatedness (Soloman *et al.,* 2000). Students have a role in classroom decisions, collaborate on challenging academic tasks, and read high-quality literature as a basis for discussion of ethical and social issues (Developmental Studies Center, 1996). In a research trial across 12 elementary schools with diverse compositions, findings revealed positive effects on students' sense of the school and classroom as a community when CDP was implemented as designed (Soloman *et al.,* 1996; Solomon *et al.,* 1997). Analyses showed that the positive impact on sense of community was related to increased empathy and self-esteem (Solomon *et al.,* 1996b).Additional positive effects were found for students' social and academic attitudes and behaviors (Solomon *et al.,* 2000), with the strongest findings in high-poverty schools (Battistich *et al.,* 1995).

School-level: Protective factors. Defined as "the quality and consistency of interpersonal interactions within the school community that influence children's cognitive, social-emotional, and psychological development" (Haynes *et al.,* 1997, p. 322), *school climate* has been the primary focus of research on school context and youth mental health (Garmezy, 1991). Research on school climate has multiple methodological and theoretical challenges. Researchers must account for the dynamic and interactional nature of school environments and the nested nature of school-level data (*i.e.,* students nested within classrooms nested within schools) in their study designs. Many studies operate without a theoretical framework to guide interpretation of results, as well as lack the statistical power or type of data necessary to test for powerful moderating or mediating influences of distal and proximal contexts. Some of these difficulties may relate to specific constituents comprising the broader construct 'school climate', such as intricacies associated with measuring the perceptions of participants across all levels of school involvement. Perhaps as a response to measurement and methodological encumbrances of school climate, some research reflects increasing empirical focus on **academic press.** Academic press is a term used to encapsulate specific research-supported components of school climate including high expectations for all students, emphasis of academic achievement, clearly articulated school goals, and safety.

Even in the context of challenges, however, studies find effects of schools on achievement (Haynes, Emmons, & Ben-Avie, 1997) and social-emotional functioning (Kuperminc, Leadbeater, & Blatt, 2001). Positive school climate has been linked to children's feelings of school connectedness (*i.e.,* the extent to which students feel accepted, respected, and supported by the school environment), a factor that has gained prominence within the mental health promotion literature (Bhana, 2000). More than three decades ago, Rutter and colleagues (1979) found that schools that promoted academic and social competence and fostered high self-esteem had positive effects on student's emotional and behavioral functioning. More recently, in their book, *Trust in Schools,* based on research in Chicago schools, Bryk and

Schneider (2002) documented that trusting relationships accompanied by academic press support and promote student success. On a smaller scale, a study of low-income third graders in six schools found that children's ability to adapt to their surroundings was related to both previous and current experiences of school support (Elias & Haynes, 2008). Taken together, these suggest that schools that promote individual self-esteem, efficacy, and competence, *as well as* an overall environment in which students perceive and experience supportive relationships and academic expectations, foster mental health and school success.

School-level: School practices. The same challenges to studying school-level predictors of resilience are present in the examination of school-level interventions to promote positive mental health. One intervention that has been implemented widely and targets the combination of support and press described above is School-wide Positive Behavioral Intervention and Supports (PBIS; Lewis & Sugai, 1999). A school-wide proactive approach to behavior management, PBIS offers a three-tiered public health approach to discipline that involves: (a) Clearly defined expectations for student behavior, (b) Active teaching of rules within various school settings, (c) Public and positive acknowledgment of appropriate behavior, (d) A system of corrective responses to address problem behavior, and (e) team-based formative evaluation to improve implementation and impact (Horner *et al.,* 2005).

Rather than a specific and prescribed school program, PBIS offers a set of guiding principles founded in behavioral analysis and organizational behavior management (Sulzer-Azaroff & Mayer, 1994), as well as emphasizes a match between the intensity of service and the intensity of the presenting problem that is based in a person-centered philosophy (Burke, Burke, Martin, Boon, & Kirkendoll, 2005).

Although the methodological rigor of the evaluation studies varies, research generally reveals that when implemented with fidelity, PBIS reduces student disciplinary referrals and suspensions (Lohrman-O'Rourke *et al.,* 2000; Luiselli, Putnam, & Sunderland, 2002; Taylor-Greene & Kartub, 2000). Lower rates of disciplinary referrals appear to be related to changes in disruptive behaviors in school settings such as the playground and hallway (Cushing, in press). Recent research points toward increases in school organizational health in PBIS schools, including such areas as staff relationships and academic press (Bradshaw, Koth, Thornton, & Leaf, 2009), as well as improved student achievement (Horner *et al.,* 2009). Elementary schools in middle-income communities have implemented PBIS to high standards (*e.g.,* Kartub, 2000; Lewis *et al.,* 1998), but findings on implementation quality in higher poverty school districts remain forthcoming. Thus, although PBIS is a promising approach to increasing academic press and supportive relationships in schools, it is not clear how well it is implemented in the highest poverty schools where children face the greatest risk for mental health problems.

BRIDGING FAMILY, CLASSROOM, AND SCHOOL IN RESEARCH AND PRACTICE

Mesosystemic and Multi-Level Research: A final important area of focus for both resilience research and school intervention practice is the *interactive* and *integrative* targeting of multiple levels within the ecological system. As discussed earlier, ecological theory posits that the mesosystem—interactions between the microsystems in which a child is involved—matter for children's development (Bronfenbrenner, 1979). One of the most important mesosystemic processes for elementary age children growing up in poverty is the home-school connection. An abundance of research demonstrates that external support for children and families who are facing environmental stress is critical (Condly, 2006; Garmezy, 1991; Werner, 1989). This suggests a need for schools to facilitate "supportive networks," not only between teachers and students, but also between teachers and parents. Home-school congruence in behavioral and academic expectations, and opportunities for meaningful and productive parent involvement in schooling, may be particularly critical for children in poverty (Jeynes, 2005). For example, research has shown that maternal involvement in the child's school partially mediates the effect of poverty on social adjustment (Bolger, 1995). This effect is theorized to relate to parents' increased expectations, interest in, and support for their child's social and academic performance, as well as the creation of a consistent socialization process across home and school.

Beyond family-school connections, intervention theories suggest that programs targeting protective factors across *multiple systems* (*e.g.,* individual, home, classroom, and school) may have the greatest chance to promote resilient outcomes in youth (see Nation *et al.,* 2003). Resilience as a dynamic process is based on the notion of increased opportunities to both minimize the existence and/or effect of risk factors as well as increase and enhance protective factors within the individual and across multiple ecological levels. Longitudinal research on risk and resilience processes has documented the additive nature of protection: the more protective factors within the child and across the settings in which a child lives, the more likely that child will adapt well in the face of adversity. Research findings indicate that the potential for resilience and positive outcomes increases with the increase and/or enhancement of multiple protective factors (Fergusson & Lynskey, 1996).

Multi-Context Practices: At the most basic level, school practices to increase linkages between parents and teachers can be relatively simple and effective. The School-Home Note (Kelley, 1990), Daily Report Card (Owens *et al.,* 2005), and Good News Notes (Blechman, Taylor, & Schrader, 1981) are strategies that improve teacher-parent communication about student learning and behavior. Although generally in written format, these messages can be started orally and continued in simple and brief written charts. As one component of broader school interventions, these strategies have been shown to improve productive communication, positive teacher-parent relationships, and student achievement (*e.g.,* Kelley, 1990; Hoover-Dempsey, Walker, Jones, & Reed, 2002). Other methods that remain understudied, but target positive and productive communication between families and the school, include ongoing and varied communication (telephone, newsletter), regular school events with parent and child involvement (*e.g.,* math/literacy nights), and parent advocates who advocate for and help to empower parents (*e.g.,* Epstein; Hoover-Dempsey). These mesosystemic strategies are often embedded within comprehensive school programs, two of which are discussed below.

The Incredible Years (IY) Series: is a well-established, community-based program that uses teacher, parent, and child components to promote positive mental health for all children, as well as provides early intervention support to children with behavioral problems (Webster-Stratton & Reid, 2010). A central tenet of IY is that strong and positive adult-child relationships are the foundation for effective discipline and positive behavior. The parent component of IY targets parent communication skills, anger and stress management, and problem solving, in addition to home-school connections (Hutchings & Lane, 2005). The teacher component involves training on behavior management and parent outreach, as well as interactive lessons for young children to increase positive peer relationships and reduce aggression. Results from an experimental trial of the parental training component for low-income families revealed improvement in parents' skills and children's social competence among families assigned to the IY condition (Gross, Fogg, & Tucker, 1995; Gross, Fogg, Webster-Stratton, & Grady, 1999). Comprehensive studies of the teacher and child components have revealed positive effects on students'school readiness scores (engagement and on-task behavior) and prosocial behaviors, increased quality of teacher-parent relationships, and reductions in student aggressive behavior (Webster-Stratton & Reid, 2008).

The Fast Track Program: is another comprehensive program that combines universal intervention for all students with an indicated intervention for children identified as "high-risk" for disruptive behavior problems and poor peer relations (Conduct Problems Prevention Research Group, 2001). Based on the premise that children's mental health is influenced by multiple interacting factors, Fast Track uses a multi-level approach with child, parent, and school components to: (a) Increase positive interactions among children, within families, across the school, and between home and school; (b) Promote children's social and cognitive abilities through class-wide and small group programs; and (c) Decrease disruptive behavior at home and in school (Conduct Problems Prevention Research Group, 1992).

Results from a longitudinal randomized control study that assigned "high-risk" schools to Fast Track or a control condition found that Fast Track improved children's behavior with peers and adults and decreased classroom aggression and disruption. Similarly, parents were found to have less endorsement of physical punishment, increased warmth in parent-child interactions, and more maternal involvement in school activities (Conduct Problems Prevention Research Group, 2002). Long-term follow-up studies demonstrate that children in Fast Track from kindergarten onward had higher social competence and fewer conduct problems at the end of elementary school (Conduct Problems Prevention Research Group,

2004) and lowered mental health diagnoses for the most at-risk students at the end of 9th grade (Conduct Problems Prevention Research Group, 2007).

CONCLUSIONS

Elementary schools in high poverty communities are a critical context for mental health promotion, with an increasing range of activities being implemented toward the goal of preventing student problems and promoting adaptive functioning. However, these activities often exist in the absence of a clear theoretical or empirical framework to guide decisions about which strategies to use with which students or settings. Developmental-ecological theory and risk-resilience research have been instrumental in identifying factors within and across the individual child and the contexts in which the child lives to help to protect children from negative school trajectories. Schools may be poised to utilize this theoretical and empirical framework to help in the choice and organization of mental health activities that increase the likelihood of promoting positive development for all students. Below are a set of overarching recommendations for choosing, implementing, and evaluating school-based mental health promotion activities within the context of ecologically-driven risk and resilience research.

- First, apply the research findings described above to the choice and implementation of school-based practices that **target protective factors** that promote *social-emotional* and *academic* functioning.

- Second, consider strategies or programs that target protective factors at **more than one level** and/or select practices that may be situated to **work together** to target protective factors across levels (*e.g.,* PBIS + GBG; see discussion of classroom- and school-level practices above).

- Beyond choosing strategies *across levels* (*e.g.,* family and classroom) and strategies that target *specific protective factors*, examine the **quality of the empirical evidence** that the strategies work in similar school contexts.

- Even the best programs do not work if they are implemented incorrectly or inadequately. Thus, become familiar with the

implementation recommendations for a particular program, including the optimal *dosage* of the program (*e.g.,* number of social-emotional learning lessons or home-school notes) and *quality* of the program (*e.g.,* how the SEL lessons are taught or focus/clarity of home-school notes).

- **Internal evaluation procedures** are recommended such that school personnel collect data before and after mental health promotion practices are implemented. This procedure will enable schools to determine how well practices are working and whether adjustments are necessary.

- Finally, and importantly, using an **ecological lens** throughout the process allows consideration of: (a) *barriers to* or *facilitators of* certain programs or practices, and (b) *impact* of particular programs *on various levels* of the ecological system. For example, schools with mental health professionals may be able to activate those staff to support a peer mediation program or to help teachers create "caring communities". Schools that face barriers to family engagement due to student busing may emphasize home-based learning activities rather than school-based family involvement. In addition, by grounding internal evaluation procedures within an ecological framework, schools can detect whether practices that occur at one level have reciprocal influences at other levels. For example, if a teacher-led curriculum targeting student social-emotional skills has the unintended effect of burdening teachers and depressing school climate, adjustments may need to be made to support teachers in their work, or to replace some of the classroom curriculum with peer-, school-, or family-level initiatives.

ACKNOWLEDGEMENT

Declare none.

CONFLICT OF INTEREST

The author(s) confirm that this chapter content has no conflict of interest.

REFERENCES

Aber, J., Bennett, N., Conley, D., & Li, J. (1997). The effects of poverty on child health and development. *Annual Review of Public Health, 18,* 463-483.

Adelman, H. & Taylor, L. (2005). Classroom climate. In S. W. Lee (Ed.), *Encyclopedia of school psychology*. Thousand Oaks, CA: Sage.

Adelman, H. & Taylor, L. (2006). Mental health in schools and public health. *Public Health Reports*, *121,* 294-298.

Adler Lent S. & Figueira-Mcdonough, J. (2002). Gender and poverty: Self-esteem among elementary school children. *Journal of Children and Poverty, 8(1),* 5-22.

Albee, G. (1996). Revolutions and counterrevolutions in prevention. *American Psychologist, 51(11),* 1130-1133.

Alexander, K. & Entwisle, D. (1988). Achievement in the first two years of school: Patterns and processes. *Monographs of the Society for Research in Child Development, 53(2).*

Anthony, J. (1974). The syndrome of the psychologically invulnerable child. In E. J. Anthony & C. Koupernik (Eds.), *The Child in his Family: Children at Psychiatric Risk, International Yearbook* (Volume 3, pp. 201-230). New York: Wiley.

Arnold, D. (1997). Co-occurrence of externalizing behavior problems and emergent academic difficulties in young high-risk boys: A preliminary evaluation of patterns and mechanisms. *Journal of Applied Developmental Psychology, 18,* 317-330.

Bagwell, C. L., Schmidt, M. E., Newcomb, A. F. & Bukowski, W. M. (2001). Friendship and peer rejection as predictors of adult adjustment. In D. W. Nangle & C. A. Erdley (Eds.), *The role of friendship in psychological adjustment. New directions for child and adolescent development*(pp. 25-49). San Francisco, CA, US: Jossey-Bass.

Baker, J. (1999). Teacher-student interaction in urban at-risk classrooms: Differential behavior, relationship quality, and student satisfaction with school. *The Elementary School Journal, 100(1),* 57-70.

Baker, J. A., Grant, S., & Morlock, L. (2008). The teacher-student relationship as a developmental context for children with internalizing or externalizing behavior problems. *School Psychology Quarterly*, *23(1),* 3–15.

Bandura, A. (1977). Self-efficacy: Toward a unifying theory of behavior change. *Psychological Review, 84,* 191–215.

Barkley R, Fischer M., Edelbrock C., & Smallish L. (1990). The adolescent outcome of hyperactive children diagnosed by research criteria: An 8-year prospective follow-up study. *Journal of the American Academy of Child and Adolescent Psychiatry, 29(4),* 546-57.

Barrish, H., Saunders, M., & Wolf, M. (1969). Good Behavior Game: Effects of individual contingencies for group consequences on disruptive behavior in a classroom. *Journal of Applied Behavior Analysis, 2,* 119-124.

Barth, J., Dunlap, S., Dane, H., Lochman, J., & Wells, K. (2004). Classroom environment influences on aggression, peer relations, and academic focus. *Journal of School Psychology, 42,* 115–133.

Battistich V., Solomon D., Kim D., Watson M., & Schaps, E. (1995). Schools as communities, poverty levels of student populations, and student attitudes, motives, and performance: A multilevel analysis. *American Educational Research Journal, 32(3),* 627-58.

Battle, E. & Rotter, J. (1963). Children's feelings of personal control as related to social class and ethnic group. *Journal of Personality, 31,* 482-90.

Berger, K. (2009). *The developing person through childhood and adolescence*. NY: Worth Publishers.

Bernat, D. & Resnick, M. (2006). Healthy youth development: Science and strategies. *Journal of Public Health Management and Practice*, *12*(6), S10-S16.

Berndt, T. J. (1996). Exploring the effects of friendship quality on social development. In W. M. Bukowski, A. F. Newcomb& W. W. Hart-up (Eds.). *The company they keep: Friendship in childhood and adolescence* (pp. 346–365). Cambridge, England: Cambridge University Press.

Bierman, K. (2002). Evaluation of the first 3 years of the Fast Track prevention trial with children at high risk for adolescent conduct problems. *Journal of Abnormal Child Psychology, 30(1),* 19-35.

Blechman, E. A., Taylor, C. J., & Schrader, S. M. (1981). Family problem solving *versus* home notes as early intervention with high-risk children. *Journal of Consulting and Clinical Psychology, 49,* 919-926.

Bolger, K., Patterson, C., Thompson, W., & Kupersmidt, J. (1995). Psychosocial adjustment among children experiencing persistent and intermittent family economic hardship. *Child Development, 66,* 1107-1129.

Bond, L., Glover, S., Godfrey, C., Butler, H. & Patton, G. (2001). Building capacity in schools: Lessons from the Gatehouse project. *Special issue on policy and system level approaches to health promotion in Australia. Health Education and Behavior*, *28 (3),* 368-383.

Bradley, R. & Corwyn, R. (2002). Socioeconomic status and child development. *Annual Review of Psychology*, *53,* 371-399.

Bradshaw, C., Koth, C., Thornton, L., & Leaf, P. (2009). Altering school climate through school-wide positive behavioral interventions and supports: Findings from a group-randomized effectiveness trial. *Prevention Science, 10,* 100-115.

Bronfenbrenner, U. (1986). Ecology of the family as a context for human development: Research perspectives. *Developmental Psychology, 22(6),* 723-742.

Bronfenbrenner, U. (1979). *The ecology of human development.* Cambridge, MA: Harvard University Press.

Bronfenbrenner, U. & Morris, P. (1998). The ecology of developmental processes. In W. Damon & R. Lerner (Eds.). *Handbook of Child Psychology* (5th ed., Vol. 1, pp. 992-1028). New York: Wiley.

Bronfenbrenner, U. & Morris, P. (2006). The bioecological model of human development. In W. Damon & R. M. Lerner (Eds.). *Handbook of child psychology* (pp. 793-828). New York: John Wiley & Sons.

Brooks-Gunn, J. & Duncan, G. (1997). The effects of poverty on children. *The Future of Children: Children and Poverty*, *7,* 55-71.

Brooks-Gunn, J., Duncan, G. J., Klebanov, P., & Sealand, N. (1993). Do neighborhoods influence child and adolescent development? *American Journal of Sociology*, *99,* 353-395.

Brooks-Gunn, J., Klebanov, P., & Liaw, F. (1995). The learning, physical, and emotional environment of the home in the context of poverty: The infant health and development program. *Children and Youth Services Review*, *17,* 251-276.

Brooks-Gunn, J., Klebanov, P., Liaw, F., & Spiker, D. (1993). Enhancing the development of low-birth-weight premature infants: Changes in cognition and behavior over the first three years. *Child Development*, 64, 736-753.

Brown, J., Jones, S., LaRusso, M., & Aber, J. (2010). Improving classroom quality: Teacher influences and experimental impacts of the 4Rs program. *Psychology Faculty Publications.* Paper 90. http: //fordham. bepress. com/psych_facultypubs/90.

Buckner, J. & Bassuk, E. (1997). Mental disorders and service utilization among youths from homeless and low-income housed families. *Journal of the AmericanAcademy of Child and Adolescent Psychiatry, 36,* 890-899.

Burrell, N., Zirbel, C., & Allen, M. (2003). Evaluating peer mediation outcomes in educational settings: A meta-analytic review. *Conflict Resolution Quarterly, 21(1),* 7-26.

Byrd, R. & Weitzman, M. (1994). Predictors of early grade retention among children in the United States. *Pediatrics, 93(3),* 481-487.

Bryk, A. & Schneider, B. (2002), *Trust in Schools: A Core Resource for Improvement.* New York, NY: Russell Sage Foundation.

Cappella, E., Frazier, S., Atkins, M., Schoenwald, S., & Glisson, C. (2008). Enhancing schools' capacity to support children in poverty: An ecological model of school-based mental health services. *Administration and Policy in Mental Health and Mental Health Services Research, 35,* 395–409.

Cardenas, J., Harris, R., del Refugio Robledo, M., & Supik, J. (1991). *Valued youth program dropout prevention strategies for at-risk students.* Paper presented at the annual meeting of the American Education Research Association, Chicago, IL.

Chavkin, N., & Williams, D. (1988). Critical issues in teacher training for parent involvement. *Educational Horizons, 66,* 87-89.

Cicchetti, D. & Garmezy, N. (1993). Prospects and promises in the study of resilience. *Development and Psychopathology, 5(4),* 497-502.

Cohen, P., Kulik, J., & C. L. Kulik, C. (1982). Educational outcomes of tutoring: A meta-analysis of findings. *American Educational Research Journal, 19 (2),* 237–248.

Cole, P., Michel, M., & Teti, L. (1994). The development of emotion regulation and dysregulation: A clinical perspective. *Monographs of the Society for Research in Child Development, 59,* 73-100.

Condly, S. J. (2006) . Resilience in children: A review of literature with implications for education. *Urban Education, 41(3)* , 211.

Conduct Problems Prevention Research Group. (1999) . Initial impact of the Fast Track prevention trial for conduct problems: II. Classroom effects. *Journal of Consulting and Clinical Psychology, 67,* 648-657.

Conduct Problems Prevention Research Group. (2002) . Evaluation of the first 3 years of the Fast Track prevention trial with children at high risk for adolescent conduct problems. *Journal of Abnormal Child Psychology, 30,* 19–35.

Conduct Problems Prevention Research Group. (2010) . The Effects of a Multiyear Universal Social–Emotional Learning Program: The Role of Student and School Characteristics. *Journal of Consulting and Clinical Psychology, 78(2)* .

Conrad, M. & Hammen, C. (1993) . Protective and resource factors in high- and low-risk children: A comparison with unipolar, bipolar, medically ill, and normal mothers. *Development and Psychopathology, 5,* 593-608.

Creemers, B. P. M. & Reezigt, G. J. (1999) . The role of school and classroom climate in elementary school learning environments, In: Freiberg, H. J. (Eds) , *School climate: Measuring, improving and sustaining healthy learning environments* (pp. 30-48) . Hampshire: Falmer.

Cushing, L. S. (in press) . Validation and congruent validity of a direct observation tool to assess student social climate at school. *Journal of Positive Interventions*.

Delquadri, J., Greenwood, C., Whorton, D., Carta, J., & Hall, R. (1986) . Classwide peer tutoring. *Exceptional Children, 52,* 532-542.

Dolan, L., Kellam, S., Brown, C., Werthamer-Larsson, L., *et al.,* (1993) . The short-term impact of two classroom-based preventive interventions on aggressive and shy behaviors and poor achievement. *Journal of Applied Developmental Psychology. 14(3)* , 317-345.

Donnellan, M., Conger, K., McAdams, K., & Neppl, T. (2009) . Personal Characteristics and Resilience to Economic Hardship and Its Consequences: Conceptual Issues and Empirical Illustrations. *Journal of Personality, 77(6)* , 1645-1676.

Dornfeld, M. & Kruttschnitt, C. (1992) . Do the stereotypes fit? Mapping gender-specific outcomes and risk factors. *Criminology, 30,* 397-419.

Duncan, G. J., Brooks-Gunn, J., & Klebanov, P. K. (1994) . Economic deprivation and early childhood development. *Child Development, 65,* 296-318.

Duncan, G., Dowsett, C., Claessens, A., Magnuson, K., Huston, A., Klebanov, P., Pagani, L., Feinstein, L., Engel, M., Brooks-Gunn, J., Sexton, H., Duckworth, K., & Japel, C. (2007) . School readiness and later achievement. *Developmental Psychology, 43,* 1428–1446.

Eamon, M. & Zuehl, R. (2001) . Maternal depression and physical punishment as mediators of the effect of poverty on socioemotional problems of children in single-mother families. *American Journal of Orthopsychiatry, 71,* 218-226.

Eccles, J., Lord, S., & Roeser, R. (1996) . Round holes, square pegs, rocky roads, and sore feet: The impact of stage/environment fit on young adolescents' experiences in schools and families. In S. L. Toth D. Cicchetti (Eds) , Adolescence: Opportunities and Challenges, (Vol. 7, pp. 49-93) . New York: University of Rochester Press.

Elias, M., & Haynes, N. (2008) . Social competence, social support, and academic achievement in minority, low-income, urban elementary school children. *School Psychology Quarterly, 23(4)* , 474-495.

Embry, D. (2002) . The Good Behavior Game: A best practice candidate as a universal behavioral vaccine. *Clinical Child & Family Psychology Review, 5(4)* , 273-297.

Entwisle, D. & Hayduck, L. (1988) . Lasting effects of elementary school. *Sociology of Education, 42,* 387–409.

Esposito, C. (1999) . Learning in urban blight: school climate and its effect on the school performance of urban, minority, low-income children. *School Psychology Review, 28(3)* , 365–377.

Epstein, J. & Van Voorhis, F. (2001) . More than minutes: Teachers' roles in designing homework. *Educational Psychologist, 36(3)* , 181-194.

Evans, G. W. (2006) . Child development and the physical environment. *Annual Review of Psychology, 57,* 423-451.

Evans, G. & Kantrowitz, E. (2002) . Socioeconomic status and health: The potential role of environmental risk exposure. *Annual Review of Public Health, 23,* 303-31.

Fergusson, D. & Lynskey, M. (1996) . Adolescent resiliency to family adversity. *Journal of Child Psychology & Psychiatry & Allied Disciplines, 37,* 281-292.

Fischer, M., Barkley R., Edelbrock C., & Smallish, L. (1990) . The adolescent outcome of hyperactive children diagnosed by research criteria: II. Academic, attentional, and neuropsychological status. *Journal of Consulting and Clinical Psychology, 58(5)* , 580-8.

Flaherty, L., & Osher, D. (2003) . History of school-based mental health service in the United States. In M. Weist, S. Evans, & N. Lever (Eds) , *Handbook of school mental health advancing practice and research* (pp. 11-22) . New York, New York: Springer Science.

Fraser, M., Richman, J., & Galinksy, M. (1999) . Risk, Protection, and Resilience: Toward a Conceptual Framework for Social Work Practice. *Social Work Research*, *23,* 131-144.

Fraser, M. (1997) Risk and resilience in childhood: An ecological perspective. Washington, DC: NASW Press.

Frick, P. J., Christian, R. E., & Wootton, J. M. (1999) . Age trends in the association between parenting practices and conduct problems. *Behavior Modification, 23,* 106-128.

Fuchs, L. S., Fuchs, D., Phillips, N. B., Hamlett, C. L., & Karns, K. (1995) . Acquisition and transfer effects of class wide peer-assisted learning strategies in mathematics for students with varying learning histories. *School Psychology Review, 24,* 604-620.

Garmezy, N. (1974) . The study of competence in children at risk for severe psychopathology. In E. J. Anthony & C. Koupernik (Eds) , *The child in his family: Children at psychiatric risk*, (Vol. 3, pp. 77-97) . New York: Wiley.

Garmezy, N. (1985) . Stress-resistant children: The search for protective factors. In J. E. Stevenson (Ed) , Recent research in developmental psychopathology (pp. 213-233) . New York: Pergamon Press.

Garmezy, N. (1991) . Resilience in children's adaptation to negative life events and stressed environments. *Pediatric Annals, 20, 9,* 459-466.

Goodenow, C. (1992) . Strengthening the links between educational psychology and the study of social contexts. *Educational Psychologist*, *27,* 177–196.

Gordon, K. A. (1996) . Resilient Hispanic youths' self-concept and motivational patterns. *Hispanic Journal of Behavioral Sciences, 18, 1,* 63-73.

Graham, B. C. & Pulvino, C. (2000) . Multicultural conflict resolution: Development, implementation, and assessment of a program for third graders. *Professional School Counseling*, *3,* 172-181.

Graziano, P., Reavis, R., Keane, S., & Calkins, S. (2007) . The role of emotion regulation in children's early academic success. *Journal of School Psychology*, *45(1)* , 3-19.

Greenberg, M. T., Domitrovich, C. E., & Bumbarger, B. (2001) . The prevention of mental disorders in school-aged children: Current state of the field. *Prevention & Treatment*, *4(1)* , 1-62.

Greenberg, M. & Kusche, C. (2006) . Building social and emotional competence: The PATHS curriculum. In S. R. Jimerson & M. Furlong (Eds) , *Handbook of school violence and school safety: From research to practice*, (pp. 395-413) . Mahwah, NJ, US: Lawrence Erlbaum Associates Publishers.

Greenwood, C., Carta, J., & Hall, R. (1988) . The use of peer tutoring strategies in classroom management and education instruction. *School Psychology Review, 17,* 258-275.

Gregory, A. & Cappella, E. (2008) . Working with socio-emotional challenges: School violence. In H. L. K. Coleman & C. J. Yeh (Eds) , *Handbook of school counseling* (pp. 693-715) . Mahwah, NJ: Lawrence Erlbaum.

Gross, D., Fogg, L., & Tucker, S. (1995) . The efficacy of parent training for promoting positive parent-toddler relationships. *Research in Nursing and Health, 18,* 489-499.

Gross, D., Fogg, L., Webster-Stratton, C., & Grady, J. (1999,) . Parent training with low-income multi-ethnic parents of toddlers. Paper presented at the Society for Research in Child Development, Albuquerque, New Mexico.

Gumora, G. & Arsenio, W. (2002) . Emotionality, emotion regulation, and school performance in middle school children. *Journal of School Psychology, 40,* 395-413.

Hagan-Burke, S., Burke, M., Martin, E., Boon, R., Fore, C., & Kirkendoll, D. (2005) . The internal consistency of the Effective Behavioral Support Survey. *Education and Treatment of Children, 28,* 400-413.

Halpern, R. (2000) . The promise of after school programs for low-income children. *Early Childhood Research Quarterly, 15(2)* , 185–214.

Hamre, B. K., & Pianta, R. C. (2001) . Early teacher-child relationships and the trajectory of children's school outcomes through eighth-grade. *Child Development, 72(2)* , 625-638.

Hanson, T., McLanahan, S., & Thomson, E. (1997) . Economic resources, parental practices, and children's well-being, In G. J. Duncan & J. Brooks-Gunn (Eds) , *Consequences of growing up poor* (pp. 190-287) . New York: Russell Sage Foundation.

Hartman, J. L., Turner, M. G., Exum, M. L., Daigle, L. E., & Cullen, F. T. (2008) . *Exploring the gender differences in protective factors: Implications for understanding resilience.* Cincinnati, OH: Academy of Criminal Justice Sciences.

Hartup, W. (1996) . The company they keep: Friendships and their developmental significance. *Child Development, 67(1)* , 1 - 13.

Haynes, N., Emmons, C., & Ben-Avie, M. (1997) . School climate as a factor in student adjustment and achievement. *The Journal of Educational and Psychological Consultation, 8,* 321-329.

Hodges, E., Boivin, M., Vitaro, F., & Bukowski, W. (1999) . The power of friendship: Protection against an escalating cycle of peer victimization. *Developmental Psychology, 35,* 94–101.

Hoover-Dempsey, K., Battiato, A., Walker, J., Reed, R., Dejong, J., & Jones, K. (2001) . Parental involvement in homework. *Educational Psychologist, 36,* 195-210.

Hoover-Dempsey, K., Walker, J., Jones, K., & Reed, R. (2002) . Teachers Involving Parents (TIP) : An in-service teacher education program for enhancing parental involvement. *Teaching and Teacher Education, 18(7)* , 843-867.

Horner, R., Sugai, G., Smolkowski, K., Eber, L., Nakasato, J. & Todd, A. (2009) . A randomized, wait-list controlled effectiveness trial assessing school-wide positive behavior support in elementary schools. *Journal of Positive Behavior Interventions, 11,* 133-144.

Horner, R., Sugai, G., Todd, A., & Lewis-Palmer, T. (2005) . School-wide positive behavior support. In L. Bambara & L. Kern (Eds) , *Individualized supports for students with problem behaviors: Designing positive behavior support plans* (pp. 359-390) . New York: Guilford Press.

Hutchings, J. & Lane, E. (2005) . Parenting and the development and prevention of child mental health problems. *Current Opinion in Psychiatry, 18,* 386-391.

Hymel S. & Ford, L. (2003) . School completion and academic success: The impact of early social-emotional competence. In R. E. Tremblay, R. G. Barr, & R. D. Peters (Eds) , *Encyclopedia on early childhood development* (pp. 1-7) . Montreal, Quebec, Canada: Centre of Excellence for Early Childhood Development.

Ialongo, N., Poduska, J., Werthamer, L., & Kellam, S. (2001) . The distal impact of two first grade preventive interventions on conduct problems and disorder in early adolescence. *Journal of Emotional and Behavioral Disorders, 9(3)* , 146–60.

Izard C., Fine, S., Schultz, D., Mostow, A., Ackerman, B., & Youngstrom, E. (2001) . Emotion knowledge as a predictor of social behavior and academic competence in children at risk. *Psychological Science, 12,* 18–23.

Institute of Medicine. (1994) . *Reducing risks for mental disorders: Frontiers for preventive intervention research*. Washington, DC: National Academy Press.

Jencks C. (1991) . Is the American underclass growing? In P. E. Peterson (Ed) , *The Urban Underclass*, (28-100) . Washington. DC: Brookings Inst.

Jenkins, J. M. and Smith, M. A. (1990) . Factors protecting children living in disharmonious homes. *Journal of the American Academy of Child and Adolescent Psychiatry*, *29,* 60-69.

Jeynes, W. (2005) . The effects of parental involvement on the academic achievement of African American youth. *Journal of Negro Education, 74(3)* , 260-274.

Johnson, D. & Johnson, R. (2001) . Peer mediation in an inner-city elementary school. *Urban Education*, *36,* 165-178.

Jones, S., Brown, J., & Aber J. (2008) . Classroom Settings as Targets of Intervention and Research. In M. Shinn & H. Yoshikawa (Eds.) *Toward Positive Youth Development: Transforming Schools and Community Programs* (pp. 58-77) . UK: Oxford University Press, Inc.

Jones, T. & Brinkman, H. (1994) . Teach your children well: Recommendations for peer mediation programs. In J. Folger & T. Jones (Eds) , *New directions in mediation: Communication research and perspectives* (pp. 159-174) . Beverly Hills, CA: Sage.

Juby, C. & Rycraft, J. R. (2004) . Family preservation strategies for families in poverty. *Families in Society*, *85(4)* , 581-587.

Kam, C., Greenberg, M., & Kusche, C. (2004) . Sustained effects of the PATHS curriculum on the social and psychological adjustment of children in social and psychological adjustment of children in special education. *Journal of Emotional & Behavioral Disorders, 12(2)* , 66-78.

Kartub, D., Taylor-Greene, S., March, R., & Horner, R. (2000) . Reducing hallway noise: A systems approach. *Journal of Positive Behavior Intervention, 2,* 179-182.

Kellam, S., Rebok, G., Ialongo, N., & Mayer, L. (1994) . The course and malleability of aggressive behavior from early first grade into middle school: Results of a developmental epidemiologically based preventive trial. *Journal of Child Psychology and Psychiatry*, *35,* 259–81.

Kelley, M. L. (1990) . *School-home notes: Promoting children's classroom success.* NY: Guilford.

Keyes, C. L. M. (2004) . Risk and resilience in human development: An introduction. *Research in Human Development, 1(4)* , 223-227.

Knight, C. (2007) . A resilience framework: perspectives for educators. *Health Education*, *107(6)* , 543-555.

Kuperminc, G., Leadbeater, B., & Blatt, S. (2001) . School social climate and individual differences in vulnerability to psychopathology among middle school students. *Journal of School Psychology*, *39(2)* , 141-159.

Kumpfer, K. & Hopkins, R. (1993) . Recent advances in addictive disorders. Prevention: Current research and trends. *Psychiatric Clinician of North America*, *16(1)* , 11-20.

La Paro, K., Pianta, R., & Stuhlman, M. (2004) . The Classroom Assessment Scoring System: Findings from the pre-kindergarten year. *The Elementary School Journal, 104(5)* , 409-426.

Lassen, S., Steele, M., & Sailor, W. (2006) . The relationship of school-wide positive behavior support to academic achievement in an urban middle school. *Psychology in the Schools, 43(6)* , 701-712.

Lee, K. (2005) . Effects of experimental center-based child care on developmental outcomes of young children living in poverty. *Social Service Review, 79(1)* , 158-180.

Leve, L., Kim, H., & Pears, K. (2005) . Childhood temperament and family environment as predictors of internalizing and externalizing trajectories from ages 5 to 17. *Journal of Abnormal Child Psychology, 33,* 505-520.

Lewis, T. & Sugai, G. (1999) . Effective behavior support: A systems approach to proactive school-wide management. *Focus on Exceptional Children, 31(6)* , 1-24.

Lohrman-O'Rourke, S., Knoster, T., Sabatine, K., Smith, D., Horvath, B., & Llewellyn, G. (2000) . School-wide application of PBS in the Bangor Area school district. Journal of *Positive Behavior Interventions, 2(4)* , 238-240.

Llewellyn, G. (2000) . School-wide application of PBS in the Bangor area school district. *Journal of Positive Behavior Interventions, 2(4)* , 238-240.

Lowry-Webster, H., Barrett, P., & Dadds, M. (2001) . A universal prevention trial of anxiety symptomatology during childhood: Results at 1-year follow-up. *Behavior Change, 20,* 25-43.

Luiselli, J., Putnam, R., & Sunderland, M. (2002) . Longitudinal evaluation of behavior support intervention in a public middle school. *Journal of Positive Behavioral Interventions, 4(3)* , 182-188.

Luthar, S. (1995) . Social competence in the school setting: Prospective cross domain associations among inner-city teens. *Child Development, 66,* 416-429.

Luthar, S. (2006) . Resilience in development: A synthesis of research across five decades. In D. Cicchetti (Ed) , *Developmental psychopathology: Risk, disorder and adaptation* (2nd Ed., Vol. 3, pp. 739-795) . Hoboken, NJ: John Wiley and Sons

Luthar S., Cichetti D., & Becker B. (2000) . The construct of resilience: a critical evaluation and guidelines for future work. *Child Development, 71(3)* , 543-62.

Luthar, S., Doernberger, C., & Zigler, E. (1993) . Resilience is not a unidimensional construct: Insights from a prospective study of inner-city adolescents. *Development and Psychopathology, 5(4)* , 703-717.

Luthar, S. & Zigler, E. (1991) . Vulnerability and competence: A review of research on resilience in childhood. *American Journal of Orthopsychiatry, 61,* 6-22.

Magnuson, K. A. & Duncan, G. J. (2002) . Parents in poverty. In M. H. Bornstein (Ed) , *Handbook of parenting: Vol. 4: Social conditions and applied parenting* (2nd ed., pp. 95-121) . Mahwah, NJ: Lawrence Erlbaum Associates Publishers.

Magnusson D. & Stattin H. (2006) . The person in the environment: Towards a general model for scientific inquiry. In W. Damon & R. M. Lerner (Eds) , *Handbook of child psychology(pp.* 793-828) . New York: John Wiley & Sons.

Masi, R, & Cooper, L. (2006) . Children's mental health: Facts for policymakers. National Center for Children in Poverty. Columbia University, Mailman School of Public Health. Retrieved on April 28, 2010 from http: //nccp. org/publications/pub_687. html

Masten, A. (1994) . Resilience in individual development: Successful adaptation despite risk and adversity. In M. Wang & E. Gordon (Eds) , *Risk and resilience in inner city America: Challenges and prospects* (pp. 3-25) . Hillsdale, NJ: Erlbaum.

Masten, A. (2001) . Ordinary magic: Resilience processes in development. *American Psychologist, 56,* 227-238.

Masten, A. (2004) . Regulatory processes, risk, and resilience in adolescent development. *Annals of the New York Academy of Sciences1021,* 310–319.

Masten, A. (2006) . Developmental psychopathology: Pathways to the future. *International Journal of Behavioral Development, 31,* 47-54

Masten, A. & Coatsworth, J. (1998) . The development of competence in favorable and unfavorable environments. *American Psychologist, 53(2)* , 205-220.

Masten, A. & Powell, J. L. (2003) . A resilience framework for research, policy, and practice. In S. S. Luthar (Ed) , *Resilience and vulnerability: Adaptation in the context of childhood adversities* (pp. 1-25) . New York: Cambridge University Press.

Masten A., Roisman G., Long J., Burt K., Obradovic J., Riley J., Boelcke-Stennes K., & Tellegen A. (2005) . Developmental cascades: Linking academic achievement and externalizing and internalizing symptoms over 20 years. *Developmental Psychology, 41,* 733-746.

McCloskey L. & Stuewig, J. (2001) . The quality of peer relationships among children exposed to family violence. *Development and Psychopathology, 13(1)* , 83-96.

McCubbin, H., Fleming, W., Thompson, A., Neitman, P., Elver, K., & Savas, S. (1998) . Resiliency and coping in "at risk" African-American youth and their families. In H. I. McCubbin, E. A. Thompson, A. I. Thompson, & J. A. Futrell (Eds) , *Resiliency in African-American families* (pp. 287-328) . Thousand Oaks, CA: Sage.

McCubbin, H., McCubbin, M., Thompson, A., Han S., & Allen, C. (1997) . Families under stress: What makes them resilient? *Journal of Family and Consumer Sciences, 89,* 2-11.

McKay, M., Atkins, M., Hawkins, T., Brown, C. & Lynn, C. (2003) . Inner-city African American parental involvement in children's schooling: Racial socialization and support from the family. *American Journal of Community Psychology, 32,* 107-114

McLeod, J. & Shanahan, M. (1993) . Poverty, Parenting, and Children's Mental Health. *American Sociological Review, 58,* 351-366.

Menesses, K. & Gresham, F. (2009) . Relative efficacy of reciprocal and nonreciprocal peer tutoring for students at-risk for academic failure. *School Psychology Quarterly, 24(4)* , 266-275.

Miles, S. & Stipek, D. (2006) . Contemporaneous and longitudinal associations between social behavior and literacy achievement in a sample of low-income elementary school children. *Child Development, 77(1)* , 103-117.

Mistry, R., Vandewater, E., Huston, A., & McLoyd, V. (2002) Economic well-being and children's social adjustment: The role of family process in an ethnically diverse low-income sample. *Child Development, 73,* 935–951.

Morrison, F., & Connor, C. M. (2002) . Understanding schooling effects on early literacy *Journal of School Psychology, 40(6)* , 493-500.

Mrazek, P. & Haggerty, R. (Eds) . (1994) . Reducing risks for mental disorders: Frontiers for preventive intervention research. Washington, DC: NationalAcademy Press.

Nation, M., Crusto, C., Wandersman, A., Kumpfer, K., Seybolt, D., Morrissey-Kane, E. & Davino, K. (2003) . What works in prevention: Principles of effective prevention programs. *American Psychologist, 58,* 449-456

New Freedom Commission on Mental Health: Achieving the Promise: Transforming Mental Health Care in America (2003) . Final Report. DHHS pub no SMA-03–3832. RockvilleMd, Department of Health and Human Services, 2003. Retrieved April 26, 2010 at www. mentalhealthcommission. gov/reports/finalreport/fullreport-02. htm

Noam, G. & Hermann, C. (2002) . Where education and mental health meet: Developmental prevention and early intervention in schools. *Developmental Psychopathology, 14(4)* , 861-75.

O'Connor, E. E., Cappella, E., Rodriguez, E. T., & McClowry, S. G. (unpublished manuscript) . Evaluating the effectiveness of INSIGHTS: Parallel and collaborative models.

Oden, S. (1987) . Alternative perspectives in children's peer relationships. In T. D. Yawkey & J. E. Johnson (Eds) , *Integrative Processes and Socialization: Early to Middle Childhood.* (pp. 139-165) . Elmsford, New Jersey: Lawrence Erlbaum, Inc.

Orthner, D., Jones-Sanpei, H., & Williamson, S. (2004) . The resilience and strengths of low-income families. *Family Relations*, *53,* 159–167.

Owens, J., Richerson, L., Beilstein, E., Crane, A., Murphy, C., & Vancouver, J. (2005) . School-based mental health programming for children with inattentive and disruptive behavior problems: First-year treatment outcomes. *Journal of Attention Disorders, 9,* 261-274

Pajares, F. & Schunk, D. (2001) . Self-beliefs and school success: Self-efficacy, self concept, and school achievement. In R. Riding & S. Rayner (Eds.) , *Perception,* (pp. 239-266) . London: Ablex Publishing.

Parker, J., Rubin, K., Erath, S., Wojslawowicz, J., & Buskirk, A. (2006) . Peer relationships and developmental psychopathology. In D. Cicchetti & D. Cohen (Eds) , *Developmental Psychopathology: Risk, Disorder, and Adaptation* (2nd edition) , Vol. 2. (pp. 419-493) . New York: Wiley.

Patrick, H., Ryan, A. M., & Kaplan, A. (2007) . Early adolescents' perceptions of the classroom social environment, motivational beliefs, and engagement. *Journal of Educational Psychology*, *99(1)* , 83-98.

Patterson, C., Kupersmidt, J., & Vaden, N. (1990) . Income level, gender, ethnicity, and household composition as predictors of children's school-based competence. *Child Development*, *61,* 485-494.

Petras, H, Chilcoat, H., Leaf, P., Ialongo, N., & Kellam, S. (2004) . Utility of TOCA-R scores during the elementary school years in identifying later violence among adolescent males. *Journal of the American Academy of Child & Adolescent Psychiatry*, *43(1)* , 88-96.

Pettit, G., Bates, J., & Dodge, K. (1997) . Supportive parenting, ecological context, and children’s adjustment. *Child Development, 68,* 908-923.

Pettit G., Bates J., Dodge K., & Meece, D. (1999) . The impact of after-school peer contact on early adolescent externalizing problems is moderated by parental monitoring, perceived neighborhood safety, and prior adjustment. *Child Development, 70(3)* , 768-78.

Pianta, R., Belsky, J., Houts, R., Morrison, F., & the National Institute of Child Health and Human Development Early Child Care Research Network. (2007) . Opportunities to learn in America’s elementary classrooms. *Science, 315,* 1795-1796.

Pianta, R., La Paro, K., Payne, C., Cox, M., & Bradley, R. (2002) . The relation of kindergarten classroom environment to teacher, family, and school characteristics and child outcomes. *The Elementary School Journal, 102,* 225-238.

Pianta, R. & Stuhlman, M. (2004) . Conceptualizing risk in relational terms: Associations among the quality of child-adult relationships prior to school entry and children’s developmental outcomes in first grade. *Educational and Child Psychology, 21(1)* , 32-45.

Pianta, R. & Walsh, C. (1998) . Applying the construct of resilience in schools: Caution from developmental systems perspective. *School Psychology Review*, *27,* 407-419.

Pollard, J., Hawkins, J., & Arthur, M. (1999) . Risk and protection: Are both necessary to understand diverse behavioral outcomes in adolescence? *Social Work Research*, *23(3)* , 145-158.

Reyes, O., Gillock, K., Kobus, K. & Sanchez, B. (2000) . A longitudinal examination of the transition into senior high school for adolescents from urban, low-income status, and predominantly minority backgrounds. *American Journal of Community Psychology, 28(4)* , 519-544.

Robinson, D., Schofield, J., & Steers-Wentzell, K. (2005) . Peer and cross-age tutoring in math: Outcomes and their design implications. *Educational Psychology Review, 14(4)* , 327-362.

Rohrbeck, C., Ginsburg-Block, M., & Fantuzzo, J. (2003) . Peer-assisted learning interventions with elementary school students: A meta-analytic review. *Journal of Educational Psychology, 95,* 240–257.

Rudasill, K., Gallagher, K., & White, J. (2010) . Temperamental attention and activity, classroom emotional support, and academic achievement in third grade. *Journal of School Psychology*, *48(2)* , 113-134.

Rutter, M. (1979) . Protective factors in children's responses to stress and disadvantage. In M. W. Kent & J. E. Rolf (Eds) , *Primary prevention of psychopathology: Social competence in children* (pp. 49-62) . Hanover, NH: University Press of New England.

Rutter, M. (1990) . Psychosocial resilience and protective mechanisms. In J. Rolf, A. Masten, D. Cicchetti, K. Nuechterlein, & S. Weintraub (Eds) , *Risk and Protective Factors in the Development of Psychopathology*. New York: CambridgeUniversity Press.

Rutter, M., & Maughan, B. (2002) . School effectiveness findings, 1979– 2002. *Journal of School Psychology*, *40,* 451–475.

Sameroff, A. J. and Chandler, M. J. (1975) . Reproductive risk and the continuum of caretaking causality. In F. D. Horowitz (Ed) *Review of child development research* (Vol. 4) (pp. 187-244) . Chicago: University of Chicago Press.

Sampson, R. & J. Laub (1994) . Urban poverty and the family context of delinquency. *Child Development, 65,* 523–40.

Sampson, R., Morenoff, J., & Gannon-Rowley, T. (2002) . Assessing neighborhood effects: Social processes and new directions in research. *Annual Review of Sociology 28,* 443–78.

Sektnan, M., McClelland, M., Acock, A., & Morrison, F. (2010) . Relations between early family risk, children's behavioral regulation, and academic achievement. *Early Childhood Research Quarterly*. DOI: 10. 1016/j. ecresq. 2010. 02. 005.

Schaps E. & Solomon D. (2003) . The Role of the school's environment in preventing student drug use. *Journal of Primary Prevention, 23(3)* , 299–328.

Shields, A., Dickstein, S., Seifer, R., Giusti, L., Magee, K., & Spritz, B. (2001) . Emotional competence and early school adjustment: A study of preschoolers at risk. *Early Education & Development*, *12(1)* , 73-96.

Shields, A. & Ciccheti, D. (2001) . Parental maltreatment and emotion dysregulation as risk factors for bullying and victimization in middle childhood. *Journal of Clinical Child Psychology. 30(3)* , 349-63.

Solomon, D., Battistich, V., & Watson, M. (1997) . Classroom practices associated with students' sense of community. *School Psychology of Education*, *2(1)* , 1-33.

Solomon, D., Battistich, V., Watson, M., Schaps, E., & Lewis, C. (2000) . A six-district study of educational change: Direct and mediated effects of the child development project. *Social Psychology of Education*, *4(1)* , 3-51.

Sroufe, L. A. (1997) . Psychopathology as an outcome of development. *Development and Psychopathology*, *9,* 251-268.

Stormshak, E., Bierman, K., McMahon, R., & Lengua, L. (2000) . CPPRG parenting practices and child disruptive behavior problems in early elementary school. *Journal of Clinical Child Psychology, 29,* 17–29.

Sulzer-Azaroff, B., & Mayer, G. R. (1994) . *Achieving educational excellence: Behavior analysis for achieving classroom and schoolwide behavior change*. San Marcos, CA: Western Image.

Surgeon General of the United States, *Report of the Surgeon General's Conference on Children's Mental Health: A National Action Agenda* (2001) . (Washington, D. C. Department of Health and Human Services, Office of the Surgeon General, 2001) . Retrieved March 29, 2010, from http: //www. surgeongeneral. gov/cmh/cmhreport. pdf.

Taylor-Greene, S. & Kartub, D. (2000) . Durable implementation of school-wide behavior support: The high five program. *Journal of Positive Behavior Interventions, 2,* 233-245.

Thomas, R. (1993) . Cross-age and peer tutoring. *ERIC Clearinghouse on Reading, English, and Communication,* Digest 78.

Thomas, A. & Sawhill, I. (1995) . For love and money? The impact of family structure on family income. *The Future of Children, 15(2) ,* 57-74.

Topping, K. & Ehly, S. (2001) . Peer assisted learning: A framework for consultation. *Journal of Educational and Psychological Consultation, 12,* 113-132.

Trentacosta, C. & Izard, C. (2007) . Kindergarten children's emotion competence as a predictor of their academic competence in first grade. *Emotion, 7,* 77-88.

Vanderbilt, E., & Shaw, D. S. (2008) . Conceptualizing and re-evaluating resilience across levels of risk, time, and domains of competence. *Clinical Child and Family Psychology Review, 11,* 30-58.

U. S. Census Bureau. (1998) . Trap door? Revolving door? Or both? *Current Population Reports Series,* 70-63.

U. S. Department of Health and Human Services: Mental Health. (2001) . *Culture, Race, and Ethnicity, Supplement to Mental Health: A Report of the Surgeon General.* Rockville, Md, Center for Mental Health Services, Substance Abuse and Mental Health Services Administration, NIMH, NIH. Retrieved April 2, 2010, from http: //www. consumerstar. org/pubs/SurgeonGeneralsReport2001. pdf.

U. S. Department of Health, Human Services (U. S. DHHS) . (1999) . *Mental health: A Report of the Surgeon General.* Rockville, Md. Substance Abuse and Mental Health Services Administration, Center for Mental Health Services, National Institutes of Health, National Institute of Mental Health.

Waller, R. J. (Ed) (2006) . *Fostering child and adolescent mental health in the classroom.* Thousand Oaks, CA: Sage.

Webster-Stratton, C., Mihalic, S., Fagan, A., Arnold, D., Taylor, T., & Tingley, C. (2001) . Blueprints for violence prevention, Book Eleven: The Incredible Years: parent, teacher and child training series. Boulder, CO: Center for the Study and Prevention of Violence. Retrieved on May 6, 2010, from http: //www. colorado. edu/cspv/blueprints/model programs/IYS. html.

Webster-Stratton, C., Reid, J., & Stoolmiller M. (2008) . Preventing conduct problems and improving school readiness: Evaluation of the Incredible Years Teacher and child training programs in high-risk schools. *Journal of Child Psychology and Psychiatry, and Allied Disciplines, 49(5) ,* 471-88.

Weinstein, R. (2002) . *Reaching higher: The power of expectations in schooling.* Cambridge, MA: Harvard University Press.

Weist, M., Sander, M., Lowie, J., & Christodulu, K. (2002) . The expanded school mental health framework. *Childhood Education, 78,* 269-273.

Weisz, J. R. , Weiss, B. , & Donenberg, G. R. (1992) . The lab *versus* the clinic: Effects of child and adolescent psychotherapy. *American Psychologist, 47(12) ,* 1578-1585

Welsh, M., Parke, R., Widaman, K., & O'Neil, R. (2001) . Linkages between children's social and academic competence: A longitudinal analysis. *Journal of School Psychology, 39*, 463-482.

Werner, E. (1989) . High risk children in young adulthood: A longitudinal study from birth to 32 years. *American Journal of Orthopsychiatry*, *59,* 72-81.

Werner, E. (1993) . Risk, resilience, and recovery: Perspectives from the Kauai longitudinal study. *Development and Psychopathology*, *5,* 503-515.

Werner, E. (2005) . What can we learn about resilience from large scale longitudinal studies? In S. Goldstein & R. Brooks (Eds) , *Handbook of resilience in children* (pp. 91 -106) . New York: Kluwer Academic Publishers.

Werner, E. & Smith, A. (1993) . *Overcoming the odds: High risk children from birth to adulthood.* Ithaca, NY: Cornell University Press.

World Health Organization [WHO] (2007) . *Mental Health: Strengthening Mental Health Promotion.* Retrieved May 6, 2010, from http: //www. who. int/mediacentre/f actsheets/fs220/en/

CHAPTER 9

Culturally Responsive Education: Promoting the Mental Health of All Students for Stronger, Inclusive Communities

JoEtta Gonzales*

Equity Alliance at Arizona State University, Tempe, AZ 85287-6103, USA

Abstract: Meeting the challenge of educating all students within the U.S. has taken on a new meaning in this age of accountability. There is a plethora of data that points to a crisis that is neither silent nor invisible. One example includes dropout rates which are high for all students, but when we look at data for our culturally and linguistically diverse students in particular, we find that our nation's schools have failed to hold on to more than 50% of all students who are African American, Latino, and/or Native American (Orfield, Losen, Wald, & Swanson, 2004; Swanson, 2004). Improvement efforts at many of these schools have focused on technical pedagogical solutions that have come up short on impacting national trends. A better approach includes systemic, comprehensive, and transformative interventions embraced simultaneously by educators at all levels of the school system. This chapter, focuses on culturally responsive education, emphasizes the need for educators to understand and build upon cultural identity in order to embrace the key features of culturally responsive education. The content will assist readers in applying their new knowledge to begin planning for and creating everyday culturally responsive practices within their own settings.

Keywords: Beliefs, cultural identity, empowered, systemic change, values, education, power, privilege, inclusive, responsive, leadership, equitable opportunities, disposition, equitable access, outcomes.

INTRODUCTION

What is Culturally Responsive Education? Culturally responsive education is broadly considered a promising approach for improving learning opportunities and increasing the academic achievement of culturally and linguistically diverse youth in U.S. schools. This educational approach requires a shift in instructional methods, curricular materials, and teacher dispositions. It also involves a style of leadership that brings together the thoughts and ideas of teachers and staff so that a consensus can emerge about how to make the school a more inclusive place for

***Address correspondence to Joetta Gonzales:** Equity Alliance at Arizona State University, Interdisciplinary B353, PO Box 876103, Tempe, AZ 85287-6103, USA; Tel: 480-965-2486; E-mail: joetta@asu.edu

Raymond J. Waller (Ed)

everyone. Teacher leaders serve as a driving force for the shift toward culturally responsive practice, and serve as a model helping students, staff, and parents to think and act more inclusively. The growing diversity of students in schools paired with the persistent homogeneity of educators across our country creates the impetus for culturally responsive educational practice.

An education that is culturally responsive requires significant changes in the way culturally and linguistically diverse youth are served, taught, and involved in U.S. schools. Several patterns of achievement highlight this imperative. One example involves our nation's lowest performing schools. The lowest-performing schools are located in every state; in urban, suburban, rural, and small-town America. They exist in large schools and small, and are present in all grade spans K-12. Their one unifying characteristic is that they disproportionately serve our nation's culturally and linguistically diverse students. In many schools, discourse around race, culture, language, and difference has been a missing element during professional development and staff meetings. In others, the conversations promote focus on perceived student and family deficits which impede efforts for change and reform.

Gay (2000) wrote that culturally responsive teaching connects students' cultural knowledge, prior experiences, and performance styles to academic knowledge and intellectual tools in ways that legitimize what students already know. By embracing the cultural backgrounds and histories of students through culturally responsive teaching,teachers enhance the opportunities students have to connect to the curriculum, engage meaningfully in school, and recognize academic potential. In so doing, teachers actively negotiate classroom routines and cultures with their students that reflect the communities where students develop, grow, and live. In order for teachers to become culturally responsive, they must recognize and transcend their own cultural biases and preferences to establish and develop patterns for learning and communicating that engage and sustain student participation and achievement.

Culturally responsive education involves creating a supportive environment where the strengths students bring to school are acknowledged, nurtured and used to promote student academic and social achievement. Culturally responsive schools are built on the kind of interactions that occur among educators and students.

These interactions are shaped by teachers' and students' cultural identities and the contexts surrounding the school community.

IDENTITY AND CULTURE IN EDUCATION

Teachers bring their life experiences, histories, and cultures into classrooms and schools. They also bring their assumptions and beliefs about what quality teaching is and what good teachers do. Their knowledge and understanding of theory, research, and human development as they relate to education impacts their practice, as does their love and knowledge of content area and learning. Inevitably, teachers bring their personalities and teaching styles that are shaped by social and cultural interactions and daily experiences in the classroom and throughout the world. The longer teachers teach, the more their beliefs, knowledge, and dispositions are reorganized and sculpted by experience.

The experiences, cultures, and personalities that contribute to the identity of teachers show up in classrooms and schools across the U.S. Many teachers from dominant cultural backgrounds (white, middle class teachers in the United States), are not immediately aware of their own culture because it fits so seamlessly with widespread opinions, beliefs, values, and expectations about behavior, education, and life choices. However, many choices that teachers make are determined more from their cultural background than from individual beliefs. In many instances, the expectations that teachers hold for teaching and learning are grounded in cultural beliefs that are unfamiliar to students and families from non-dominant cultures.

Teachers express their cultural backgrounds and understandings in many ways; the danger lies in being unaware of this expression. Building understanding of the ways in which one's beliefs, experiences, values, and assumptions are linked to culture is an essential feature of culturally responsive practice. Culturally responsive education requires teachers to acknowledge and understand their own cultural values and how they impact their own teaching practice.

Many times, when individuals from different cultures interact, cultural disconnects occur. This is not different in schools. In so many schools across the U.S., the cultural backgrounds of teachers differ significantly from their students due to ethnic, racial, linguistic, social, religious, or economic reasons. Students in these schools are especially vulnerable to cultural disconnect, and as a result, may perform poorly on school-related tasks. For example, consider a situation in which both a teacher and the family of one of her students value education. The teacher's beliefs include ideas about what parent and family involvement in learning should look like. Her beliefs include parent attendance at school events, including parent-teacher conferences, student performances, and other organized family activities. The family, however, supports student learning at home and for various reasons, does not attend school functions. For the family, their role in education includes establishing routines for their children, encouraging homework reading at home, and fostering a sense of work ethic. They do not see the importance in attending school events, and as a result, conflict arises between the teacher and the students' family even though both value education.

Situations such as this occur frequently in schools, and in many cases judgments are made about a lack of concern by parents such as these. However, who is to say one is right and the other is wrong? In many cases like this, the dominant cultural perspective prevails. Teachers, students, and families may disagree on the nature and value of schoolwork, school attendance and punctuality, the level of family engagement, and a host of other things related to the role of home, family, and community, but unless teachers are able to create space to discuss and explore a variety of values, beliefs, and expectations of families, cultural disconnects will continue to be common.

In understanding and valuing their own cultural identities, teachers are able to create the possibility for deeper connections with their students and families. They understand that notions of culture are complex and work to develop a strong understanding of self and others so that different norms are respected, rather than one set of values being imposed on all. Teachers who are culturally responsive build robust learning environments in which students and teachers can build an appreciation for one another.

VALUES AND BELIEFS SHAPE THE CULTURALLY RESPONSIVE TEACHER

Ensuring that every student feels a sense of belonging and membership in the school community are necessary building blocks toward creating a community that considers the development of competence in *all* children significant. These values and beliefs are reinforced by federal laws that require schools to monitor the progress of all students, including many who have been marginal members of a school community; students with disabilities, students who have diverse cultural and ethnic heritages, students whose native languages are not English, students who bring rich experiences to school but may not have been exposed to the learning experiences that are often presumed in the school curriculum. Teachers are required to provide additional services and supports to students who may need them while ensuring that these students continue to learn with their peers in general education environments. The teacher's attitudes about student learning today, more than ever, shape the school environment.

In order to address the diverse needs of students, it is critical for teachers to explore their own personal histories and experiences, as well as the history and current experiences of their students and families. With self-knowledge comes a better understanding of others, and a healthier appreciation of differences. When teachers are equitable in their teaching and knowledgeable about themselves and their students, they can be more responsive to the needs of all their students.

SPECIFIC ACTIVITIES FOR BECOMING A REFLECTIVE TEACHER LEADER FOR CULTURALLY RESPONSIVE SCHOOLS

The following endeavor shave been proposed for assisting educational professionals in their efforts to enhance culturally responsive thinking in the school setting (Gay, 2002; Villegas & Lucas, 2002).

1. ***Engage in Reflective Thinking and Writing:***Teachers must reflect on their actions and interactions as they try to discern the personal motivations that govern their behaviors. Understanding the factors that contribute to certain behaviors (*e.g.,* racism, ethnocentrism) is the first step toward changing these behaviors. This process may be facilitated by autobiographical and reflective writing, usually in a journal.

2. ***Explore Personal and Family Histories:***Teachers need to explore their early experiences and familial events that have contributed to their understanding of themselves as racial or nonracial beings. As

part of this process, teachers can conduct informal interviews of family members (*e.g.,* parents, grandparents) about their beliefs and experiences regarding different groups in society. The information shared can enlighten teachers about the roots of their own views. When teachers explore the historical shaping of their values, they can better relate to other individuals.

3. ***Acknowledge Membership in Different Groups:*** Teachers must recognize and acknowledge their affiliation with various groups in society, and the advantages and disadvantages of belonging to each group. For example, for white middle-class female teachers, membership in that group affords certain privileges in society; at the same time being a female presents many challenges in a male-dominated world. Moreover, teachers need to assess how belonging to one group influences how one relates to and views other groups.

4. ***Learn About the History and Experiences of Diverse Groups:*** It is important that teachers learn about the lives and experiences of other groups in order to understand how different historical experiences have shaped attitudes and perspectives of various groups. Further, by learning about other groups, teachers begin to see differences between their own values and those of other groups. To learn about the histories of diverse groups, particularly from their own perspectives, teachers can read literature written by those particular groups as well as personally interact with members of those groups.

5. ***Visit Students' Families and Communities:*** It is important that teachers get to know their students' families and communities by actually going into the students' home environments. This allows teachers to relate to their students as more than just "bodies" in the classroom but also as social and cultural beings connected to a complex social and cultural network. Moreover, by becoming familiar with students' home lives, teachers gain insight into the influences on the students' attitudes and behaviors. Additionally, teachers can use the families and communities as resources (*e.g.,* classroom helpers or speakers) that will contribute to the educational growth of the students.

6. ***Visit or Read About Successful Teachers in Diverse Settings:*** Teachers need to learn about successful approaches to educating children from diverse backgrounds. By actually visiting classrooms of successful teachers of children from diverse backgrounds and/or reading authentic accounts of such success, teachers can gain exemplary models for developing their own skills.

7. ***Develop an Appreciation of Diversity:*** To be effective in a diverse classroom, teachers must have an appreciation of diversity. They must view difference as the "norm" in society and reject notions that any one group is more competent than another. This entails developing respect for differences, and the willingness to teach from this perspective. Moreover, there must be an acknowledgment that the teachers' views of the world are not the only views.

8. ***Participate in Reforming the Institution:*** The educational system has historically fostered the achievement of one segment of the school population by establishing culturally biased standards and values. The monocultural values of schools have promoted biases in curriculum development and instructional practices that have been detrimental to the achievement of students from culturally and linguistically diverse backgrounds. Teachers need to participate in reforming the educational system so that it becomes inclusive. As the direct link between the institution and the students, teachers are in a pivotal position to facilitate change. By continuing a traditional "conform-or-fail" approach to instruction, teachers perpetuate a monocultural institution. By questioning traditional policies and practices, and by becoming culturally responsive in instruction, teachers work toward changing the institution.

CULTURALLY RESPONSIVE LEADERSHIP

Culturally responsive education honors independence and interdependence. Independence is stressed when we encourage teachers and students to use resources and tools to help themselves in a cycle of continuous improvement to learn, grow, and develop new skills in which there is substance and interest. Interdependence, on the other hand, involves learning to live more collaboratively with others, and includes making choices which foster a sense of belonging and community. Culturally responsive education demonstrates respect for student voice, and elicits involvement from all school community members. It embraces a systemic approach to change, unifying teachers, staff, students, families and communities to promote the practice of collaborative and shared leadership. In a culturally responsive school, every child, regardless of his or her intelligence, ability, or ethnicity is offered opportunities for success (Sands, Kozleski & French, 2000).

One characteristic of culturally responsive education is equity. In a culturally responsive school, all students and all staff members are treated with respect and dignity; all voices are honored and all contributions are seen as valuable. Another common characteristic is collaboration. Students in culturally responsive schools are connected to each other, to the immediate neighborhood, to the larger community, and to curriculum and instruction that relates to life experience and student-centered interests. Consider the example of Nina's classroom:

> *Entering Nina's classroom during learning time is a step into poised energy. Excellent lesson design and organized routines are immediately evident, lending a sense of calm predictability. This structure is critical for children in order to eliminate distractions from the true purpose of school – learning, growing, and having fun while doing so!*
>
> *Within this sense of calm is an underlying energy. Children are primed to expect the novel. Nina approaches serious learning with a sense of playfulness and an element of surprise. Students have to pay close attention so they don't miss the exciting next step. During one particular visit to Nina's class, her third grade students were reading scary stories they had written. It was immediately after recess, the hour before school was to let out for vacation, when most students are anxiously anticipating their break. The students gathered quietly into a circle with all the lights out. They took turns passing around a flashlight to read their stories aloud to one another. You could hear a pin drop as students listened attentively and waited their turn.*

Nina had an expectation for every student to produce and share a story that incorporated an element of suspense. She worked with students individually and in small groups to ensure their success. Students supported one another by offering suggestions regarding ideas, content, and word-choice, and they rehearsed with one another using voice and tempo for effect. Mutual respect was evident that day, and is evident every day, as Nina instills a true sense of community within her classroom. Her gentle and joyful approach helps students learn that school is a place for peace and fun.

When teachers join together to improve their practices through becoming culturally responsive, they do so for a variety of reasons. Key to this collaborative spirit is the idea that schools are enhanced when they reflect the diversity of society and when *all* learners become active members of the learning community. When schools create learning communities that reflect democratic and socially just principles, all students will be valued and seen as important members of the school including: students from all racial and ethnic groups, students new to the school and community, students using English as a second or third language, students who identify as gay/lesbian/bisexual/transgendered, and students marginalized for having differences in learning. Increased and improved opportunities for parents, staff, and students to participate and be meaningfully involved within the school environment is a natural outcome of an inclusive learning environment, and comprehensive site governance structures allow individuals to bond with the school while participating in problem solving, decision-making, and goal-setting.

Culturally Responsive Teacher Leaders…

- **Serve as models for other teachers** by demonstrating an enjoyment of teaching all students and by holding the highest expectations of what each student is capable of achieving. An awareness of the individual needs, interests, and capacities of each of their students is a characteristic of the teacher leader, as is challenging students accordingly through inspiration, motivation, correction, and support so that all students achieve their potential.

- **Treat all students honestly, justly and equitably** by acknowledging and welcoming the range of values held by students as well as within families, groups, cultures, and the wider school community.

- **Exemplify the values and beliefs that they seek to inspire in their students**, including authenticity, academic inquisitiveness and rigor, tolerance, justice, self-confidence, respect for self and others, compassion, appreciation of diversity, and celebration of cultural differences.

- **Show commitment to their own professional learning**, looking to extend their awareness, sharpen their judgment, expand their repertoire of instructional techniques, and adapt their teaching to culturally responsive practices.

- **Exercise educational leadership** by working collaboratively with peers to develop policies, curriculum, and professional learning opportunities that help to ensure that the interconnected goals of creating an inclusive learning community are being met.

- **Reflect on practice** and critique the impact of their teaching and professional values upon students, colleagues, and others in the wider learning community. The proficient teacher leader has a keen awareness of the role their own background plays, including educational, social, cultural, religious, and financial experiences. They have a deepened awareness and understanding of how these experiences may have helped to shape their own values, their approach to teaching, and their assumptions about education.

Stephan is a teacher that exemplifies the spirit of culturally responsive leadership. Read about his responsibilities, and consider the ways in which he contributes to his school community:

Stephan Greene has a magical way of involving parents in his classroom and in the school as a whole. As an active leader in the PTSA and school leadership team, he stirs a whirlwind of energy that is contagious. His leadership is valued, helping to make the school both popular and successful.

Stephan's responsibilities within the school include mentoring new teachers at his grade level, providing a model classroom in which other teachers observe, and facilitating lesson design at the team level. Mr. Greene has a reputation of being caring, loyal, and supportive of teachers and students alike. Everyone who knows Stephan knows he will act as their advocate when appropriate. Staff members understand that he works closely with the principal in leading school improvement efforts. They respect his expertise as well as his sense of commitment.

For student assessment and classroom instruction, Stephan works from a depth of content knowledge and professional expertise. Other teachers look to Stephan for suggesting strategies that include authentic classroom experiences for students. He is masterful at structuring the work at hand so students can engage in meaningful content that connects their lives to the academic curriculum. He presents lessons in such a way that all students are challenged to do their best, and assures goals will be accomplished with dignity and pride. Mr. Greene recognizes the importance of his own learning, and in fact, insists he learns as much from his students and other teachers as they learn from him.

Stephan's classroom offers a sanctuary for students struggling with hardship. He works hard to ensure that all students in the school feel a true sense of belonging. If someone in the school were to be aware of an incident that prevented students from concentrating on doing their best socially and academically at school, it would be Stephan. Children throughout the school both respect and love him. Parents always have confidence in the extent that Stephan values their children as individuals. Stephan's vision for community building has started something powerfully strong and good for his school; his school looks and feels much more positive because of his culturally responsive contributions.

Part of the tradition of teaching is that teachers have the role of guiding students through a journey of rich learning experiences leading to an acquisition of knowledge, skills, and dispositions necessary to be contributing adult citizens. When the cultural backgrounds, beliefs, and expectations about what is deemed important enough to teach compete with other compelling realities, teachers lose their esteemed status as knowledge brokers. Becoming culturally responsive means that teachers, as well as students, have to negotiate and agree upon new standards and norms that acknowledge the differences and the similarities among and between individuals and groups (Kozleski, 2009). Students from all backgrounds learn the value in similarities, uniqueness, and differences and gain perspective on inclusive, participatory society. Ultimately, promoting practices that benefit students benefit the community at large.

Teachers are integral in helping students make meaning of the social and academic curriculum, written or unwritten, that is present at the school. When teachers build upon the ideas and experiences that students have knowledge and understanding about, they are able to help learning come alive for students. In *mediating* the curriculum, they help students connect background knowledge to frameworks and models for thinking and organizing information that are commonly embedded within disciplines such as literacy, mathematics, social studies, arts, and the sciences. Culturally responsive teachers recognize that not all students learn in the same way, and embrace practices that offer variety, choice, and student input. They understand that mastering academic knowledge involves understanding complex organizational systems that offer multiple avenues for students to understand and access information. Careful consideration of the ways in which teachers might incorporate diverse perspectives into the curriculum is an essential part of culturally responsive teaching.

The way that instruction is *facilitated* is also an integral part of culturally responsive education. When teachers structure classrooms to foster academic excellence and a sense of community, students become skilled at facilitating their own learning as well as that of their peers. In order to create this type of learning community, teachers need to carefully plan and explicitly teach routines for various learning scenarios in order for students to take leadership for their learning. Likewise, explicit teaching around social interactions is important so students can feel comfortable exploring differences of opinion, and accept that they may need help from their classmates in order to be successful. This style of teaching helps students learn to see participation in collaborative learning groups as opportunities to expand their repertoire of academic and social skills. Thus, they are helped to see new learning from more than one perspective, which fosters a sense of empowerment to identify potential difficulties that come from assumptions of privilege, the distribution of power, and the assessment of performance and competence.

STUDENTS IN CULTURALLY RESPONSIVE CLASSROOMS

Students in culturally responsive classrooms often engage with one another, sharing ideas, creating rules, and making decisions about their learning and their environment. Often, students are empowered to direct their own learning, and the teacher may serve more of a facilitative role. Culturally responsive teachers have the confidence to encourage students to respectfully challenge authority, understanding that negotiation skills are best taught in a safe environment. They are interested in reaching and encouraging all students, and are well equipped to adapt materials and situations to maximize student success. A teacher interested in making their classroom more culturally responsive might ask the following questions:

- Who determines classroom rules? What is my influence on the governance of our class? How are procedures articulated and enforced? Is there a hierarchy of governance within the student population or do all students have an equal voice?

- What does the classroom environment look like? What is the general feeling one gets as they walk into the room? Does the space appear to include ample room for student movement? Does the arrangement of furniture promote collaboration?

- Who makes decisions regarding curriculum? Does the teacher select topics that reflect the cultural backgrounds of all students in the class? Do students participate in decisions regarding instructional delivery, including which materials to use, and whether to work individually, in pairs, or small groups?

- How is equity and mutual respect fostered? How are actions of discrimination and/or prejudice addressed? In what ways are students encouraged to think critically about issues of justice?

Consider the ways in which Marcus' students are empowered to direct their own learning. Notice also the ways in which Marcus and Belinda share the responsibilities of classroom facilitation:

> *Marcus teaches in an urban high school, and has many students in his classes who are learning English. During three of his classes, a special education teacher, Belinda co-teaches with him. Before the start of school, Marcus and Belinda spent a great deal of time discussing the individual needs of all the students in their classes in order to support their learning while maintaining high standards for academic proficiency. One strategy they decided to use is heterogeneous student grouping across learning styles, proficiencies and preferences. They also take race, gender, and primary language into consideration when grouping students. Small groups provide students opportunities to rehearse answers before responding to the entire class. To demonstrate learning, students choose to be assessed through a written test, or verbal response using a student designed graphic organizer. Marcus uses the strategies from his co-taught classes in all of his classes because he believes it helps support all learners.*
>
> *Marcus begins each of his ninth-grade classes by having all the students create a time capsule of what they think are the most important artifacts from the past. Students are allowed to bring in artifacts from home, re-create models of significant items by drawing or building, or use representations found on the internet. In small groups, the students' task is to put down on paper why they chose the items they did. In this way, the students explicitly articulate their underlying assumptions of what constitutes historical significance. Students' responses are pooled, and he*

writes them on a large poster that he hangs on the classroom wall. This poster, which Marcus calls "Rules for Determining Historical Significance," becomes a lightning rod for class discussions throughout the year, undergoing revisions and elaborations as students become better able to articulate their ideas.

In having students participate in the time capsule activity, Marcus immediately learns about student background, understanding, and perspective. In using their ideas in establishing the "Rules for Determining Historical Significance" as the starting point for group discussions, students automatically draw upon their background knowledge and use their new learning to build upon understanding, and in the course of discussion, they are actively practicing their newly acquired academic language. Marcus uses the information students' determined as historically significant to design assessments, and because the students have ownership of this information, and choice in assessment style, they perform exceptionally.

WHAT CULTURALLY RESPONSIVE TEACHER LEADERS DO

Student learning is heavily dependent on teacher quality, therefore it makes sense that teachers would be involved in the efforts to help make their schools more culturally responsive. Teachers at all levels are assuming greater roles of responsibility and leadership. Roland Barth (2001), a strong supporter of teacher leadership in schools, notes that there are at least ten areas, all of them having an impact on a school's inclusive practices, in which teacher leadership is essential to the strength of a school:

1. Choosing textbooks and instructional materials;
2. Shaping curriculum;
3. Setting standards for student behavior;
4. Deciding whether students are tracked into special classes;
5. Designing staff development and in-service programs;

6. Setting promotion and retention policies;
7. Deciding on school budgets;
8. Evaluating teacher performance;
9. Selecting new teachers; and
10. Selecting new administrators.

These areas of teacher leadership correspond with the practitioner and school levels of the systemic change framework, which was designed by the National Institute for Urban School Improvement to assist school leadership teams in establishing goals for culturally responsive change. This framework serves as the starting point for schools and districts working with the Equity Alliance to embrace culturally responsive initiatives.

There are several arenas that frame activity and everyday practice in schools. These arenas provide a way for educators to assess where their school is as well as to identify leadership issues that may exist within any of these arenas.

PRACTITIONER LEVEL ELEMENTS

- **Teaching Design and Practices**: These include not only the lesson planning activities and content delivery processes, but how curricula are selected, whether thematic units are used, how extension and remediation activities are determined, and how teachers interact with students during a lesson. In a culturally responsive classroom, teachers pay close attention to instructional models that engage all students.

- **Group Practice and Professional Learning**: This includes not only the professional learning that is provided by the school and district, but how teachers learn from one another and the accepted norms for sharing lesson planning, observing classes, and coordinating activities. Culturally responsive teachers share effective lesson plans and ideas with one another. They also take a lead in helping to design professional learning priorities and activities.

- **Family Participation and Partnerships**: Contact with families and community groups should go far beyond Open House night and parent-teacher conferences. Schools benefit greatly from ongoing parent input into curriculum decisions, lesson planning, identifying resources, and partnerships with local Boys & Girls Clubs, churches, and businesses. These relationships should be developed both at the school and at the classroom level. Culturally responsive teachers seek creative approaches to involve parents in the classroom and throughout the school.

SCHOOL LEVEL ELEMENTS

- **Governance, Leadership, and Accountability**: The ways that decisions are made in a school have a strong impact on the school's culture, and the interaction between leadership and accountability help to determine the success of a school. In a culturally responsive school, teachers help in decision making by providing diverse perspectives. Educators concerned with equity ensure all decisions made take into consideration what is best for all students.

- **Culture of Change and Improvement**: This component includes not only professional learning, but the school's culture and practices around sharing ideas and learning from one another. This is a vital component of creating culturally responsive schools; change is constant, and schools need to be able to embrace change and use it to improve practice. Teachers can help create a culture of change and improvement by using collaborative approaches to designing instruction, planning professional learning experiences, and incorporating team reflection as a regular part of the work week.

- **School/Community Participation and Partnerships**: These are at the heart of successful culturally responsive schools. Families, churches, and community centers all contribute to students' daily lives and are stakeholders in their education. Effective communication with these stakeholders will provide insights into students' interests, talents, and challenges. Developing ongoing partnerships with families and community groups will strengthen schools' relationships with students and improve students' performance. Schools that fail to connect to their communities often struggle with resistance from families and students who don't feel valued. Teacher leaders go the extra mile to ensure parents and community members are involved. They actively seek opportunities to work with local businesses, have local citizens as guest speakers, and plan events that bring the community together during times when school may not be in session.

- **Structure and Use of Space and Time**: The way that learning spaces are organized sets the tone for the learning. Paint color, desk arrangement, temperature, and noise can all affect students' performance. In addition, the placement of classrooms often indicates the value of the staff and students in those classrooms. Teacher leaders can assist with the planning of school schedules and in creating a warm learning environment in the entire school. They can create learning niches throughout the school, so students can engage with literacy in various places, including the front office, the cafeteria, the playground, and while visiting the school nurse.
- **Inquiry on Equity in Schooling**: Educators, as a general rule, truly care about students and want to treat all children equitably. However, good intentions are not enough; without ongoing dialogue about the effectiveness of teaching practices, we will not be able to effectively serve our students. If students are not making sufficient progress, teacher leaders need to mentor others so they can examine what they are doing, identify the types of activities that students respond well to, and brainstorm new ways of delivering instruction. Culturally responsive educators make sure conversations throughout the school include professional, student-first language.

WHY IS SYSTEMIC CHANGE ESSENTIAL FOR CULTURALLY RESPONSIVE EDUCATION?

Systemic change is change that penetrates all aspects of the school system and offers greater opportunity for sustainability as a result. Often there is a strong desire by culturally responsive educators to transform their school, but they have struggled in their efforts because of a focus on one program-at-a-time approaches. In a challenging educational environment, reforms focusing on only one system component (*e.g.*, assessment, curriculum materials, professional learning, instructional design, or accountability measures) have little likelihood of lasting impact. As isolated initiatives, they are easily overwhelmed by the dysfunction of the larger system.

Similarly, reforms focused at either the school or classroom level seldom achieve notable success because the means are lacking to extend the reform throughout the system. The development of the systemic change framework, therefore, is essential to articulate reform that spans many layers from policy to classroom practice and throughout the many related systems of the district and community. Eckel, Hill and Green (1998, p.3) define this type of systemic change as one that:

1. Alters the culture of the system by changing select underlying assumptions and institutional behaviors, processes, and products;
2. Is deep and pervasive, affecting the whole system;
3. Is intentional; and
4. Occurs over time.

We know the old paradigm for schooling cannot get us to where we need to go in creating culturally responsive educational systems. Fixing the parts of the school systems which were designed for success in the Industrial - Age does not serve today's students well. Instead, new school systems that are completely aligned with the needs and requirements of diverse student populations in this era are the needed. The challenge is to break away from ways of the past - in other words, the ways in which we ourselves were educated - and embrace practices that are unfamiliar and often met with resistance.

CULTURALLY RESPONSIVE EDUCATORS AFFECT SCHOOL CULTURE

Claudia is an outstanding teacher leader - someone who communicates and inspires a strong vision for academic excellence for all students. Her passion lies in the area of cultural literacy. Her leadership skills, creativity, and enthusiasm provide a strong model and sense of direction for staff and students in the area of instruction. Her commitment is visible in the standards she sets for quality and in the passion she expresses by assisting and mentoring teachers, which helps them achieve success.

Claudia is a strong advocate for children, especially culturally and linguistically diverse learners. She has on many occasions shared her thoughts and inspired ideas about ways to conquer the achievement gap. She knows what is necessary to take students, and the teachers that work with them, into the future. However, not all teachers at her school are as experienced, and at times her ideas have been met with resistance.

Claudia's had to step back at times, and re-examine her role as teacher leader. While she is well versed in best instructional practices, and can easily balance the art and science of quality teaching, other teachers have had difficulty keeping up with all the changes. For example, when Claudia and several other teachers designed a multi-cultural gardening unit in which the entire school would participate, several teachers argued that they could not fit it in to their routines. This frustrated Claudia, as she knew the unit was well articulated at each grade level with the standards teachers were intended to teach any way, and she had difficulty understanding the reasons behind the opposition to such a well-planned and thought out unit that involved the collaboration of parents and local businesses in constructing and maintaining a newly planned school garden. She understood the sense of community that would result as the school embraced the common theme, and was adamant about students learning cultural and historical lessons which could help ground them in their own identities.

After careful deliberation, Claudia and the other teachers working on the unit decided to meet with the group of teachers resisting the change. In order to discern the challenges associated with the unit, it would be important to understand the range of perspectives. The conversation was lively, and at times intense, but ultimately led to a better understanding of the teachers' needs. As it turns out, the biggest concern with the unit was the lack of comfort teachers had in facilitating lessons on cultures different from their own. What they wanted and requested was additional training to help them lead rich and engaging dialogue amongst students.

Together the teachers discovered they did indeed have the goal of strong and sustained academic achievement in common. They also came to a shared understanding about the prerequisites necessary for initiatives such as this. Claudia was able to facilitate a process in which teachers engaged in honest discourse to solve a problem and move forward with the schools' vision. She learned that leading change in her school needs to be approached much like she teaches, with a culturally responsive style and attitude.

Culture includes the way things are done within the school. A culturally responsive school culture involves the standards, expectations, habits or customs that lead to practices that benefit all students. Many times the culture of a school is determined by visitors immediately as they enter the building. The welcome visitors receive as well as the kinds of banners or signs that cover the walls make a difference in the way they feel within the school. Culture is perpetuated by the types of teacher conversations taking place in the lounge and the ways in which students are engaged in classrooms and throughout the school.

When the culture of a school is open, tolerant, and compassionate, culturally responsive education is cultivated. However, when a school culture is competitive, and authoritative, teachers will find it challenging to lead culturally responsive initiatives. Promoting a safe, affirming, and robust school culture may be the most difficult task of the culturally responsive educator, but leads to satisfaction as it exemplifies the courage and integrity involved in doing what is good and right for children.

Culturally responsive teachers and leaders working collaboratively to build an inclusive school culture embrace parent and community involvement; inviting them to visit classrooms, assist with projects, and serve as guest speakers. They take the time to recognize volunteers and regularly celebrate the accomplishments of students as well as families in the community. Culturally responsive teachers find clever ways to involve families in the traditions of the learning community, and look to participate as contributing members to a school culture that is all-encompassing of the community in which the school exists.

Culturally responsive teachers can influence the inclusive culture of the school by helping to develop policies and practices that embrace culturally responsive approaches and philosophies. Specifically, teachers can help with the development of:

- A school philosophy or mission statement that supports culturally responsive education;
- Professional learning opportunities that reflect a culturally responsive philosophy and inclusive practices;
- A common language that reflects the philosophy of inclusive education (*e.g.*, "our students" *vs*. "your students" or "my students");
- Practices where students with a wide range of needs and abilities are educated throughout the school (not concentrated in one or two classrooms, or a different school all together);
- An array of curricular adaptations and modifications offered to all learners; and
- Professional learning opportunities offering effective instructional strategies that support a culturally responsive curriculum.

Teachers interested in creating change in their schools can review this list and determine areas of need. Once these areas are identified, teachers can work within the leadership team to develop a plan for school improvement. There are many tools, strategies, and protocols that can be used to help create change and inspire progress at www.equityallianceatasu.org

WHY SHOULD CULTURALLY RESPONSIVE TEACHING BE THE NORM?

The achievement gap in the US often separates groups of students by drawing distinctions between White, middle class students and their peers who may be American Indian, African-American, and/or Latino/a. There are many harmful effects of looking at performance in terms of gaps particularly because the gaps that are noticed often situate deficits within students deficits in students rather than on deficits in opportunities to learn. The focus on gaps also tends to privilege some kinds of knowledge over others. While the path leading to a university education is based on stockpiling specific types of information and using it to demonstrate aptitude, we must remember that practical and indigenous ways of knowing offer vast insight into everyday life that may have ecological and social significance (Kozleski, 2009).

Culturally responsive teaching helps to bridge the experiences of culturally and linguistically diverse students who may have different ways of knowing and learning, and meaningfully engages them in demonstrating proficiency in language usage, grammar, mathematical knowledge and other tools used to navigate their everyday lives. Further, by understanding the features of this knowledge, all students are empowered to translate the logical structures of their knowledge and by seeing themselves and their experiences within the school curriculum.

WHAT ARE KEY FEATURES OF CULTURALLY RESPONSIVE TEACHING?

Communicate High Expectations: Culturally responsive teachers make explicit expectations for student engagement, performance, and achievement at high levels, rather than making excuses for why some students don't participate at optimal levels at times. They develop relationships with students that inspire confidence, helping all students reach their potential.

Actively Engage Students in Learning: Culturally responsive teachers coach students to think critically, question what is taught, and consult original sources for information. They find ways to help students connect learning to their own lives and experiences, while ensuring active participation throughout the school day. Student engagement means complex expository, creative and reflective writing, reading a variety of genres across the disciplines, the use of advanced graphic organizers for establishing relationship between multifaceted ideas, and taking on a variety of facilitation roles in collaborative student learning groups. Culturally responsive teachers get to know their students and show genuine concern for their decisions so that the disappointments that come from trying and not quite succeeding inspire them to continue learning and taking risks.

***Facilitate Learning*:** Culturally responsive teachers work to build students' capacity to handle new material, solve complex problems, and develop new skills by scaffolding their learning from what they already know through a series of increasingly complex experiences that shift the locus of control from the teacher to the learner. They use strategies for incorporating comprehensible input that is appropriate for all learners in the classroom, and structure learning opportunities that help students take responsibility for their own outcomes.

***Anchor Curriculum in the Everyday Lives of Students*:** Culturally responsive teachers structure curriculum in ways that connect the knowledge and skills necessary for new content knowledge to the background experiences of the learners within their class. They work from a backward design model, ensuring that the most important aspects of the content are taught, emphasized, and experienced by students in a variety of different formats. They work to make the curriculum meaningful, by helping students see the relevance of standard content, and helping them inquire about the aspects that matter most to them personally.

Select Participation Structures for Learning that Reflect Students' Ways of Knowing and Doing: Culturally responsive teachers actively seek opportunities to participate in situations and group roles where they're not dominant, and learn from experiences where they might feel uncomfortable. They spend time in the community in which they teach, and get to know the customs and routines of the people within the neighborhood. They attend local events and visit with families to gain a deeper understanding of how things work. They suspend judgment in order to reflect upon their own cultural knowledge and understandings, then use their reflections to help them structure ways to include and engage students for more meaningful participation.

Building the capacity of schools to become culturally responsive involves broadening our view of who leaders are and what leadership means. Teachers have a responsibility to work with principals, parents, community members, and students in creating the conditions necessary for change to occur and culturally responsive practices to take hold. Educators committed to culturally responsive education value diversity, push the boundaries of traditional thinking, and lead by example. While following that lead may take teachers down an unfamiliar path, what occurs along the journey can transform not only schools, but the individuals within them. By learning together, taking risks, supporting each other, and weathering the challenges along the way, schools can emerge as successful culturally responsive learning communities that cultivate the success of *all* learners.

ACKNOWLEDGEMENT

Declare none.

CONFLICT OF INTEREST

The author(s) confirm that this chapter content has no conflict of interest.

REFERENCES

Artiles, A. J. & Kozleski, E. B. (2007). Beyond convictions: Interrogating culture, history, and power in inclusive education. *Language Arts*, *84*, 351-358.

Artiles, A. J. (2003). The dilemma of difference: Enriching the disproportionality of discourse with theory and context. *The Journal of Special Education, 32,* 32-36.

Artiles, A. J., Kozleski, E. B., Dorn, S., & Christensen, C. (2007). Learning in inclusive education research: Re-mediating theory and methods with a transformative agenda. *Review of Research in Education, 30*, 65-108.

Artiles, A. J., Trent, S. C., & Palmer, J. (2004). Culturally diverse students in special education: Legacies and prospects. In J.A. Banks & C. M. Banks (Eds.), *Handbook of research on multicultural education* (2nd Ed.) (pp. 716-735). San Francisco, CA: Jossey Bass.

Barnett, J. & Fallon, G. (2007). Conflicting views of school community: The dichotomy between administrators and teachers. *International Journal of Education Policy and Leadership,2(1).* Retrieved January 11, 2008 from http://www.ijepl.org/.

Barth, R.S. (1990). *Improving schools from within: Teachers, parents, and principals can make the difference.* San Francisco, CA: Jossey-Bass.

Barth, R.S. (2001). Teacher leader. *Phi Delta Kappan, 82(6),*443-446.

Bazron, B., Osher, D., & Fleischman, S. (2005). Creating culturally responsive schools. *Educational Leadership,63(1),* 83-84.

Capper, C.A., Frattura, E., & Keyes, M. W. (2000). *Meeting the needs of students of all abilities. How leaders go beyond inclusion.* Thousand Oaks, CA: Corwin Press.

Eckel, P., Hill, B. & Green, M. (1998). *On Change: En Route to Transformation.* Washington, D.C., American Council on Education.

DuFour, R. (2004). What is a "professional learning community"? *Educational Leadership, 61(8),* 6-11.

DuFour, R., DuFour, R., Eaker, R., & Karhanek, G. (2004). *Whatever it takes: how professional learning communities respond when kids don't learn.* Bloomington, IN: National Educational Service.

Falvey, M., Givner, C., & Kimm, C. (1995). What is an inclusive school? In R. Villa & J. Thousand (Eds.), *Creating an inclusive school* (pp. 1-12). Alexandria,VA: Association for Supervision and Curriculum Development.

Ferguson, D.L., Meyer, G., Jeanchild, L., Juniper, L., Zingo, J. (1992). Figuring out what to do with the grownups: how teachers make inclusion 'work' for students with disabilities. *Journal of the Association for Persons with Severe Handicaps, 17(4),*218-26.

Fullan, M.G. (1992). Visions that blind. *Educational Leadership, 49(5),* 19-20.

Gay, G. (2000). *Culturally Responsive Teaching: Theory, Practice, & Research.* New York: Teachers College Press.

Gay, G. (2002). Preparing for culturally responsive teaching. *Journal of Teacher Education, 52(2),* 106-116.

Haberman, M. (2004). Can star teachers create learning communities? *Educational Leadership, 61(8),* 52-56.

Huffman, J. (2003). The role of shared values and vision in creating professional learning communities. *NASSP Bulletin, 87(637),* 21-34.

Irvine, J.J. (2003). *Educating teachers for a diverse society: Seeing with the cultural eye.* New York, NY: Teachers College Press.

Kluth, P. (2005). *Is your school inclusive? Toward more inclusive classrooms and communities.* From http://www.paulakluth.com/articles/schoolinclusive.html.

Kouzes, J. M., & Posner, B. Z. (2006). *A leader's legacy.* San Francisco, CA: Jossey-Bass.

Kozleski, E. (2009). *Culturally Responsive Teaching and Learning Matter.* From http://www.equityallianceatasu.org/pdf.culturallyresponsiveteaching

Larson, C.L., & Murtadha, K. (2002). Leadership for social justice. In J. Murphy (Ed.), *The educational leadership challenge: Redefining leadership for the 21st century* (pp. 134-161). Chicago: University of Chicago Press.

Lee, C. D. (2007). *Culture, literacy, and learning: Taking bloom in the midst of the whirlwind.* New York: Teachers College Press.

Orfield, G., Losen, D., Wald, J., & Swanson, C. (2004). *Losing our future: How minority youth are being left behind by the graduation rate crisis*, Cambridge, MA: The Civil Rights Project at Harvard University.

Palmer, P. J. (1998) *The Courage to Teach.* San Francisco, CA: Jossey-Bass.

Sands, D.J., Kozleski, E.B., & French, N.K. (2000). *Inclusive education for the 21st century.* Belmont: Wadsworth.

Salisbury, C. & McGregor, G. (2005). *Principals of Inclusive Schools.*From http://www.urbanschools.org/pdf/principals.inclusive.LETTER.pdf?v_document_name=Principals%20of%20Inclusive%20Schools

Sergiovanni, T. J. (1990). *Value-added leadership: How to get extraordinary performance in schools.* Orlando, FL: Harcourt Brace Jovanovich.

Sergiovanni, T. J. (1992). *Moral leadership: Getting to the heart of school improvement.* San Francisco, CA: Jossey-Bass.

Sergiovanni, T.J. (1994). *Building community in schools.* San Francisco: Jossey-Bass.

Udvari-Solner, A. (1997). Inclusive education. In C. A. Grant & G. Ladson- Billings (Eds.), *Dictionary of multicultural education* (pp. 141-144). Phoenix, AZ: Oryx Press.

Villa, R., Thousand, J., Stainback, W., & Stanback, S. (1992). *Restructuring for caring and effective education: An administrative guide to creating heterogeneous schools.* Baltimore: Paul H. Brokes.

Villegas, A. M., & Lucas, T. (2002). *Educating culturally responsive teachers.* Albany, NY: State University of New York Press.

CHAPTER 10

System of Care for Children with Severe Emotional Disturbance: A Framework of Mental Health Promotion Based on Students Most in Need

Denise M. Green[1,*] **and Sarah E. Twill**[2]

[1]Department of Human Services, Social Work, and Rehabilitation, 107 McCartha Hall, Troy University, Troy, USA and [2]Department of Social Work, Wright State University, 270 Millett Hall, 3640 Colonel Glenn Hwy, Dayton, OH 45435, USA

Abstract: The purpose of this chapter is to provide the reader with information concerning current definitions of the term Severe Emotional Disturbance, a brief history of public care provisions for children with Severe Emotional Disturbance, a historical review of the System of Care movement defining the model as a Best Practices Model of service delivery for children with Severe Emotional Disturbance, and an example case study utilizing a System of Care model. Also, the most common mental health conditions typically diagnosed in school-aged children are discussed. It is hoped that dialogue regarding students with the highest level of need, will provide the reader with a broad perspective on the mental system of care resources available for children and adolescents. Creative collaboration among involved—and other potential system of care members—can be tantamount in pursuit of effective mental health promotion provided that participants adhere to principals discussed previously in this text and avoid detrimental philosophy and intervention strategies such as coercive control techniques.

Keywords: Diagnosis, disorders, most in need, severe emotional disturbance (SED), system of care.

INTRODUCTION

Defining Severe Emotional Disturbance (SED): The definition of severe emotional disturbance (SED) has been varied. Four commonly used definitions have been included as parts of federal legislation or initiatives. One of the earliest definitions of emotional disturbance came from the Individuals with Disabilities Education Act (IDEA) (P.L. 94-142) as reviewed in Narrow, and colleagues(1998). This definition is:

***Address correspondence to Denise M. Green:** Department of Human Services, Social Work, and Rehabilitation, 107 McCartha Hall, Troy University, Troy, AL 36311, USA; Tel: 334-670-3366; Email: dmgreen@troy.edu

Raymond J. Waller (Ed)

> A condition exhibiting one or more of the following characteristics over a long period of time and to a marked degree that adversely affects a child's educational performance: an inability to learn than cannot be explained by intellectual, sensory, or health factor; an inability to build or maintain satisfactory interpersonal relationships with peers and teachers; inappropriate types of behavior or feelings under normal circumstances; a general pervasive mood of unhappiness or depression; or a tendency to develop physical symptoms or fears associated with personal or school problems (section 300.7).

This definition of SED is applicable to educational settings and does not translate to other settings such as community mental health services. Further, the IDEA definition of SED is considered by some to be vague and outdated (Narrow, *et al.,* 1998). As such, states and local school entities have transformed the SED definition into a more practice friendly definition. In 1992, the Alcohol, Drug Abuse, and Mental Health Administration Reorganization Act of 1992 (P.L. 102-321) included a definition of SED that took into account mental health diagnosis and functional impairment. Narrow and colleagues (1998) summarized the act as follows:

> Children with a serious emotional disturbance are persons from birth to age 18 who currently or at any time during the past year have had a diagnosable mental, behavioral, or emotional disorder of sufficient duration to meet diagnostic criteria specified within the DSM-III-R that resulted in functional impairment which substantially interferes with or limits the child's role or functioning in family, school, or other support services (p. 1602).

However, the United States Senate Committee on Appropriations in the appropriations bill for the Department of Health and Human Services (FY 1993) and the National Advisory

Mental Health Council (1993) substantially narrowed the definition. Also as referenced in Narrow and colleagues (1998), Severe Emotional Disturbance was defined by these organizations as:

> through diagnosis, disability, and duration, and included disorders with psychotic symptoms such as schizophrenia, schizoaffective disorder, manic depressive disorder, autism, as well as other disorders such as major depression, panic disorder, and obsessive compulsive disorder (p. 1602).

It should be noted that this definition was intended to apply to all citizens, children and adults, with mental health issues.

The Community Mental Health Services (CMHS) initiative defined SED based on age, diagnosis, disability, multi-agency need, and duration and intensity. The current federal government eligibility definition (SAMHSA, 2000, Data Collection Procedure Manual, Section 5), is as follows:

> Limited to children and adolescents under 22 years of age and their family. Client eligibility requires the presence of an emotional, behavioral, or mental disorder diagnosable under DSM-IV diagnostic categories or their ICD-9-CM equivalents of subsequent revisions (with the exception of DSM-IV "V" codes, substance use disorders, and developmental disorders, unless they co-occur with another diagnosable serious emotional disturbance). Client eligibility should be defined based on the basis of degree or level of functioning. Inability to perform in the family, school, and/or community is the basic factor that determines the need for services. Children and adolescents must have service needs involving two or more community agencies, such as mental health, substance abuse, health, education, juvenile justice, or child welfare. The disability must be present for at least one year or, on the basis of diagnosis and intensity, be expected to last more than 1 year (p. 3).

DEFINING MENTAL DISORDERS

In the previous section, four definitions of SED were explored. Some of the definitions required a mental health diagnosis before being considered SED. In this section, the scope of mental health issues will be discussed. In addition, four commonly diagnosed disorders in youth will be articulated. The four disorders to be outlined are attention deficit hyperactivity disorder, conduct disorder, oppositional defiant disorder, and mood disorders. Attention is given to the disorder prevalence, diagnostic criteria, impairment across the life spheres, and predicted life outcomes. Identifying and counting the number of American children suffering with an emotional disorder is a difficult and complex task. The definition of an emotional disorder has varied (*i.e.,* diagnosis based on the Diagnostic and Statistical Manual (DSM-IV-TR), functional impairment based on standardized measures such as the Child Behavior Checklist (CBCL) or the Child and Adolescent Functional Assessment Scale (CAFAS), or criteria specified in federal legislation).

Multiple studies indicate that between 23% and 61% of children meet criteria for a psychiatric disorder during at least one wave of assessment (Kashani, McGee, Clarkson, Anderson, Walton, Williams, Silva, Robbins, & McKnew, 1983; Anderson, Williams, McGee, & Silva, 1987; McGee, Feehan, Williams, Patridge, Silva, & Kelly, 1990; Fergusson, Horwood, & Lynskey, 1993; Velez, Johnson, & Cohen, 1989; Cohen, Cohen, Kasen, Velez, Hartman, Johnson, Rojas, Brook, & Streuning, 1993; Reinhert, Giaconia, Lefkowitz, Pakiz, & Frost, 1993; Lewinsohn, Rhode, Klein, & Seeley, 1999). Costello, Mustillo, Erkanli, Keller, and Angold (2003) in a study on psychiatric prevalence found that 36.7% of youth met criteria for at least one disorder by age sixteen. By the time the youth reached age sixteen, 79% of diagnosed boys and 58% of diagnosed girls additionally met the criteria of having a severe emotional disturbance (SED). Further, 25.5% of the sample had two or more mental health disorders.

Within the population of children suffering with a mental illness, some youth are identified as having a severe emotional disturbance (SED). SED eligibility is limited to children and adolescents under 22 years of age and their family. Eligibility requires the presence of an emotional, behavioral, or mental disorder diagnosable under DSM-IV diagnostic categories or their ICD-9-CM equivalents of subsequent revisions (with the exception of DSM-IV "V" codes, substance use disorders, and developmental disorders, unless they co-occur with another diagnosable serious emotional disturbance). Eligibility should be defined based on the degree or level of functioning of the student. Inability to perform in the family, school, and/or community is the fundamental factor that determines the need for services. Children and adolescents must have service needs involving two or more community agencies, such as mental health, substance abuse, health, education, juvenile justice, or child welfare. The disability must be present for at least one year or, on the basis of diagnosis and intensity, be expected to last more than 1 year (SAMHSA, 2000, Data Collection Procedure Manual, Section 5-Page 3).

In a multiple site evaluation of prevalence, it was estimated that between 4% - 17% of youth had a domain specific SED and between 4% - 7.4% had global impairment SED (Costello, Messer, Bird, Cohen, & Reinherz, 1998).

Numerically, three to four million children and adolescents between the ages of 4-17 have significant impairment. Of youth classified as having SED, only one in four received specialized mental health care as specified by the block grant funding in P.L. 102-321 (Costello, Messer, Bird, Cohen, & Reinherz, 1998). It is necessary to consider the DSM-IV-TR (American Psychiatric Association, 2000) criteria for disorders usually first diagnosed in infancy, childhood, or adolescence. In the following section, the most common disorders of childhood-attention deficit hyperactivity disorder, conduct disorder, oppositional defiant disorder, and mood disorders are reviewed. Consideration is given to the disorder prevalence, diagnostic criteria, impairment across the life spheres, and predicted life outcomes.

ATTENTION DEFICIT HYPERACTIVITY DISORDER

Prevalence rates for Attention Deficit Hyperactivity Disorder (ADHD) range from 1.9% - 14.4% (Scahill & Schwab-Stone, 2000). The DSM-IV-TR reports estimates of ADHD at 3% - 7% (American Psychiatric Association, 2000). There is difficulty in capturing an accurate measure of ADHD prevalence as the methodologies have varied in definition of the disorder, data collection techniques (*i.e.,* case file review *versus* semi-structured interviews with teachers and care givers), and age groups sampled (Scahill & Schwab-Stone, 2000). Further, prevalence rates vary based on culture (Verhulst, Achenbach, Ferdinand, & Kasius, 1993) and if the sample was urban, suburban, or rural (Zahner, Jacobs, Freeman, & Trainor, 1993). In spite of variations in prevalence rates, ADHD is thought to be "chronic and enduring" disorder (Keller, Lavori, Beardslee, & Wunder, 1992). Inattention, hyperactivity, and impulsivity characterize ADHD (American Psychiatric Association, 2000). Characteristics of inattention include making careless mistakes in schoolwork, work, or other activities, having difficulty sustaining attention in task or play activities, difficulty organizing tasks and activities, and being easily distracted by extraneous stimuli. Characteristics of hyperactivity include fidgeting with hands and feet, talking excessively, and having difficulty remaining in seat or assigned area when expected.

Characteristics of impulsivity include having difficulty taking turns and interrupting others.

Adolescents diagnosed with ADHD experience problems across life spheres. It is theorized that youth diagnosed with ADHD have difficulty in their interpersonal relationships because some of the behaviors affiliated with ADHD interfere with appropriate prosocial behavior, such as interrupting others, disorganization, or not taking turns. As such, families with youth with ADHD are often characterized as negative and frustrated (Befera & Barkley, 1985).

Similarly, adolescents diagnosed with ADHD experience difficulty in peer relationships. Adolescents diagnosed with ADHD also experience more problems in educational settings compared to their non-diagnosed peers (Faraone, Beiderman, Lehman, Spencer, Norman, Deidman, Kraus, Perrin, & Chen, 1993; Frick, Kamphaus, Lahey, Loeber, Christ, Hart, & Tannenbaum, 1991).

ADHD is often diagnosed with other mental health disorders. It is estimated that between 30% - 80% of youth diagnosed with ADHD also have a diagnosis of conduct disorder (CD) or oppositional defiant disorder (ODD) (Biederman, Newcorn, & Sprich, 1991; Klein & Mannuzza, 1991; Babinski, Hartought, & Lambert, 1999; Mannuzza, Klein, Bessler, Malloy, & LaPadula, 1998). Also, 50%-60% of children ages 6-18 who are diagnosed with Tourette's Disorder have ADHD (Cohen & Leckman, 1989). Learning disorders appear more frequently in youth diagnosed with ADHD compared to youth without the diagnosis (Semrud-Clikeman, Biederman, Sprich-Buckminster, & Lehman, 1992; Cantwell & Baker, 1991). Finally, youth diagnosed with ADHD are at risk for developing a substance abuse disorder (Klein & Mannuzza, 1991; Hoegerman, Resnick, & Schnoll, 1993; Rounsaville, Anton, Carroll, Budde, Prusoff, & Gawin, 1991; Gittelman, Mannuzza, Shenker, & Bonagura, 1985). Keller, Lavori, Beardslee, and Wunder

(1992) claimed ADHD was a "chronic and enduring" disorder. Between 20-70% of youth diagnosed with ADHD continue to experience symptoms as adults (Althoff, Rettew, & Hudzaik, 2003). As such, adolescents diagnosed with ADHD are at risk for experiencing negative life outcomes. Follow-up studies of youth diagnosed with ADHD indicate that individuals experience lower academic and professional achievement and are at increased risk for developing antisocial behaviors (Klein & Mannuzza, 1991). Mannuzza, Klein, Bessler, Malloy, and LaPadula (1993) found that adolescents diagnosed with ADHD experience higher rates of criminal activity, incarceration, and substance abuse. Likewise, studies of adult cocaine users indicate that childhood histories of ADHD were present at higher rates (Hoegerman, Resnick, & Schnoll, 1993; Rounsaville, Anton, Carroll, Buddle, Prusoff, & Gawin, 1991).

CONDUCT DISORDER

The estimates of the number of persons under the age of 18 years old diagnosed with conduct disorder range from 1% -16% (American Psychiatric Association, 1994, 2000; Bauermeister, Canino, & Bird, 1994; Esser, Schmidt, & Woermer, 1990; Kashani, Carlson, Beck, & Hoeper, 1987). Prevalence rates have varied as the Diagnostic and Statistical Manual of Mental Disorders (DSM) has under-gone changes, due to data differences across studies, and because of differences in the manifestation of the disorder across the developmental process. Conduct disorder is more common in boys than in girls (Loeber, Burke, Lahey, Winters, & Zera, 2000). Conduct disorder, especially with onset before the age of ten years old, has a profound impact on adolescent outcomes.

The DSM-IV-TR defines conduct disorder as 'a repetitive and persistent pattern of behavior in which the basic rights of others or major age-appropriate societal norms or rules are violated' (American Psychiatric Association, 2000, p. 99). Behaviors such as physical fighting, cruelty to people and animals, fire setting, destruction of property, and theft are some typical behaviors of youth with conduct disorder. It should be noted that conduct disorder and oppositional defiant disorder (ODD) cannot be diagnosed together. However, the younger that ODD is diagnosed, the greater the severity of ODD related behaviors, the increased number of physical fights, along with parental substance abuse and lower socioeconomic status, the higher the risk that ODD will progress and become consistent with the conduct disorder diagnosis (Loeber, Green, Keenan, & Lahey, 1995). Conduct disorder and other disorders can be comorbid. Conduct disorder and attention deficit hyperactivity disorder (ADHD) often coexist (Loeber, Burke, Lahey, Winters, & Zera, 2000; Cantwell & Baker, 1989; Walker, Lahey, Hynd, & Frame, 1987). These studies indicated that when conduct disorder and ADHD are comorbid, the severity of the conduct disorder is worse when compared to youth diagnosed only with conduct disorder. Likewise, substance abuse disorders and conduct disorder are often comorbid. The temporal relationship between the two disorders is uncertain; it is possible that either the substance abuse leads to further delinquent behavior or that the impulsivity and flaunting of societal norms drives one to partake in illicit substance use (Brook, Whiteman, & Finch, 1992). Reebye, Moretti, and Lessard (1995) found that over 50% of youth diagnosed with conduct disorder also met criteria for substance use disorder. Additionally cited in this research, youth between the ages of 10-13 had higher rates of comorbidity; and, 40% to 60% of arrested male juveniles have drugs and alcohol in their bloodstream, suggesting a relationship between substance use and further delinquency. A diagnosis of conduct disorder, especially when made at an early age, with severity of behaviors, and comorbid with another diagnosis, can predict severe impairment across life spheres. For example, preschool children diagnosed with conduct disorder have a highly stable diagnosis, and thus, stable behavioral problems over time (Lavigne, Cicchetti, Gibbons, Binns, Larson, & Devito, 2001). Youth diagnosed with conduct disorder are more immature in cognition and moral reasoning (Lee & Prentice, 1988), have fewer problem solving strategies than their non-diagnosed peers (Webster-Stratton & Lindsay, 1999), are unable to assume the point of view of another (Short & Simeonsson, 1986), pay greater attention to aggressive environmental cues (Kendall, 1993), and view others as adversaries and respond with hostility (Guerra & Slaby, 1989). The aforementioned lead to difficulty in maintaining appropriate peer and family relationships, thus causing difficulty in multiple settings such as at school, home, and in the community. Youth diagnosed with conduct disorder often experience difficulty into adulthood.

This is especially true when conduct disorder is diagnosed at an early age and the behaviors are severe (American Psychiatric Association, 1994; Cohen, Cohen, Kasen, Velez, Hartmark, Johnson, Rojas, Brook, & Streunonh, 1993). Robbins and Ratcliff (1979) concluded that 23%- 41% of antisocial youth became antisocial adults, 17%- 28% of antisocial youth did not become antisocial adults, and the remaining youth could not be classified as either antisocial or not antisocial. They found that early diagnosis of antisocial behaviors, drug use prior to age fifteen, out of home placement, and poverty predicted antisocial behaviors as adults. Further, youth who display aggressive behaviors were more likely to continue to exhibit behaviors consistent with conduct disorder (Stewart & Kelso, 1987). Likewise, aggressive behaviors, fire setting, family deviance, and inattention all predicted continuous antisocial behaviors (Stewart & Kelso, 1987). Early conduct problems are, too often, related to involvement with the adult criminal justice system (Lewis, Yeager, Lovely, & Stein, 1994; Lewis, Yeager, Cobham-Porterreal, & Klein, 1991; Lewis, Lovely, Yeager, & della Femina, 1989; Hechtman & Offord, 1994).

In summary, youth diagnosed with conduct disorder face an array of life challenges in the absence of effective intervention. For example, youth diagnosed with conduct disorder have difficulty in maintaining appropriate peer and family relationships, thus causing difficulty in multiple settings such as at school, home, and in the community. In this section, the diagnostic criteria for conduct disorder, issues of dual diagnosis, and impairment across the life sphere were discussed. The scope of oppositional defiant disorder will be considered in the next section.

OPPOSITIONAL DEFIANT DISORDER

Oppositional defiant disorder (ODD) occurs in 2% - 16% of youth (American Psychiatric Association, 2000). The diagnosis is twice as common in males as in females. ODD generally appears in youth starting at age eight years. Typically the ODD behaviors appear first in the home setting with adults and peers with whom the effected youth is most acquainted (American Psychiatric Association, 2000). The DSM-IV-TR criteria for ODD include "a pattern of negativistic, hostile, and defiant behavior lasting at least 6 months" (American Psychiatric Association, 2000, p. 102). Behaviors such as refusing to comply with adults' requests or rules, deliberately annoying people, losing temper, blaming others for mistakes, and being spiteful are some typical behaviors of youth with ODD. Youth diagnosed with ODD display behaviors more serve and frequent than typically observed in other youth of comparable age and developmental level (American Psychiatric Association, 2000). In the literature, ODD and conduct disorder are often addressed together, as many either surmise that ODD is the precursor of conduct disorder (Green & Doyle, 1999; Kuhne, Schachar, & Tannock, 1997) or discuss both disorders as "conduct problems" (Biderman, Faraone, Milberger, Jetton, Chen, Mick, Green, & Russell, 1996; Hinshaw, Lahey, & Hart, 1993; Kim-Cohen, Caspi, Moffitt, Harrington, Milne, & Poulton, 2003). However, Greene, Biederman, Zerwas, Monuteaux, Goring, and Faratone (2002) attempted to isolate children diagnosed only with ODD and compare them to youth diagnosed with conduct disorder and other psychiatric disorders. The authors found that youth diagnosed with ODD had poorer family cohesion and higher family conflict than the other groups. Moreover, youth diagnosed with ODD had more impaired social interactions across environments, such as at school, with peers and siblings, and at home, than the youth diagnosed with conduct disorder or other psychiatric disorders. Finally, youth diagnosed with ODD were twice as likely as the other groups to have a comorbid diagnosis of a mood disorder.

MOOD DISORDERS

Each year, 1.3 million youth between the ages of 15-19 experience depression (Angold, Costello, & Worthman, 1998). In a study of 1,710 high school students, 9.6% met criteria for a current mood disorder, 33% had experienced a depression related disorder over their lifetime, and 31.7% had experienced another mental health disorder (Lewinsohn, Hops, Roberts, Seeley, & Andrews, 1993). Prevalence rates for adolescents with depression are 15-20%, which is similar to adult prevalence rates (Kessler, McGonagle, Zhao, & Nelson, 1994; Lewinsohn, Duncan, Stanton, & Hautzinger, 1986; Lewinsohn, Hops, Roberts, Seeley, & Andrews, 1993; Lewinsohn, Rodhe, Seeley, & Fisher, 1993). One inference that could be drawn from the similarity in prevalence is that depression may begin during the adolescent years and persist over the life span.

The DSM-IV-TR distinguishes depression as either depressed mood or loss of interest or pleasure (American Psychiatric Association, 2000). Adolescents suffering with a mood disorder experience impairment across numerous life spheres. Youth who are diagnosed with major depression often have difficulty in interpersonal relationships with family and friends (Fleming & Offord, 1990; Kashani, Carlson, Beck, & Hoeper, 1987; Kolvin, Barrett, Bhate, & Berney, 1991). Difficulty with concentration and thinking are diagnostic, and these may spur poor school performance, including a drop in grades or attendance (Kovacs, Paulauskas, Gastonis, & Richards, 1988). Finally, suicide is the third leading cause of death among adolescents; adolescents with a depressive disorder are at an increased risk as compared to the non diagnosed population (Rao, Weissman, Martin, & Hammond, 1993). The impact to health and functioning often resulting from depression cannot be understated.

Depression is, like the mental health issues discussed above, often comorbid with other psychiatric disorders. Twenty percent of youth diagnosed with a mood disorder have a comorbid diagnosis of substance abuse (Weller &Weller, 1990). Between 36-80% of youth diagnosis with depression are also diagnosed with conduct disorder (Ferro, Carlson, Grayson, & Klein, 1994; Kovacs *et al.,* 1988). Similarly, more than 50% of adolescents diagnosed with a mood disorder were also diagnosed with either conduct disorder or oppositional defiant disorder (Bird, Canino, Rubio-Stepec, & Gould, 1988). Though depression is dangerous, the risk is exacerbated by the presence of a comorbid condition. For example, youth diagnosed with depression and a comorbid diagnosis of a disruptive disorder have worse short term outcomes, higher rates of adult involvement with the justice system, more suicide attempts, and higher levels of family conflict (Harrington, Fudge, Rutter, & Pickles, 1990; Harrington, Fudge, Rutter, & Pickles, 1991; Kutcher, Marton, & Korenblum, 1989; Puig-Antich, Goetz, Davies, & Kaplan, 1989).

Prognosis for youth diagnosed with a mood disorder does not improve as they become young adults. Approximately 20-40% of adolescents diagnosed with major depression develop bipolar I within five years of the onset of depression (Geller, Fox, & Clark, 1994; Rao, Ryan, Birmaher, Dahl, Williamson, Kaufman, Rao, & Nelson, 1995; Kovacs, Gatsonis, Paulaiskas, & Richards, 1989). Lewinsohn, Rohde, Klein, and Seeley (1999) compared youth diagnosed with major depression to other adolescents with either non-affective mental health disorders or no reported psychiatric history. Adolescents with a history of depression had higher rates (9% compared to 5.6% with non-affective disorders and 3.7% with no disorders) of depression in young adulthood. Further, youth who had experienced a major depression episode were at higher risk for developing substance abuse disorders and Axis II psychopathology as young adults. Thus, effective intervention for mood disorders is an important public health concern and a paramount concern for long-term positive outcomes.

As evidenced by the multiple definitions of Severe Emotional Disturbance and the complexity of mental health disorders often found to accompany this diagnosis, it is not difficult to surmise the issues surrounding diagnosis, treatment and service delivery to these children and their families. The next section discusses the historical development of public sector acknowledgement of the severity of these issues and the policies enacted to address the issues faced by children and their families in search of services.

HISTORY OF MODERN CHILDREN'S MENTAL HEALTH PUBLIC CARE PROVISIONS: LONG, SLOW PROGRESS IN MEETING CHILDREN'S NEED

Community Mental Health Movement. The Community Mental Health Movement began in the early 1960's with the release of the Joint Commission's report, Action for Mental Health (1960), and the Celebrezze Task Force Report (1962), both of which proposed types of community based treatment centers (Grob, 1991). While children's mental health needs had been rudimentarily addressed in the community by the child guidance movement and by the child welfare and juvenile justice systems, the psychiatric treatment needs of adults was limited to services provided while a resident of a state hospital. As many adults with psychiatric illness were deinstutionalized, communities needed to deliver appropriate mental health care. Federal legislation followed that addressed this issue for both adults and children in need of mental health treatment (Grob; Hartley, Bird, Lambert, & Coffin, 2002).

FEDERAL COMMUNITY MENTAL HEALTH CENTER ACT

To help communities deliver services to chronically mentally ill adults who had been deinstitutionalized, Congress passed the Mental Retardation Facilities and Community Mental Health Center Construction Act of 1963 (P.L. 88-164). The purpose of the act was to create and build community mental health centers (CMHC). Each catchment area, serving between 75,000-200,000 people, was to provide five services: short term inpatient care, outpatient treatment, emergency services, crisis stabilization (*i.e.,* partial hospitalization), and consultation and education. Additionally, for a CMHC to have the 'comprehensive' designation, an additional five services -- rehabilitation, diagnosis, pre and aftercare, research, and training-- needed to be provided (Hartley *et al.,* 2002; Grob, 1991).

The act did not specifically include or exclude the treatment of children and adolescents. No requirements were made of CMHC programs to design treatment addressing the needs of youth. As such, only about half of the CMHCs offered any services for children (Ad Hoc Committee, 1971). In 1971, approximately 500,000 people were being served under CMHC programs; 20%, (or 100,000), of them were children. Two factors influenced the limited offering of children's services. First, psychiatry tended to emphasise adult treatment. Less was known about the unique mental health needs of children and adolescents. Furthermore, the needs of the adult population were so great as to warrant exclusive resource allocation. For example, between 33-40% of the individuals being served were identified as functionally psychotic and 16% were former residents of state psychiatric institutions. Second, children's mental health services are expensive, in part due to 'indirect' services involved in provision of care (Hartley *et al.,* 2002; Grob, 1991).

The Mental Retardation and Community Mental Health Center Construction Act of 1963 (P.L. 88-164) provided eight years of federal funding. When the federal funding was no longer available, state monies that had been previously allocated for hospitals and institutions and reimbursements from public and private insurance, filled the gap. Adults with mental illness had billable insurance in the form of Medicaid, Medicare, and Supplemental Security Income (SSI). That is, CMHCs were reimbursed for the services provided to adults with chronic mental illness. Unfortunately, children had less coverage, and thus, received less care (Hartley *et al.,* 2002; Grob, 1991). Further, children required more 'indirect' services. While the federal funding was available, CMHCs were able to bill some children's case management services, such as consulting with the schools working with other service providers who treat the parents or other family members, under the educational provision of the act. For example, CHMC staff spent 25% of consulting and education service time engaged with schools. However, once the federal money was gone, these case management services were no longer eligible for insurance reimbursements. About half of the CMHCs that had been providing children's services could no longer afford them and discontinued services.

PART F OF THE COMMUNITY MENTAL HEALTH CENTER ACT

Child advocates were frustrated that the Mental Retardation and Community Mental Health Center Construction Act of 1963 (P.L. 88-164) did not require services for youth in need of mental health treatment. They lobbied Congress and, in 1972, an amendment to the act was added. It is known as Part F of the Community Mental Health Center Act and was designed to address children's mental health needs. Under Part F, a third of CMHCs (about 400) developed specific children's mental health programs (Hartley *et al.,* 2002; Grob, 1991). The children's programs implemented as a result of Part F of the Community Mental Health Center Act were determined to be necessary and successful (Hartley *et al.,* 2002; Grob, 1991). As a result, the act was again amended in 1974 to require all CMHCs to provide children's services (P.L. 94-63). However, in addition to requiring children's mental health services, the act also required six other treatment services --wider community screening, services to the elderly, alcohol and drug treatment, transitional housing, discharge and follow-up care-: beginning to be provided. This raised the requirements of the act from five to twelve. No additional funding was included as part of the amendment and the seven new required services were under funded.

JOINT COMMISSION ON THE MENTAL HEALTH OF CHILDREN

The aforementioned legislation attempted to address the shortcomings of services to children with mental health issues, but their effectiveness was yet to be assessed. The Mental Health Study Act of 1955 (P.L. 182) required a national study of how mental illness affected human and economic problems. As a result of the act, the Joint Commission on Mental Illness and Health was established. This act globally assessed conditions of mental health. It was not until 1965 that the Joint Commission on the Mental Health of Children specifically addressed the special needs of children and adolescents (P.L. 8997). In 1970, the Joint Commission on the Mental Health of Children published a report, *Crisis in Child Mental Health*, detailing the problems with mental health services for children. The main conclusion of the report was that a large number of emotionally and socially disabled children did not receive necessary or appropriate services (Hartley *et al.,* 2002; Grob, 1991).

The recommendations of the Joint Commission influenced future legislation (*i.e.,* Education for All Handicapped Children Act, Mental Health Systems Act, the State Comprehensive Mental Health Services Plan Act). The aforementioned legislation, while good intentioned, cannot be said to have met the needs of youth with mental health needs and multiple social problems. In the next section, the historical development of the system of care movement will be described and the body of the model will be discussed.

SYSTEM OF CARE MOVEMENT

The System of Care (SOC) movement gained momentum in the late 1970's. In 1977, President Carter appointed First Lady Rosalynn Carter as the honorary chair of the President's Commission on Mental Health (Hartley *et al.,* 2002; Grob, 1991). The lessons learned from the child guidance movement and the community mental health center movement were heeded, as the children's mental health system and the youth it served were in crisis. Ultimately, *Unclaimed Children*, a report by Knitzer (1982) and the Children's Defense Fund detailed the failings of previous movements and legislation, and lead to Stroul and Freidman's System of Care Model (1986).

NATIONAL PLAN FOR MENTAL HEALTH

The President's Commission on Mental Health (1978) released a report detailing the state of mental health in America (Hartley *et al.,* 2002; Grob, 1991). The Commission identified two underserved population: adults with chronic mental illness and children with severe emotional disturbances (SED). As a result of these findings, the federal government attempted to improve services to these populations. Adults with chronic mental illness were served under the Community Supports Program (CSP) (Morriseey & Goldman, 1984; Morrissey & Goldman,

1985). CSP's purpose was to develop local and state efforts to provide rehabilitative services, such as housing, social skills training, community adaptive skills, for adults with persistent mental illness (U.S. Department of Health and Human Services, 1999). These programs were better funded than children's services and successful in providing treatment to adults with significant mental health needs (Green, 2005).

MOST-IN-NEED PROGRAM

As a result of the findings of The President's Commission on Mental Health (1978), children with severe emotional disturbances were identified as needing additional services. To remedy this deficit, the Most-In-Need Program (MIN) was developed. The program was designed to incorporate the recommendations of the Joint Commission, while allowing local communities to address the unique needs of youth they served. However, MIN was barely funded. Essentially, in regards to youth with SED, the findings of The President's Commission on Mental Health were ignored and the subsequent MIN program was unsuccessful in addressing the needs of SED youth (Hartley *et al.,* 2002; Grob, 1991).

MENTAL HEALTH SYSTEM ACT

The Mental Health Systems Act (P.L. 96-398) was passed in 1980, a month before President Carter lost reelection to President Reagan (Hartley *et al.,* 2002; Green, 2005; Grob, 1991). This law intended to address the needs of underserved populations, specifically adults with chronic mental illness and youth with serve emotional disturbances, by improving the linkages between federal, state, and local governments through the restructuring of the community mental health center program. CMHCs were mandated under the act to provide services to underserved populations (U.S. Department of Health and Human Services, 1999). Among the mandates that affected children were grants to serve youth with SED, grants for education and consulting needs (*i.e.,* CMHCs could again receive reimbursement for case management services for children), and a call for consumer involvement in treatment.

BLOCK GRANT PROGRAM

The anticipated improvements in children's mental health as authorized under the Mental Health Systems Act were not realized. When President Ronald Regan took office, the priorities, agenda, and policies of the administration changed. The Omnibus Budget Reconciliation Act of 1981 (P.L. 97-35) was passed (Hartley *et al.,* 2002). Roll back many provisions that affected the successfulness of CMCHs (Minkoff, 1987). First, the Mental Health Systems Act was repealed, removing the mandates of providing services to youth with SED, funding of education and consulting, and the call for client involvement in treatment (Hartley *et al.,* 2002). Second, CMHCs lost direct federal funding. It was replaced with funding from Alcohol, Drug Abuse and Mental Health (ADM) block grants to the states. This marked a return to the states having control over how and to whom mental health treatment services were delivered, which, the astute reader may recall, had already largely ignored the specific mental health needs of children.

The shift from federal to state control of mental health monies directly affected the youth in need of mental health treatment services (Minkoff, 1987). Because there were not specific provisions requiring services to youth in the Omnibus Budget Reconciliation Act of 1981, states were free to allocate their mental health funds as they deemed appropriate, though Congress directed states to use between 10-25% of block grant money to fund children's services. However, the use of such funds was not monitored or strictly enforced, and, as a result, well intentioned legislation again failed to meet the needs of youth with SED (Hartley *et al.,* 2002).

UNCLAIMED CHILDREN REPORT

Jane Knitzer (1982) published Unclaimed Children: The Failure of Public Responsibility to Children and Adolescents in Need of Mental Health Services for the Children's Defense Fund. This sentinel work detailed the lack of appropriate services for children. The report highlighted five main problems with children's mental health services. First, both residential and outpatient services were inadequate in meeting the needs of children. Second, while inpatient care was the most accessible, it was the most costly and most restrictive placement. Third, states lacked a way to track children in the mental health system. Similarly, the juvenile justice system, the education system, the child welfare system, and the mental health system failed to coordinate appropriate care for the children who were jointly served. Finally, related to children's mental health, under the

Education for All Handicapped Children (P.L. 94-142) youth with SED were underserved. To address these shortcomings, four recommendations were made to improve mental health service delivery. First, strategies and efforts needed to be developed to identify youth who were either in need of service or were inappropriately served. Second, agencies needed to be offered incentives for coordinating services. Third, a child advocacy system needed to be developed to coordinate juvenile justice, education, child welfare, and mental health services. Finally, mental health service providers needed to apply for federal Alcohol, Drug Abuse & Mental Health (ADM) block grant funds for children's services. This report seems to have provided the impetus for commitment to the mental health needs of children to a degree that had not been observed before.

CHILD AND ADOLESCENT SERVICE SYSTEM PROGRAM

The Child and Adolescent Service System Program (CASSP) was developed in 1984 to address the concerns raised in the *Unclaimed Children* report (Hartley *et al.,* 2002). Specifically, the CASSP sought to remedy the lack of attention, lack of services, and lack of interagency coordination for youth with SED (Hartley *et al.,* 2002). The CASSP was initially housed within the National Institute of Mental Health. In 1992, under the Alcohol, Drug Abuse, and Mental Health Services Reconciliation Act (P.L. 102-321) it became part of the new Center for Mental Health Services. While CASSP has had multiple homes and names, the essence of the program has been unwavering. The goals of the program have been:

- To improve access to and the availability of a continuum of care for children and adolescents with serious emotional disturbances and their families,

- To develop leadership capacity and increase funding priority for child and adolescent mental health services,

- To promote more and better coordination and collaboration among child-serving agencies,

- To promote full family participation in all aspects of planning and service delivery,

- To ensure that services are structured and delivered so as to maximize their efficacy within the cultural context of the client, and
- To evaluate the progress of states and communities in improving systems of care for this population (Hartley et.al., 2002).

The Child and Adolescent Service System Program finally addressed the unique needs of youth with SED. The CASSP and its successes lead to the development of the Comprehensive Community Mental Health Services Program for Children and their Families (Grob, 1991). To date, it is the largest mental health program serving youth with SED (SAMHSA, 2003).

COMPREHENSIVE COMMUNITY MENTAL HEALTH SERVICES PROGRAM

The Comprehensive Community Mental Health Services Program for Children and their Families, built on the earlier success of the CASSP. In 1992, the program which is administered by The Center for Mental Health Services by the Child, Adolescent and Family Branch, was authorized to provide funding to communities to develop and build the infrastructure needed to deliver multi-agency and multi-disciplinary services to youth with SED (SAMHSA, 2003). Six year grants were made available to states, communities, Territories and Indian tribes, or tribal organizations to improve or expand services. To receive funding, agencies needed to serve the target population, youth with SED. The Comprehensive Community Mental Health Services Program SAMHSA, 2000, Data Collection Procedure Manual, Section 5, defined SED as:

> Limited to children and adolescents under 22 years of age and their family. Client eligibility requires the presence of an emotional, behavioral, or mental disorder diagnosable under DSM-IV diagnostic categories or their ICD-9-CM equivalents of subsequent revisions (with the exception of DSM-IV "V" codes,substance use disorders, and developmental disorders, unless they co-occur with another diagnosable serious emotional disturbance). Client eligibility should be defined based on the basis of degree or level of functioning. Inability to perform in the family, school, and/or community is the basic factor that determines the

> need for services. Children and adolescents must have service needs involving two or more community agencies, such as mental health, substance abuse, health, education, juvenile justice, or child welfare. The disability must be present for at least one year or, on the basis of diagnosis and intensity, be expected to last more than 1 year (page 3).

Further, to receive funding, grant recipients needed to develop non-federal match funds (SAMHSA, 2003). In the initial phase of the grant, communities needed to provide $1 for every $3 federal dollars. Over time, communities were responsible for $2 match funds for every $1 of federal money. Additionally, communities needed to agree to provide the following services: diagnosis and evaluation, outpatient treatment, emergency services, intensive home based treatment, day treatment services, transitional and case management services, and respite care (SAMHSA, 2003). The goals of the CMHS Comprehensive Community Mental Health Services Program were to:

- Expand the service capacity in communities that have developed an infrastructure for a community based, interagency approach to serving children and adolescents in the target population,

- Provide a broad array of mental health services that are community based, family centered and tailored to meet the needs of the child or adolescent through an individualized service planning process, and

- Ensure the full involvement of families in the development of local services and in the care of their children and adolescents (SAMHSA, 2003).

The Comprehensive Community Mental Health Services Program for Children and their Families espoused a four point philosophy that guided treatment for youth with SED. The program specified that:

- Mental health service systems should be driven by the needs and preferences of the child and family, and address these needs through a strength-based approach,

- The focus and management of services should occur within a multi-agency collaborative environment and be grounded in a strong community base,

- The services offered, the agencies participating, and the programs generated should be responsive to the cultural context and characteristics of the populations served, and

- Families should be partners in the planning, implementing and evaluating of the system of care (SAMHSA, 2004).

Since its inception in 1992, the program has funded ninety-two sites across the nation (SAMHSA, 2003). These sites have operated under the system of care model developed by Stroul and Freidman (1986). The system of care model provides the sites, the social service providers, and the program participants with a philosophical lens with which to view service delivery.

EDUCATIONAL MOVEMENT AFFECTING YOUTH MENTAL HEALTH

At the same time as services to youth with SED were being evaluated within the mental health arena, the public educational system was reconsidering how to meet the needs of students with special educational needs (Minkoff, 1987). In 1975, the Department of Health, Education, and Welfare commissioned the Project on the Classification of Exceptional Children. The study concluded that "services for all kinds of children remain a tangled thicket of conceptual confusions, competing authorities, contrary purposed, and professional rivalries, leading to the fragmentation of services and the lack of sustained attention to the needs of individual children and their families" (Hobbs, 1975 as cited in Dougherty, Saxe, Cross, & Silverman, 1987, p. 20). The authors recommended that all disabled students, including those with emotional disabilities, be educated in the public school system. Further, the commission suggested that in an attempt to reduce labeling, disabilities be categorized, not students. Finally, services needed to be planned and coordinated. The commission felt that because they served all children, schools were obvious leaders and advocates (Minkoff, 1987).

As a result of the findings of the Project on the Classification of Exceptional Children, the Education for All Handicapped Children Act (P. L. 94-142) passed in 1975. This historic legislation guaranteed that students with special education needs received a free and appropriate education in the least restrictive environment. The act, and its successor, the Individuals with Disabilities Education Act (P.L. 107-476) of 1990, and its amended version, such as Individuals with Disabilities Education Act of June of 1997 (IDEA '97) (P.L. 105-17), mandated Individualized Education Programs (IEP) to address the unique needs of each student. The IEP process also integrated multiple service providers, such as mental health workers, speech therapists, and regular education teachers, together to coordinate a plan of service for a child. Further, the IEP process required parental involvement (National Dissemination Center for Children with Disabilities, 2001).

All of the aforementioned legislation provided important protections to youth with emotional and behavioral disorders. School districts had to make accommodations, such as smaller class size or behavior management systems, to address difficulties in learning. The students were not only guaranteed of an appropriate education, but school officials now had to consider the affect a student's disability had on his or her behavior (National Dissemination Center for Children with Disabilities, 2001). For example, if an inappropriate behavior was related to the disability (*i.e.,* emotional outbursts if diagnosed with intermittent explosive disorder) the youth could not be expelled from school or excessively suspended.

Perhaps most important to youth with SED, Individuals with Disabilities Education Act of 1997 (IDEA '97) required schools to provided 'related services' that students needed to be successful (Section 300.347 (a) (3)). Related services could include: speech-language pathology, audiology services, psychological services, physical and occupational therapy, therapeutic recreation, early identification and assessment of disabilities, counseling services, orientation and mobility services, medical services for diagnostic evaluation purposes, school health services, social work services in schools, parent counseling and training, and transportation (Section 300.24 (a)). If the IEP team determined that a youth needs related services, the school district must provide the services to the child free of charge. It should be noted that the law does not prohibit the school district or its contract agencies from billing Medicaid or other insurances for provided services as long as parents do not incur co-pays or limitation of lifetime benefits (National Dissemination Center for Children with Disabilities, 2001).

Schools were now mandated to address the mental health needs of students whose need level precluded their school success by providing services typically thought to be mental health services. In fact, subsequent ratification *expanded* the definition of psychological services schools may be obligated to provide to include:

- Administering psychological and educational tests;
- Interpreting assessment results,
- Obtaining, integrating, and interpreting information about a student's behavior and conditions related to learning,
- Consulting with other staff members in planning school programs to meet the special needs of children as indicated by psychological tests, interviews, and behavioral evaluations, and
- Planning and managing a program of psychological services, including psychological counseling for students and parents, and assisting in developing positive behavioral intervention strategies (Section 300.24 (b) (9)).

TRUE INTERDISCIPLINARY COLLABORATION BEGINS...

Because IDEA '97 specifications required involving delivery of related services, specifically those related to mental health treatment, school districts and mental health service providers became necessary allies in serving youth with SED. School educators, social workers, school counselors, and school psychologists could address some of the aforementioned tasks, but the duration, intensity, and specialization of services, such as consultation with a psychiatrist or extensive training in therapeutic techniques, required to work with youth with SED require a partnership with community mental health providers. The philosophies of IDEA regarding parental involvement, service delivery in the least restrictive environment, individualized plans, and collaboration and coordination with other providers mirrors some of the assumptions of current mental health legislation. Following the requirements of IDEA '97, schools were primed to partner with mental health agencies in serving youth with SED (National Dissemination Center for Children with Disabilities, 2001). IDEA '97 allows for necessary related services to be contracted out to appropriate agencies and service providers, such as local mental health centers and the social workers and therapists they employ. As a result of the partnership, school districts and mental health centers collaborated to serve emotionally and behaviorally disturbed youth. In part, the youth served could be identified as SED because they had a persistent mental illness and were served by two agencies, and, thus were eligible to receive treatment in a system of care model.

THE SYSTEM OF CARE MODEL

In the previous section, the evolution of modern children's mental health history were reviewed. Many policies, reports, and programs lead to the development and use of the system of care model. In this section, the philosophies of the system of care model will be explored.

Stroul and Freidman (1986) developed the system of care model. The model consists of three core values and ten guiding principles. The core values are:

1. The system of care should be child centered and family focused, with the needs of the child and the family dictating the types and mix of services provided.

2. The system of care should be community based, with the locus of services as well as the management and decision making responsibility resting at the community level.

3. The system of care should be culturally competent, with agencies, programs, and services that are responsive to the cultural, racial, and ethnic differences of the population they serve.

The ten guiding principles are:

1. Children with emotional disturbances should have access to a comprehensive array of services that address their physical, emotional, social, and educational needs.

2. Children with emotional disturbances should receive individualized services in accordance with the unique needs and potentials of each child and guided by an individualized service plan.

3. Children with emotional disturbances should receive services within the least restrictive, most normative environment that is clinically appropriate.

4. The families and surrogate families of children with emotional disturbances should be full participants in all aspects of planning and delivering services.

5. Children with emotional disturbances should receive services that are integrated, with linkages between child-serving agencies and programs and mechanisms for planning, developing, and coordinating services.

6. Children with emotional disturbances should be provided with case management or similar mechanisms to ensure that multiple services are delivered in a coordinated and therapeutic manner and that they can move through the system of services in accordance with changing needs.

7. Early identification and intervention for children with emotional disturbances should be promoted by the system of care in order to enhance the likelihood of positive outcomes.

8. Children with emotional disturbances should be ensured a smooth transition to the adult service system as they reach maturity.

9. The rights of children with emotional disturbances should be protected and effective advocacy efforts for children and adolescents with emotional disturbances should be promoted.

10. Children with emotional disturbances should receive services without regard to race, religion, national origin, sex, physical disability, or other characteristics, and services should be sensitive and responsive to cultural differences and special needs (pp. 3-15).

In addition to the core values and guiding principles, the authors articulated the mental health services to be provided within the system of care model. The outpatient services range from prevention programs to children's day treatment to crisis stabilization. Residential services include living situations like therapeutic foster and group homes, residential treatment centers, and the most restrictive environment, inpatient. The SOC model recognized the multiple layers and complex needs that may occur in a child's life and attempted to provide some integration in service coordination The SOC model sought to provide additional linkages at the mesosystem level by holding interagency staffings and requiring a unified treatment plan (Stroul & Freidman, 1986).

Consider the example of a student not attending school regularly because of poor academic functioning. A system of care worker may recognize that the student avoids school because he has a learning disability that has not been properly diagnosed. The caseworker helps bring together the student, family, special educators, and mental health providers to match access to assistance with level of need. In this case, goodness of fit is achieved by the student, school representatives, and others coming together to address the attendance problem by way of appropriate special education service provision. Youths' needs for goodness of fit (Bronfenbrenner, 1979; Germain & Gitterman, 1980) are addressed in the system of care model through the guiding principles of providing individualized services (principle #1), coordination of integrated services (principles #5 and #6), and advocacy efforts (principle #9) (Stroul &Freidman, 1986). Natural Environment/Life Space (Assumption #3-5). An example of *disregarding* SOC principles and assumptions might be said to occur when a youth who lives in the inner city and is sent to a wilderness program instead of being served in his or her natural environment.

DOES A SYSTEM OF CARE IMPROVE TREATMENT OUTCOMES?

This section will review community based treatment services. Providing treatment in a home community is purported to be beneficial to the individual and is required by law (Grob, 1989; Fields & Ogle, 2002; Keisler, 1993; Minkoff, 1987; Munetz & Geller, 1993). The concepts embodied in deinstitutionalization (Grob, 1989) and IDEA (P.L. 94-142, P.L. 107-476, & P.L. 105-17) promoted service delivery in the most appropriate and least restrictive environment (Stroul & Freidman, 1986). The research involving outpatient settings, home based programs, children's day treatment, and case management services eventually led to the concept of "bundling" services in a system of care model.

Outpatient Treatment: Outpatient services can be defined as "an intervention designed to decrease distress, psychological symptoms, and maladaptive behavior or to improve adaptive and prosocial functioning" (Kazdin, 1991, p. 785). Psychotherapy is perhaps the outpatient intervention preference of mental health professionals has shown mixed results with children and adolescents. Youth involved in this type of treatment conducted in controlled laboratory settings, mostly university training centers, have reportedly fared better than their counterparts who did not receive treatment (*e.g.,*a meta-analysis conducted by Weisz, Donenberg, Han, & Kauneckis, 1995). It should be noted that no treatment modality (*i.e.,* behavior interventions, social skills training, art and play therapy) was used universally in the studies that were included in the meta-analysis. However, once outpatient treatment was delivered in the 'real world setting' of mental health clinics, the results were not as promising. Multiple investigations have concluded that there were no clinical differences between the treatment and control groups either during or following outpatient treatment (*e.g.,*Weisz & Jenson, 1999; Antonuccio, Danton, & DeNelsky, 1995; Salzar, Bickman, Lambert, 1999).

Home Based Programs: Home based services include intervention strategies referred to by a variety of designations such as family preservation services, in-home services, family centered services, family based services, or intensive family services (Kutash & Robbins Rivera, 1996). Treatment is characterized by providing services in the home or other environments that fit the need of the family, flexible service delivery hours to meet the needs of families, small caseloads, an emphasis on family empowerment, and coordinating services in the community (Stroul & Goldman, 1990). The costs associated with delivering home based services are appreciable but less than placing children out of the home. Cost comparisons, suggesting expenditure differentials, such as the estimate that home based services cost between $3,000 -$5,000, whereas out of home placements-- foster care, group home, detention, residential treatment, and psychiatric hospitalization-- range from $5,000 to $40,000 (Henggeler, Melton, & Smith, 1992; Kinney Haapala, & Booth, 1991; Behar, 1990), clearly indicate that home based services can make economic sense. Home based services have also been shown to be effective in producing positive clinical outcomes. One example of an effective home based approach is Multisystemic Treatment (MST).The Surgeon General, in the 2001 report on youth violence, named MST as a best practices model. MST has consistently demonstrated positive results with chronic juvenile offenders (Henggeler, Schoenwald, Borduin, Rowland, & Cunningham, 1998; Henggeler, 1996; Henggeler, Melton, & Smith, 1992; Henggeler, Melton, & Smith, Schoenwald, & Hanley, 1993). When compared to youth who received traditional outpatient services, youth involved with MST had fewer arrests and a general decrease in symptomology. Families also reported fewer behavior problems and more family cohesion following MST.

For example: Homebuilders is a well-known family preservation program (Forsythe, 1992; Kinney, Haapala, & Booth, 1991). Those receiving this home based care were not only more likely to have their family intact at a one year follow-up than were recipients of other methods, they also experienced positive outcomes such as decreases in delinquent behavior and increases in school adjustment, behavioral improvement at home, and increased participation and parental supervision.

Children's Day Treatment: Children's Day Treatment (CDT) is the one of the most intensive nonresidential program available (Stroul & Friedman, 1986). Treatment can take place in either a special educational classroom or partial hospitalization setting. In both settings, treatment is characterized by an emphasis on behavior modification, interpersonal skills building, educational and vocational training, and group, individual, and family counseling. Costs descriptions range from $10,000- $15,000 per year for full day CDT (Grizenko & Papineau, 1992; Parker & Knoll, 1990; Kiser, Acherman, & Pruitt, 1987) to $41 per day for three hours of service (Robinson, Dow, & Nicholas, 1999) and do not clearly support a strong economic argument for CDT. The authors offering the above cost comparison suggested that the daily costs of CDT are less expensive than hospitalization, but acknowledged that youth stay in CDT longer than hospitalized youth.

The existing research generally supports the notion that CDT produces modest positive clinical outcomes (*e.g.,* Robinson & Rapport, 2002; Vernberg, Jacobs, Nyre, Puddy, Roberts; 2004; Kostrun, Brown, & Brown; 1990; Canton & Weiss, 1994). The aforementioned studies all involved youth with SED who were treated either at school or in partial hospitalization settings. To offer a specific example, Robinson and Rapport conducted a study of a CDT program (N=142) held in a public school. They found that participants improved with nine months of treatment. Fifty percent had symptom reduction and nearly a quarter of participants score in 'normal' range on the Youth Outcomes Questionnaire.

Case Management Services: The Social Work Dictionary defined case management as "a procedure to plan, seek, and monitor services from different social service agencies or staff on behalf of a client." (Barker, 1995, p. 47). Case management typically involves multidimensional assessment, linking and brokering services, and coordination of resources. Stroul and Friedman (1986) referred to case management as the "backbone of the system of care" (p. 265). There are many ways in which case management can be implemented. Robinson (1991) conceptualized four models of case management, while Burns, Gwaltney, and Bishop (1995) identified seven. The comprehensiveness of case management varies within each model. Given there is no universally accepted way in which case management services are delivered and the multiple models that dictate intensity of services provided, no cost comparisons were reported (Kutash & Robbins Rivera, 1996) and would be difficult. However, the Fort Bragg project reported a daily cost of $53 for case management services (Bickman, Guthrie, Foster, Lambert, Summerfelt, Breda, & Heflinger, 1995).

Findings regarding the effectiveness of case management services are varied. Burns, Farmer, Angold, Costello, and Behar (1995) examined the use of therapist case managers compared to case managers who coordinated a treatment team. Participants were labeled with SED and received services from a community mental health center. The case manager/treatment team approach resulted in an increase in desired case management service outcomes such as outreach, monitoring, linking, and advocacy, and positive parental regard towards the mental health system. However, there were no functional differences between the groups on outcomes as measured by the Child and Adolescent Functional Assessment (CAFAS).

In conclusion, the journey to provide comprehensive care to children with SED and their families has spanned decades. The SOC model has risen to the top as a best practices model for several pivotal reasons. First, it is a philosophy that engages all service providers to coordinate care and share resources. Second, it places the child and family as the point of focus. System of Care embraces the community, acknowledges the least restrictive level of care, and breaks down 'silos of communication' existing in bureaucratic public sector services. Finally, SOC demonstrates that effective service delivery in the child and family's natural environment can be cost effective and have sustainable results. In closing out this chapter, the following case study is provided to illustrate how a SOC could function for a child with SED and his family.

SYSTEM OF CARE MODEL CASE STUDY: AN APPLIED EXAMPLE

Helping Ben to Improve Functioning at Home, School, and in the Community. Ben is a thirteen year old male. He receives special education services resulting from his evaluation results indicating he met the labeling parameters of having an emotional/behavioral disturbance. Ben was identified as needing services in the 1st grade and is currently served in a self-contained classroom setting. Ben was referred to the System of Care Program by the Juvenile Court. Ben was placed on probation as a result of being adjudicated delinquent. Ben appeared before the court on three charges: disturbing school, making threats towards a teacher and assistant principal, and assault with subsequent injury.

HISTORY OF SCHOOL PROBLEMS

Ben's mother, Crystal, reported that Ben has had problems at school all his life. Mom reported that Ben has been enrolled in special education since he was in the 1st grade. Since Ben was in the 4th grade, he has had problems controlling his anger and has been sent home on multiple occasions for hitting others, disrupting the classroom by refusing to work, and/or having a tantrum. Mom also reported that "Ben can't read." Ben was placed in a self-contained classroom for 'emotionally disturbed' students in the 4th grade. He also has an identified reading disorder.

The most recent problems at school resulted in juvenile justice involvement. Ben and Mom said the police were called and Ben had to go to court this time because he broke Miss Hill's (his teacher) wrist when he threw a desk at her. During the same incident, Ben told other staff members (Mrs. Whitley, the assistant principal; Mr. Roland, the classroom aide) that he was "going to kill them."

Ben has been suspended twice this school year -- once was for the current incident and the other for a fight on the school bus involving another student with a disability. This is the first time that the police have pressed charges and he has been adjudicated by the court. During this school year, Ben has had 14 write-ups for behavior violations. School reports indicate that Ben has spit, bitten, kicked, and hit peers and school staff. Consequences included restricted classroom privileges, loss of social lunch, recess time replaced by trash detail, in-school suspension, and a referral to the community mental health center for an assessment.

Mom reported that Ben's problems have gotten worse since he started middle school. She is worried that Ben picks fights with some of the older and larger youth. She also thinks that the middle school staff are quicker to "call the police than they should." Mom reported that Ben is more withdrawn than he has ever been. He refuses to engage with her and spends most of his time alone in his bedroom.

Ben said he acts out when "people make him mad." Ben said he does not like to be told what to do and if he "don't want to do something, nobody can make him."

When questioned about the most recent school incident, he said "Miss Hill was pissing me off. She wanted me to sit and do math. She knows I hate math and I hate her." Ben also reported, "I am always tired and people are always bothering me. I just want to be left alone. No one likes me so why should I like them….?"

Ben's teacher, Miss Hill, and the assistant principal, Mrs. Whitley, reported that Ben has difficulty with most assignments, is often off task, fails to complete homework, and reads at a 2nd grade level. Miss Hill reports that Ben escalates his and others' behaviors by first getting angry and aggressive and afterward often becoming frustrated and sad. Ben cries when he is frustrated. This behavior is often mocked by peers which perpetuates Ben's cycle of frustration. School personnel reported that Ben has impaired and immature peer interactions. He is easily frustrated and often provokes peers. He yells out in class and wanders around the classroom at will. Mrs. Whitley reports that Ben especially likes to "pick on and name call" the students with physical disabilities. This occurs primarily on the school bus. School personnel agree that Ben understands the behavior management system; however, he has little interest in working for the classroom privileges. Ben has the best relationship with Mr. Roland, one of the classroom aides.

School personnel also reported that Mom has been uncooperative. The school personnel have difficulty reaching her by phone and she lacks the transportation to pick up Ben when he is in trouble. Miss Hill reported that Mom has not attended an Individual Education Plan (IEP) meeting in three years.

RELATIONSHIPS WITH FAMILY

The family consists of the following members: Ben (age 13), Mom (Crystal, age 36), maternal grandmother (Janie, age 53), and half-brother, Elijah (age 20). Elijah does not live with the family as he is currently incarcerated for four years for possession and intent to distribute heroin. Ben reports that everyone "pretty much gets along. We go in our own rooms and watch TV. Sometimes I fight with grandma when she is drunk and turns the TV up too loud." Ben reports that they do not eat meals together. When asked about how often Ben gets in trouble at home for aggression towards Mom or other family members, Mom states, "None

– I whip his butt so he don't try that at home". Ben said he "gets his butt kicked once a week" by Mom because he "cuts the fool" by talking back or yelling at Grandma."

Ben reports that there are no family rules. He said he does not have a curfew and can go to bed whenever he wants. Ben stays awake watching TV until 2am. Ben has run away on two occasions; he returned home both times after 48 hours. Ben did "get his butt whipped" last month when he hit grandma with a wrench following a fight about the TV. Ben and Mom agreed that there are no consequences when Ben gets in trouble at school.

RELATIONSHIPS WITH PEERS

Ben says he "only has one or two friends." When asked about how his aggression impacts those friends, Ben stated "I mostly hit people I don't like." Ben said he is friends with Adam and that they play basketball when they have earned recess. Ben reports that he "does not like most people because they don't like him." Ben is capable of pointing out the flaws of others, but sees little relationship between his own behaviors and the way people treat him.

School personnel report Ben has impaired and immature peer interactions. He engages in behaviors such as name calling and picking his nose in order to antagonize other students. Ben is easily frustrated and often provokes peers when he wants their attention. Teachers described Ben as a follower.

MENTAL HEALTH NEEDS

Ben was referred by the school to the community mental health center for a psychiatric assessment. The psychiatric assessment was completed by Dr. McKenzie who diagnosed Ben with the following: Attention Deficit Hyperactivity Disorder, Oppositional Defiant Disorder, Major Depression, and a Reading Disorder. Ben was prescribed Adderall XR™ for ADHD™ and Cymbalta and Abilify™ for depression. The medications are monitored at a monthly medication check appointment.

Ben is also seen by clinical social worker, Mr. Barker, twice a month for individual therapy. Treatment goals include social skills training and cognitive restructuring to deal with symptoms of depression. Ben is also participating in a weekly anger management group as ordered by the juvenile court. Mr. Barker reports that Ben is compliant with the monthly medication checks but has missed 50% of individual and group meetings. Phone calls to Mom have gone unreturned.

Ben was hospitalized last month for suicidal ideation. Mom called the police because Ben was on the roof of the trailer threatening to jump so he "would die and everyone would leave him alone." Ben was transported to the local hospital and held for three days for observation and stabilization. He was discharged into Mom's care and follow-up care is to be provided by the mental health center.

JUVENILE COURT INVOLVEMENT

Ben was adjudicated delinquent this year as a result of the three charges (disturbing school, making threats towards a teacher and assistant principal, and assault) that occurred at school. Ben was placed on probation for a minimum of one year. Ben was assigned to probation officer, Mr. Sheeler, for monitoring. Ben was ordered to attend school and stay out of trouble, to be compliant with the recommendations of the treatment staff at the mental health center, to participate in an anger management group, to complete 20 hours of community service, and to report monthly to his probation officer.

ENVIRONMENTAL FACTORS THAT INFLUENCE FUNCTIONING

The family has minimal recourses. Mom works part-time at gas station and makes approximately $800 per month. The family receives approximately $350 in SNAP benefits. Janie, Crystal's mother who lives with them, contributes her $500 per month SSDI check. Ben has health coverage through S-CHIP and gets a free breakfast and lunch at school. Mom states that they run out of money each month and are typically behind on their bills. The family lives in a double-wide trailer in a trailer park. The family does not have a car and uses public transportation. Mom indicated that she does not like to use social services because she "don't want people in my business". Mom stated she does not have friends and does little socializing with the neighbors.

SYSTEM OF CARE INTERVENTION/RECOMMENDATIONS

Ben was admitted to the System of Care Program due to his classification as a youth with a severe emotional disturbance and his involvement with multiple social service agencies (school, mental health, juvenile court). Ben and Mom met with their System of Care case manager, Ms. Ford, to assess strengths and needs.

A unified plan of action was developed to improve functioning at home, school, and in the community. Ms. Ford began working with Mom to see how she could assist Ben. Mom is resistant to working with service providers because she is fearful they "blame me for Ben's behavior and I don't always understand what they tell me." Ms. Ford will meet with Ben and Mom at least three times per week during the initial work with the System of Care Program. Additional contact will be made with Mom *via* phone. Ms. Ford will also have weekly contact with the service providers at school, the mental health center, and the juvenile court in order to coordinate care. Ms. Ford is going to accompany Mom to appointments at school and with other providers to help model for Mom expectations and to clarify any questions she might have. This will also improve attendance at meetings and appointments since transportation will no longer be a barrier.

Ms. Ford is working with Ben and Mom to develop a behavior management plan at home which reinforces behavior at school. Ms. Ford is helping the family establish family rules and routines that will help Ben be successful at school. The plan includes having a set bed time so that Ben can be rested for the school day, and using an assignment book so that Mom and the school staff can communicate in writing about homework and other issues. Mom will sign the book each night to verify that homework is completed. Mom and Ben are also going to come up with a list of privileges that Ben will earn based on his school behavior. For example, Mom agreed to remove the TV from Ben's room until school behavior improves. Not having a TV in the bedroom should also remedy sleeping problems. If sleep hygiene does not improve, Mom will talk with Dr. McKenzie at the next medication monitoring appointment to discuss pharmacological interventions.

The System of Care Program is also going to pay for a trained behavioral aide to shadow Ben for a maximum of 20 hours a week. The hours will be split equally between school (2 hours per day 5 days a week) and home (3 hours on Tuesdays and Thursdays and 3 hours on Saturday). The behavioral aide will work on social skills with Ben. The skills will focus on having an appropriate conversation with a friend and how to express frustration in a socially acceptable manner. Opportunities to practice skills in a natural environment will be utilized. The System of Care Program will look into day camp opportunities for the summer breaks so that skills can continue to be developed.

A monthly meeting will be facilitated by the System of Care Program to discuss Ben's progress and address any barriers. Representatives from the school, mental health center, juvenile court, and the System of Care Program will be invited to participate. The participants will be encouraged to coordinate treatment plans so that they efforts of each compliment and support the work of the other agencies. Ben and Mom will be given an opportunity to share concerns with the participants at each meeting. The case plan will be monitored and modified as needed.

CONCLUSION

A system of care for promoting mental health for students, especially for students with existing mental health challenges, should not and cannot be the sole responsibility of schools. This chapter discusses a system of care for meeting the mental health requisites of students most in need for support and intervention. It necessitates the participation of many agencies and the expertise and involvement of the community to ensure that children's best interests are fully and effectively met School can serve as the logical and most therapeutic focal point for mental health promotion in children and adolescents. It clearly needs to be part of the solution of meeting their mental health needs, though should not bear the sole responsibility for clinical outcome. As the often repeated axiom reminds us, it takes a village to raise a child.

ACKNOWLEDGEMENT

Declare none.

CONFLICT OF INTEREST

The author(s) confirm that this chapter content has no conflict of interest.

REFERENCES

Ad Hoc Committee on Child Mental Health (1971). *Ad hoc committee on child mental health: Report to the director.* Rockville, MD: National Institute on Mental Health.

Althoff, R.R., Rettew, D.C., & Hudzaik, J.J. (2003). Attention-deficit/hyperactivity disorder, oppositional defiant disorder, and conduct disorder. *Psychiatric Annals, 33(4),* 245-252.

American Psychiatric Association (2000). *Diagnostic and Statistical Manual of Mental Disorders,* 4th Edition, Text Revised. Washington, D.C.: American Psychiatric Association.

American Psychiatric Association (1994). *Diagnostic and Statistical Manual of Mental Disorders,* 4th Edition. Washington, D.C.: American Psychiatric Association.

Anderson, J.C., Williams, S., McGee, R., & Silva, P.A. (1987). DSM-III disorders in preadolescence children: prevalence in a large sample from the general population. *Archives of General Psychiatry, 44(1),* 69-76.

Antonuccio, D.O., Danton, W.G., & DeNelsky, G.Y. (1995). Psychotherapy *versus* medication for depression: challenging the conventional wisdom with data. *Professional Psychology: Research and Practice, 26,* 574-585.

Babinski, L.M., Hartough, C.S., & Lambert, N.M. (1999). Childhood conduct problems, hyperactivity-impulsivity, and inattention as predictors of adult criminal activity. [Electronic version]. *Journal of Child Psychology and Psychiatry, 40(3),* 347-355.

Behar, L. (1990). Financing mental health services for children and adolescents. [Electronic version]. *Bulletin of the Menninger Clinic,* 54, 127-140.

Barker, R.L. (1995).*The Social Work Dictionary* (3rd ed.). Washington, D.C.: NASW Press.

Bauermeister, J.J., Canino, G., & Bird, H.R. (2001). Epidemiology of disruptive behavior disorders. *Child and Adolescent Psychiatry of Clinics in North American, 3,* 177-194.

Befera, M.S. & Barkley, R.A. (1985). Hyperactive and normal girls and boys: Mother-child interaction, parent psychiatric status and child psychopathology. *Journal of Child Psychology and Psychiatry, 26(3),* 439-452.

Bickman, L., Foster, M., & Lambert, W. (1996). Who gets hospitalized in a continuum of care? [Electronic version]. *Journalof the American Academy of Child and Adolescent Psychiatry, 35,* 74-81.

Bickman, L., Guthrie, P.R., Foster, E.M., Lambert, E.W., Summerfelt, W.T., Breda, C.S., & Heflinger, C.A. (1995). *Evaluating managed mental health services: The Fort Bragg experiments.* New York: Plenum Press.

Biederman, J., Faraone, S.V., Milberger, S., Jetton, J.G., Chen, L., Mick, E., Greene, R.W., & Russell, R.L. (1996). Is childhood oppositional defiant disorder a precursor to adolescent conduct disorder? Findings from a four-year follow-up study of children with ADHD. *Journal of the American Academy of Child and Adolescent Psychiatry, 35 (9),* 1193-1204.

Beiderman, J., Newcorn, J., & Sprich, S. (1991). Comorbidity of attention defect hyperactivity disorder with conduct, depressive, anxiety, and other disorders. *American Journal of Psychiatry, 148,* 564-577.

Bird, H.R., Canino, G., Rubio-Stepec, M., &Gould, M.S. (1988). Estimates of the prevalence of childhood maladjustment in a community survey in Puerto Rico: The use of combined measures. *Archives of General Psychiatry, 45(12),* 1120-1126.

Bronfenbrenner, U. (1979). *The ecology of human development: Experiments by nature and design.* Cambridge, MA: Harvard University Press.

Brooks, J.S., Whiteman, N.M., & Finch, S. (1992). Childhood aggression, adolescent delinquency, and drug use: A longitudinal study. *Journal of General Psychology, 153,* 369-383.

Burns, B.J., Gwaltney,E.A., & Bishop, G.K. (1995). Case management research: Issues and direction. In Friensen, & Poertner, J. (Eds.), *From case management to service coordination for children with emotional, behavioral, or mental disorders: Building on family strengths* (pp. 353-372). Baltimore: Paul H. Brooks Publishing Co.

Cantwell, D.P., & Baker, L. (1991). Association between attention deficit-hyperactivity disorder and learning disorders. *Journal of Learning Disabilities, 24,* 88-95.

Cantwell, D.P., & Baker, L. (1989). Stability and natural history of DSM-III childhood diagnoses. *Journal of the American Academy of Child and Adolescent Psychiatry, 28(5),* 691-700.

Catron, T., & Weiss, B. (1994). The Vanderbilt school-based counseling program: An interagency, primary care model of mental health services. [Electronic version]. *Journal of Emotional and Behavioral Disorders, 2(4),* 247-253.

Cohen, P., Cohen J., Kasen, S., Velez, C.N., Hartmark, C., Johnson, J., Rojas, M., Brook, J., & Streunonh, E.L. (1993). An epidemiological study of disorders in late childhood and adolescence, I: Age and gender specific prevalence. *Journal of Child Psychology and Psychiatry, 34 (6),* 851-867.

Cohen, D.E., & Leckman, J.F. (1989). Methylphenidate treatment of attention-deficit hyperactivity disorder in boys with Tourette's Syndrome: Commentary. *Journal of the American Academy of Child and Adolescent Psychiatry, 28(4),* 580-582.

Costello, E.J., Messer, S.C., Bird. H.R., Cohen, P., & Reinherz, H. Z. (1998). The prevalence of serious emotional disturbance: A re-analysis of community studies. [Electronic version]. *Journal of Child and Family Studies, 7(4),* 411-432.

Costello, E.J., Mustillo, S., Erkanli, A., Keller, G., & Angold, A. (2003). Prevalence and development of psychiatric disorders in childhood and adolescents. *Archives of General Psychiatry, 60(8),* 837-844.

Department of Health and Human Services: Substance Abuse and Mental Health Services Administration (2002). *National household survey on drug abuse: Volume I. Summary of national findings; Prevalence and treatment of mental health problems.*

Esser, G., Schmidt, M.H., & Woermer, W. (1990). Epidemiology and course of psychiatric disorders in school-age children: results of a longitudinal study. *Journal of Child Psychology and Psychiatry, 31(2),* 243-263.

Faraone, S.V., Beiderman, J., Lehman, B.K., Spencer, K., Norman, D., Seidman, L.J., Kraus, I., Perrin, J., & Chen, W.J. (1993). Intellectual performance and school failure in children with attention deficit hyperactivity disorder and in their siblings. *Journal of Abnormal Psychology, 102(4),* 616-623.

Fergusson, D. M., Horwood, L.J., & Lynskey, M. T. (1993). Prevalence and comorbidity of DSM-III diagnoses in a birth cohort of 15 year olds. *Journal of the American Academy of Child and Adolescent Psychiatry, 32 (6),* 1127-1134.

Ferro, T., Carlson, G.A., Grayson, P., Klein, D.N. (1994). Depressive disorders: Distinctions in childhood. *Journal of the American Academy of Child and Adolescent Psychiatry, 33(5),* 664-670.

Fields, S.A., & Ogles, B.M. (2002). The system of care for children and the least restrictive alternative: Legal origins and current concerns. [Electronic version]. *Children's Services: Social Policy, Research, and Practice, 5(2),* 75-93.

Fleming, J.E., & Offord, D.R. (1990). Epidemiology of childhood depressive disorders: A critical review. *Journal of the American Academy of Child and Adolescent Psychiatry, 29(4),* 571-580.

Forsythe, P. (1992). Homebuilders and family preservation. *Children and Youth Services Review, 14,* 37-47.

Frick, P.J., Kamphaus, R.W., Lahey, B.B., Loeber, R., Christ, M.G., Hart, E.L., & Tannenbaum, L.E. (1991). Academic under-achievement and the disruptive behavior disorders. *Journal of Consulting and Clinical Psychology, 59(2),* 289-294.

Geller, B., Fox, L.W., & Clark, K.A. (1994). Rate and predictors of prepubertal bipolarity during follow-up of 6 to 12 year old depressed children. *Journal of the AmericanAcademy of Child and Adolescent Psychiatry, 33(4),* 461-468.

Germain, C.B., and Gitterman, A. (1980). *The life model of social work practice* (2nd Ed.). New York: Columbia University Press.

Gittelman, R., Mannuzza, S., Shenker, R, & Bonagura, N. (1985). Hyperactive boys almost grown up, I: Psychiatric status. *Archives of General Psychiatry 42(10*), 937-947.

Green, D. (2005). History, Discussion and Review of a Best Practices Model for Service Deliveryfor the Homeless. *Social Work in Mental Health, 3(4),* 1-16.

Greene, R.W., Biederman, J., Zerwas, S., Monuteaux, M., Goring, J.C., & Faratone, S.V. (2002). Psychiatric comorbidity, family dysfunction, and social impairment in referred youth with oppositional defiant disorder. *American Journal of Psychiatry, 159(7),*1214-1224.

Greene, R.W., & Doyle, A.E. (1999). Towards a transactional conceptualization ofoppositional defiant disorder: implications for treatment and assessment. *Clinical Child and Family Psychology Review, 2(3),* 129-148.

Grizenko, N, & Papineau, D. (1992). A comparison of the cost-effectiveness of day treatment and residential treatment for children with severe behavior problems. *Canadian Journal of Psychiatry, 37(6),* 393-400.

Grob, G.N. (1994). *The mad among us: A history of the care of America's mentally ill.* New York: Free Press.

Guerra, N.G., & Slaby, R.G. (1989). Evaluative factors in social problem solving by aggressive boys. *Journal of Abnormal Child Psychology, 17(3),* 277-289.

Harrington, R., Fudge, H., Rutter, M., & Pickles, A. (1990). Adult outcomes of childhood and adolescent depression, I: Psychiatric status. *Archives of General Psychiatry, 47(5),* 465-473.

Harrington, R., Fudge, H., Rutter, M., & Pickles, A. (1991). Adult outcomes of childhood and adolescent depression, II: Links with antisocial disorders. *Journal of the American Academy of Child and Adolescent Psychiatry, 30(3),* 434-439.

Hartley, D., Bird, D.C., Lambert, D., & Coffin, J. (2002). *The role of community mental health centers as rural safety net providers: Working paper #30.* Portland, ME: Maine Rural Health Research Center.

Hechtman, L, & Oxford, D.R. (1994). Long-term outcome of disruptive disorders. *Child and Adolescent Psychiatry of Clinics in North America, 3,* 379-403.

Henggeler, S.W. (1996). *Treating serious anti-social behaviors in youth: The MST approach.* Washington, D.C.: Office of Juvenile Justice and Delinquency Prevention.

Henggeler, S.W., Melton, G.M., & Smith, L.A. (1992). Family preservation using Multisystemic therapy: an effective alternative to incarcerating serious juvenile offenders. [Electronic version]. *Journal of Consulting and Clinical Psychology, 60(6),* 953-961.

Henggeler, S.W., Melton, G.M., Smith, L.A., Schoenwald, S.K., & Hanley, J. H. (1993). Family preservation using Multisystemic treatment: Long-term follow-up to a clinical trial with serious juvenile offenders. *Journal of Child and Family Studies, 2(4),* 283-293.

Henggeler, S.W., Schoenwald, S.K., Borduin, C.M., Rowland, M.D., and Cunningham, P.B. (1998). Multisystemic treatment of antisocial behavior in children and adolescents. New York: Guilford.

Hinshaw, S.P., Lahey, B.B., & Hart, E.L. (1993). Issues of taxonomy and comorbidity in the development of conduct disorder. *Development & Psychopathology, 5(1-2),* 31-49.

Hoegerman, G.S., Resnick, R.J., & Schnoll, S.H. (1993). Attention defects in newly abstinent substance abusers: Childhood recollections and attention performance in thirty-nine subjects. *Journal of Addictive Diseased, 12(1),* 37-53.

Kashani, J.H., Carlson, G.A., Beck, N.C., & Hoeper, E.W. (1987). Depression, depressive symptoms, and depressed mood among a community sample of adolescents. *American Journal of Psychiatry, 144(7),* 931-934.

Kashani, J.H., McGee, R.O., Clarkson, S.E., Anderson, J.C., Walton, L. A., Williams, S., Silvia, P.A., Robins, A.J., Cytryn, L., & McKnew. (1983). Depression in a sample of 9-year old children: Prevalence and associated characteristics. *Archives of General Psychiatry, 40(11),* 1217-1223.

Kazdin, A. (1991). Effectiveness of psychotherapy with children and adolescents. Journal of *Consulting and Clinical Psychology, 59(6),* 785-798.

Keisler, C.A. (1993). Mental health policy and the psychiatric inpatient care of children. *Applied and Preventative Psychology, 2,* 91-99.

Keller, M.B., Lavori, P.W., Beardslee, W.R., & Wunder, J. (1992). The disruptive behavioral disorder in children and adolescents: Comorbidity and clinical course. *Journal of the American Academy of Child and Adolescent Psychiatry, 31(2),* 204-209.

Kendall, P.C. (1993). Cognitive-behavioral therapies with youth: Guiding theory, current status, and emerging development. *Journal of Consulting and Clinical Psychology, 61(2),* 235-247.

Kessler, R.C., McGonagle, K. A., Zhao, S., Nelson, C.B., Hughes, M., Eshleman, S., *et al.,* (1994). Lifetime and 12 month prevalence of DSM-III-R psychiatric disorders in the United States: Results from the National Comorbidity Survey. *Archives of General Psychiatry, 51(1),* 8-19.

Kim-Cohen, J., Caspi, A., Moffitt, T.E., Harrington, H., Milne, B.J., & Poulton, R. (2003). Prior juvenile diagnoses in adults with mental disorder: Developmental follow-back of a prospective-longitudinal cohort. *Archive of General Psychiatry, 60(7),* 709-717.

Kinney, J., Haapala, D., & Booth, C. (1991). Keeping families together: The Homebuilders model. New York: Aldine DeGruyter.

Kiser, L.J., Ackerman, B.J., & Pruitt, D.B. (1987). A comparison of intensive psychiatric services for children and adolescents: Cost of day treatment *versus* hospitalization. *International Journal of Partial Hospitalization, 4,* 17-27.

Klein, R.G., & Mannuzza, S. (1991). Long-term outcome of hyperactive children: A review. *Journal of the American Academy of Child and Adolescent Psychiatry, 30(3*), 383-387.

Knitzer, J. (1982). *Unclaimed children.* Washington, DC: Children's Defense Fund.

Kolvin, I., Barrett, M.L., Bhate, S.R., & Berney, T.P. (1991). The Newcastle Child Depression Project: Diagnosis and classification of depression. *British Journal of Psychiatry, 159(11),* 9-21.

Kosturn, C., Brown, N.L., & Brown, R.M. (1990). Day treatment and the behavior of emotionally disturbed children. *Journal of Social Behavior and Personality, 5(6*), 671-682.

Kovacs, M., Paulauskas, S., Gatsonis, C., & Richards, S.C. (1988). Depressive disorders in childhood, III: A longitudinal study of comorbidity with and risk for conduct disorders. *Journal of Affective Disorders, 15(3),* 205-217.

Kovacs, M., Gatsonis, C., Paulauskas, S., & Richards, S.C. (1989). Depressive disorders in childhood, IV: A longitudinal study of comorbidity with and risk for anxiety disorders. *Archives of General Psychiatry, 46(9),* 776-782.

Kutcher, S.P., Marton, D., & Korenblum, J. (1989). Relationships between psychiatric illness and conduct disorder in adolescents. *Canadian Journal of Psychiatry, 34(6),* 536-529.

Kuhne, M., Schachar, R., & Tannock, R. (1997). Impact of comorbid oppositional or conduct problems on attention-deficit hyperactivity disorder. *Journal of the American Academy of Child and Adolescent Psychiatry, 36(12),* 1715-1725.

Kutash, K., & Robbins Rivera, V. (1996). *What works in children's mental health: Uncovering answers to critical questions.* Baltimore: Paul H. Brooks Publishing Co.

Lavigne, J.V., Cicchetti, C., Gibbins, R.D., Binns, H.J., Larsen, L., & Devito, C. (2001). Oppositional defiant disorder with onset in preschool years: Longitudinal stability and pathways to other disorders. *Journal of the American Academy of Child and Adolescent Psychiatry, 40(12),* 1393-1400.

Lee, M, & Prentice, N.M. (1988). Interrelations of empathy, cognition, and moral reasoning with dimensions of juvenile delinquency. *Journal of Abnormal Clinical Psychology, 16(2),* 127-139.

Lewinsohn, P.M., Rohde, P., Klein, D.N., & Seeley, J.R. (1999). Natural course of adolescent major depressive disorders, I: continuity into young adulthood. *Journal of the American Academy of Child and Adolescent Psychiatry, 38(1),* 56-63.

Lewinsohn, P.H., Hops, H., Roberts, R.E., Seeley, J.R., & Andrews, J.A. (1993). Adolescent psychopathology, I: Prevalence and incidence of depression and other DSM-III-R in high school students. *Journal of Abnormal Psychology, 102(4),* 133-144.

Lewinsohn, P.M., Rohde, P., Seeley, J.R., & Fisher, S.A. (1993). Age-cohorts changes in the lifetime occurrence of depression and other mental disorders. *Journal of Abnormal Psychology, 102(1),* 110-120.

Lewinsohn, P.M., Duncan, E.M., Stanton, A.K., & Hautzinger, M. (1986). Age at first onset for nonbipolar depression. *Journal of Abnormal Psychology, 95(4),* 378-383.

Lewis, D.O., Yeager, C.A., Lovely, R., & Stein, A. (1994). A clinical follow-up of delinquent males: Ignored vulnerabilities, unmet needs, and the perpetuation of violence. *Journal of the American Academy of Child and Adolescent Psychiatry, 33(4),* 518-528.

Lewis, D.O., Yeager, C.A., Cobham-Porterreal, C.S., & Klein, N. (1991). A follow-up of female delinquents: Maternal contributions to the perpetuation of deviance. *Journal of the American Academy of Child and Adolescent Psychiatry, 30(2),* 197-201.

Lewis, D.O., Lovely, R., Yeager, C, & della Femina, D. (1989). Toward a theory of the genesis of violence: A follow-up study of delinquents. *Journal of the American Academy of Child and Adolescent Psychiatry, 28(3),* 431-436.

Loeber, R., Green, S.M., Keenan, K., & Lahey, B.B.(1995). Which boys will fare worse? Early predictors for the onset of conduct disorder in a six-year longitudinal study. *Journal of the American Academy of Child and Adolescent Psychiatry, 34(4),* 599-509.

Loeber, R., Burke, J.D., Lahey, B.B., Winters, A., & Zera, M. (2000). Oppositional defiant disorder and conduct disorder: A review of the last 10 years, part I. *Journal of the American Academy of Child and Adolescent Psychiatry, 39(12),* 1468-1484.

Mannuzza, S., Klein, R.G., Bessler, A., Malloy, P., & LaPadula, M. (1998). Adult psychiatric status of hyperactive boys grown up. *American Journal of Psychiatry, 50(7),* 493-498.

McGee, R., Feehan, M., Williams, S., Partridge, F., Silva, P.A., & Kelly, J. (1990). DSM-II disorders in a large sample of adolescents. *Journal of the American Academy of Child and Adolescent Psychiatry, 29(4),* 611-619.

Minkoff, K. (1987). Beyond deinstitionalization: a new ideology for the Postinstitutional era. *Hospital and Community Psychiatry, 38,* 945-950.

Morrissey, J.P., & Goldman, H.H. (1984). Cycles of reform in the care of the chronically mentally ill. *Hospital in Community Psychiatry, 35(8),* 785-793.

Munetz, M.R., & Geller, J.L. (1993). The least restrictive alternative in the postinstitional era. *Hospital and Community Psychiatry, 38,* 967-973.

Narrow, W.E., Reiger, D.A., Goodman, S.H., Rae, D.S., Roper, M.T., Bourdon, K. H., Hover, C., & Moore, R. (1998). A comparison of federal definitions of severe mental illness among children and adolescents in four communities. [Electronic version]. *Psychiatric Services, 49(12),* 1601-1608.

National Advisory Committee on Rural Health (2002*). A Targeted Look at the Rural Health Care Safety Net: A Report to the Secretary.* U.S. Department of Health and Human Services. Washington, DC: National Advisory Committee on Rural Health.

Parker, S., & Knoll, J.L. (1990). Partial hospitalization: An update. *American Journal of Psychiatry, 147,* 156-160.

Puig-Antich, J. Goetz, D., Davies, M., & Kaplan, T. (1989). A controlled family history study of prepubertal major depressive disorder. *Archives of General Psychiatry, 46(5),* 406-418.

Rao,. U., Ryan, N.D., Birmaher, B., Dahl, R.E., Williamson, D.E., Kaufman, J., Rao, R., & Nelson, B. (1995). Unipolar depression in adolescents: Clinical outcomes in adulthood. *Journal of the American Academy of Child and Adolescent Psychiatry, 34(5),* 566-578.

Rao, U., Weissman, M.M., Martin, J.A., & Hammond, R.W. (1993). Childhood depression and risk of suicide: A preliminary report of a longitudinal study. *Journal of the American Academy of Child and Adolescent Psychiatry, 32(1),* 244-253.

Reebye, P., Moretti, M.M., & Lessard, J.C. (1995). Conduct disorder and substance use disorder: Comorbidity in a clinical sample of preadolescents and adolescents. *Canadian Journal of Psychiatry, 40(6),* 313-319.

Reinherz, H.Z., Giaconia, R.M., Lefkowitz, E.S., Pakiz, B., & Frost, A. K. (1993). Prevalence of psychiatric disorders in a community population of older adolescents. *Journal of the American Academy of Child and Adolescent Psychiatry, 32(2),* 369-377.

Robbins, L.N., & Ratcliff, K.S. (1979). Risk factors in the continuation of childhood antisocial behavior into adulthood. *International Journal of Mental Health, 7,* 96-111.

Robinson, G. (1991). Choices in case management. *Community Support Network News, 7,* 1112.

Robinson, K.E., Dow, R.A., & Nichols, P.M. (1999). Expanding a continuum of care: A report on a partial-day treatment program. [Electronic version]. *Child and Youth Care Forum, 28,* 221-228.

Robinson, K.E., & Rapport, L.J. (2002). Outcomes of a school-based mental health program for youth with serious emotional disorders. [Electronic version]. *Psychology in the Schools, 39(6),* 661-675.

Rounsaville, B.J., Anton, S.F., Carroll, K., Budde, D., Prusoff, B.A., & Gawin, F. (1991). Psychiatric diagnoses of treatment-seeking cocaine abusers. *Archives of General Psychiatry 48(1),* 43-51.

Salzar, M.S., Bickman, L., Lambert, E.W. (1999). Dose-effect relationship in children's psychotherapy services. [Electronic version]. *Journal of Consulting and Clinical Psychology, 67(2),* 228-239.

Scahill, L. & Schwab-Stone, M. Epidemiology of ADHD in school-age children. *Child & Adolescent Psychiatric Clinics of North America, 9(3),* 541-555.

Semrud-Clikeman, M., Biederman, J., Sprich-Buckminster, S., & Lehman, B.K. (1992). Comorbidity between ADDH and learning disability: A review and report in a clinically referred sample. *Journal of the American Academy of Child and Adolescent Psychiatry, 31(3),* 439-448.

Short, R.J. & Simeonsson, R.J. (1986). Social cognition and aggression in delinquent adolescent males. *Adolescence, 21(81),* 159-176.

Stewart, M. & Kelso, J. (1987). A two-year follow-up of boys with aggressive conduct. *Psychopathology, 20(5),* 296-304.

Stroul, B. A., & Friedman, R. M. (1986). The system of care concept and philosophy. In Stroul, B.A., & Goldman, S.K. (1990). Study of community-based services for children and adolescents who are severely emotionally disturbed. *Journal of Mental Health Administration, 17,* 61-77.

U.S. Department of Education Office of Special Education Programs (2001). *Twenty-third Annual Report to Congress on the Implementation of the Individuals with Disabilities Education Act: Results.* U.S. Department of Education, Office of Special Education Programs.

U.S. Public Health Service Office of the Surgeon General (1999). *Mental Health: A Report of the Surgeon General.* Rockville, MD: Department of Health and Human Services, U.S. Public Health Service.

Vernberg, E.M., Jacobs, A.K., Nyre, J.E., Ruddy, R. W., & Roberts, M.C. (2004). Innovative treatment for children with serious emotional disturbance: Preliminary outcomes for a school-based intensive mental health program. *Journal of Clinical Child and Adolescent Psychology, 33(2),* 359-365.

Verhulst, F.C., Achenbach, T.M., Ferdinand, R.F., & Kasius, M.C. (1993). Epidemiological comparisons of American and Dutch adolescents' self-reports. *Journal of American Child and Adolescent Psychiatry, 32(6),* 1135-1144.

Walker, J.L., Lahey, B.B., Hynd, G.W., & Frame, C.L. (1987). Comparison of specific patterns of antisocial behavior in children with conduct disorder with or without coexisting hyperactivity. *Journal of Consulting and Clinical Psychology, 55(6),* 910-913.

Webster-Stratton, L.C., & Lindsay, D.W. (1999). Social competence and conduct disorder problems in young children: Issues in assessment. *Journal of Clinical Child Psychology, 28(1),* 25-43.

Weller, E.B., & Weller, R.A. (1990). Depressive disorders in children and adolescents. In Garfinkel, B.D. (Eds.). *Psychiatric Disorders in Children and Adolescents* (pp.3-20). Philadelphia, PA: W.B. Sanders.

Weisz, J.R., Doneberg, G.R., Han, S.S., & Kauneckis, D. (1995). Child and adolescent psychotherapy outcomes in experiments *versus* clinic: Why the disparity? [Electronic version]. *Journal of Abnormal Child Psychology, 23(1),* 83-106.

Weisz, J.R., & Jenson, P.S. (1999). Efficacy and effectiveness of psychotherapy and pharmacotherapy with children and adolescents. *Mental Health Services Research, 1,*125-157.

Zahner, G.E., Jacobs, J.H., Freeman, D.H.J., & Trainor, K.F. (1993). Rural-urban child psychopathology in a Northeastern U.S. state: 1986-1989. *Journal of American Academy of Child and Adolescent Psychiatry, 32(2),* 378-387.

www.ingramcontent.com/pod-product-compliance
Lightning Source LLC
LaVergne TN
LVHW070948210926
848482LV00002B/136

* 9 7 8 1 6 0 8 0 5 5 6 8 5 *